D0849352

27.95
80E

AGING AND
PUBLIC HEALTH

Harry T. Phillips is Professor Emeritus in the Department of Health Policy and Administration, School of Public Health, University of North Carolina at Chapel Hill. He received his M.D. and D.P.H. at the University of Cape Town, South Africa, and has worked as a public health administrator at the local, state, and institutional levels in the United States. For ten years he was actively involved in regional health planning. In 1979 he became the Director of the Program on Aging at the School of Public Health, and in 1980 he spent a half year abroad studying services for the elderly in the United Kingdom and Israel.

Susan A. Gaylord is a Research Associate of the Program on Aging, School of Public Health, University of North Carolina at Chapel Hill. She received her B.A. from the University of North Carolina at Chapel Hill and Ph.D. in Experimental Psychology from Duke University. For five years she was associated with Duke University's Center for the Study of Aging and Human Development, involved in research on psychological aspects of aging and serving as book review editor of the KWIC Index of Training and Educational Materials in Aging.

AGING AND PUBLIC HEALTH

Harry T. Phillips, M.D., D.P.H.
Susan A. Gaylord, PH.D.

Editors

Foreword by Michel A. Ibrahim, M.D.

SPRINGER PUBLISHING COMPANY
New York

Springer Publishing Company, Inc.
536 Broadway
New York, New York 10012

85 86 87 88 89 / 10 9 8 7 6 5 4 3 2 1

Library of Congress Cataloging in Publication Data
Main entry under title:
Aging and public health.
   Includes bibliographies and index.
   1. Aged—Care and hygiene—United States. 2. Aged—United States—Social conditions. 3. Aged—Services for—United States. 4. Aging—Psychological aspects. I. Phillips, Harry T. II. Gaylord, Susan A. [DNLM: 1. Aged. 2. Aging. 3. Health Services for the Aged—organization & administration—United States. 4. Public Health—United States. WT 30 A26753]
RA564.8.A397   1985   362.1'9897'00973   85-2815
ISBN 0-8261-4380-6

Printed in the United States of America

Contents

II Environmental Aspects of Aging and Public Health 101

III Psychosocial Aspects of Aging and Public Health 181

IV Health Services for the Elderly 249

Foreword

With the control of threats to life in early and middle years, public health is faced with a new and growing challenge—the aging of our society. Individuals in advanced ages are growing steadily in number and proportion to the general population. Compared to younger individuals, the elderly experience a large share of the following problems: a) chronic disease, such as atherosclerosis, cancer, stroke, diabetes, and arthritis; b) psychosocial expressions in the form of anxiety, loneliness, depression, and isolation; and c) inaccessibility to needed services. To further our understanding of these diverse problems, several disciplines such as epidemiology, health education, health care organization, environmental sciences, and public policy analysis are required.

Such disciplines form an integral part of the science and practice of public health. It is no surprise, therefore, that as the needs of the aged become urgent, the expression of interest and concern by public health professionals intensifies. The School of Public Health at the University of North Carolina has had a long history of addressing health problems of populations, not only from the more traditional physical and biological viewpoints, but also from the social and behavioral perspectives. This book applies this long-standing interest towards a further understanding of the multiple forces that impinge on the health status of aging populations, and expresses the commitment of the disciplines of public health to research and education in the service of the elderly.

The editors of this book, in collaboration with several of their colleagues, have made a timely and significant contribution both to public health and to the aging population in presenting the potential and actual contributions of a broad range of public health disciplines in promoting the well-being of our older citizens.

Michel A. Ibrahim, M.D.
Dean
School of Public Health
University of North Carolina at Chapel Hill

Acknowledgments

We are grateful for the help of outside reviewers, who enriched the authors' ideas in the early stages. The authors, editors, and reviewers met at a two-day conference to review first drafts of the chapters and to share viewpoints. Included were Mary Bethel, Carey Bostian, Janice Caldwell, Rachel Gray, Kathryn Habib, Howard Jacobson, Margaret Jones, Ronald Levine, Erdman Palmore, Ilene Siegler, Harvey Smith, Dorothy Talbot, Paul Taylor, and Peter Uhlenberg.

In addition, special thanks are due to Eva Salber, for her wise and generous contribution of ideas in developing the final versions of several chapters. We are also grateful to Ernest Schoenfeld for his ready and genial support in the production of this book. Thanks are due to the many people who participated in the typing, in particular, Bobbie Dampier, Joy Laird, and Dinah Lloyd. Finally, we appreciate the patience and dedication of Donna Cooper in typing and retyping major portions of the manuscript.

Contributors

Marie T. Fanelli is Assistant Professor in the Department of Nutrition, School of Public Health, University of North Carolina at Chapel Hill. She received her B.A. from Douglass College and both her M.S. and Ph.D. from Rutgers University. Her primary research interest focuses on the relationship of nutritional knowledge and attitudes of older adults to their dietary practices. Her activities include presenting workshops on nutritional assessment and nutritional needs of older adults.

Lisa Fredman is a graduate student in the Department of Epidemiology, School of Public Health, University of North Carolina at Chapel Hill. She received her B.A. from Swarthmore College and M.S.P.H. from the University of North Carolina at Chapel Hill. She has worked in the Department of Gerontological Services of the Hebrew Rehabilitation Center for the Aged in Boston, Massachusetts.

Bruce J. Fried is an Assistant Professor in the Health Administration Program in the Faculty of Medicine at the University of Toronto, Canada. He received his Ph.D. from the Department of Health Policy and Administration, School of Public Health, University of North Carolina at Chapel Hill; his M.A. from the University of Chicago School of Social Service Administration; and his B.S. from the State University of New York at Buffalo. His research interests include evaluation, organizational theory, and mental health policy.

Suzanne G. Haynes is Chief of the Medical Statistics Branch, Division of Health Examination Statistics, of the National Center for Health Statistics in Hyattsville, Maryland. She was formerly Research Assistant Professor of Epidemiology, School of Public Health,

University of North Carolina at Chapel Hill. She received her Ph.D. in Epidemiology from the University of North Carolina at Chapel Hill; her M.A. and M.P.H. from the University of Texas; and her B.A. from the University of Tennessee. Her research interests include type A behavior, employment status, and coronary heart disease in women. She is coeditor of a book on the epidemiology of aging, and has published several articles on the health effects of retirement.

Arnold D. Kaluzny is Professor in the Department of Health Policy and Administration, School of Public Health, University of North Carolina at Chapel Hill, and an Adjunct Professor in the Department of Health Administration at Duke University. He holds a B.A. from the University of Wisconsin and M.H.A. and Ph.D. from the University of Michigan. He is the author and coauthor of numerous articles and papers in the field of health services research.

Mildred Kaufman is Associate Professor in the Department of Nutrition, School of Public Health, University of North Carolina at Chapel Hill. She holds an M.S. in Nutrition and Public Health from Teachers College, Columbia University. She has had extensive experience as a public health nutrition consultant and administrator in local, state, and federal voluntary and official health agencies. In these capacities she has worked to develop community nutrition services for older adults.

Victor J. Schoenbach is Assistant Professor of Epidemiology, School of Public Health, University of North Carolina at Chapel Hill, and Research Associate, Health Services Research Center. An epidemiologist with varied interests, he has attended Harvard and Columbia Universities, the London School of Economics and Political Science, and the University of North Carolina at Chapel Hill; his masters degrees are in economics and public health education, and his Ph.D. is in epidemiology. Dr. Schoenbach has carried out or contributed to research projects on adolescent depression, health hazard/health risk appraisal programs, health life style behaviors of members of a large fraternal benefits organization, effect of social ties on mortality, and vitamin A and lung cancer risk. He teaches a seminar in epidemiologic considerations in health promotion/disease prevention.

Michael A. Stegman is Chairman of the Department of City and Regional Planning, University of North Carolina at Chapel Hill.

He received his B.A. in Political Science from Brooklyn College and his M.C.P. (Master of City Planning) and Ph.D. at the University of Pennsylvania. During the Carter Administration, he was Deputy Assistant Secretary for Research at the Department of Housing and Urban Development. He is currently writing a book on national housing policy.

Guy W. Steuart is Professor of Health Education, School of Public Health, University of North Carolina Chapel Hill, and was previously Professor of Public Health and Preventive Medicine, University of California at Los Angeles. He received his Ph.D. in Psychology from the University of Natal, South Africa and his M.P.H. from Yale University. His specialty is community health development and primary care, and he has consulted extensively in Europe, Africa, and the Middle East.

Patricia F. Waller is Associate Director for Driver Studies at the University of North Carolina Highway Safety Research Center and Research Professor in the Department of Health Policy and Administration, School of Public Health, University of North Carolina at Chapel Hill. She holds an A.B. and an M.S. from the University of Miami and a Ph.D. from the University of North Carolina. A psychologist, she has worked with elderly patients in psychiatric settings. More recently she has taught and conducted research in the area of injury and has authored numerous chapters, articles, and reports in this area. One of her interests has been the development and implementation of programs to meet the special needs of the growing population of older drivers and pedestrians. She is past president of the American Association for Automotive Medicine and serves on the National Highway Safety Advisory Committee as well as other national committees.

Introduction

This book primarily addresses students in public health, but should be of interest also to students, practitioners, and researchers in other fields who are interested in the well-being of the elderly. Its purpose is to demonstrate that public health can make major contributions in meeting the challenge of an aging society. To this end, writers from several sub-areas of public health show what their specialty can add to the understanding of the health of the older population; where appropriate they indicate ways in which public health can improve the collective well-being of old people.

Public health and aging are two fields of professional interest which have been converging for the last few decades. Public health came of age in 1872 when the American Public Health Association (APHA) was formed. Aging was first recognized professionally in the U.S. with the formation of the American Geriatric Association in 1942 and the Gerontological Society of America (GSA) in 1945. The APHA has 24 sections; the Gerontological Health Section was established only in 1978. (The Maternal and Child Health Section was formed in 1921. The organization of medical services was accepted as a public health concern only after a major struggle within the association, and the Medical Care Section was established in 1948.) The GSA has four sections—Biological Sciences, Clinical Medicine, Behavioral and Social Sciences, and Social Research, Planning, and Practice—the interests of the last section being closest to those of public health. Although some initial work has been done, the application of aging in public health thinking and practice is still very limited.

Broadly but briefly, the two fields of public health and aging are reviewed below.

Public Health

Two main strategies are used to safeguard the health of people. The first focuses on the individual; it is essentially the medical approach. The second, the public health approach, focuses on the group. The two strategies are of necessity strongly interdependent; they borrow knowledge and skills from each other.

Definition of Public Health

Several definitions of public health exist (Hanlon, 1974, pp. 3–4; Milbank Commission, 1976, p. 3). Drawing upon these definitions, for the purpose of this book, public health is defined as *the combined science, art, and practice directed by organized community action to promote health, prevent disease, and alleviate the burdens of illness in the population.*

Since public health practice is an activity directed and carried out *by* the community *for* the community, it implies a certain level of self-consciousness and intelligence in using community health resources to meet community health needs, as perceived by both the public and professionals. The public health ideal is a model of coordinated health services, functioning in response to demonstrated need, and accountable to legitimate representatives of the people served.

Goals and Strategies of Public Health

By definition, the broad goals of public health are to promote health, prevent disease, and alleviate the burdens of illness in the population through organized community action. More specific goals will of necessity be developed by and for each population or community. As presented by Vickers (1958), these specific goals will be set according to the perceived needs, culture, history, technology, economics, politics, and other social characteristics of the community. Consequently, public health goals can and will vary from time to time and place to place.

Public health practice therefore can be seen as a response to the question, "What do the people want to do about their health?" This response is shaped by the degree to which a situation is seen as an existing or potential problem, the desirability of acting collectively, who will benefit and how the action will be paid for, and the technical, administrative, and political feasibility of intervention.

Over the years a number of strategies have developed in public health. These strategies can be summarized as:

1. Regarding the community or population as the target group or unit of practice (McGavran, 1958; National Commission of Community Health Services, 1966).
2. Assigning highest priority to preventive action, rather than to curative measures.
3. Protecting or modifying the environment (physical, biological, and psychosocial) in order to promote the well-being of the community.
4. Providing leadership in advocating, planning, organizing, and supporting programs to meet current health needs.
5. Giving assistance to and accepting support from other organized groups with similar or related goals.
6. Encouraging and assisting the individual to do for himself what he can to promote and protect his own health.
7. Using the *collective* approach only when and where the advantages clearly outweigh the disadvantages.

It is evident that public health is both a way of thinking and a way of acting, that it requires partnerships between many actors, and that no single agency or organization has a monopoly on responsibility for the health of the public.

Targets of Public Health

Public health is an expression of community leadership and action. In this book community is broadly defined as a number of people who share common concerns and goals. The target group or community may be a neighborhood, city, county, country, or even several countries. Alternatively, the target may be selected individuals within a geographic area with shared risks or needs.

At times, public health has been oriented towards disease or injury, and focused upon communicable diseases, environmental hazards, heart disease, cancer, or other threats to health. At other times, the effort has been oriented towards people and focused on mothers and infants, minority groups, inner city dwellers, migrants, and more recently, the chronically ill and aged. Resulting interventions may not be limited to prevention; they may also provide organized rehabilitation, and long-term and terminal care services.

Since the years of the Depression, and World War II particularly, the organization and delivery of adequate health and medical care services for the general population have been seen as a *public* concern and no longer solely as a private matter. This changing perception resulted from the growth of medical science and technology, growing expectations and demands of the public, escalating costs of care, and the perceived need to reduce physical and financial barriers to care.

The Structure of Public Health Services

The goals of public health are promoted not by government or health workers alone. In their collective way, innumerable groups, public and private, serve the goals of maintaining and promoting the health of groups of people. In the United States, organization of services characteristically lacks uniformity. Recognized public health agencies operate in coalition with other human service agencies, voluntary organizations, professional practitioners, and for-profit agencies. Many programs could not operate without such partnerships. Historically, church groups and voluntary agencies have served as catalysts or initiators of innovative health programs.

The degree of centralization can be high, as in national programs such as Medicare, or low, as in the case of voluntary neighborhood support groups. The preference in the United States is for services to be delivered by the private sector (whether non-profit or for-profit), but paid for, at least in part, by public funds. However, because the weak, the poor, and the disabled often lack influence and depend on the conscience of others, a central actor in any major public health effort must, of necessity, be some level of government.

Aging

Definition

In biological terms, aging may be defined as a postmaturational process that correlates over time with increasing functional losses. People vary greatly in the rapidity with which they age. Similarly, organs within an individual age at different rates. Of primary concern are those people who exhibit functional losses that are accompanied by dependency. Dependency may be defined in physical, social, or behavioral terms, and is correlated with chronological age only in statistical terms. While some people at early ages become functionally impaired and need societal support, others maintain vigorous and independent lives well into advanced age. But dependence is difficult to measure objectively and reliably so that a usable definition can be built on functional criteria. Consequently, demographers, policymakers, and others have tended to take the easy path and use some chronological marker for this purpose, usually the age of 65 or older. Because there seems to be a much higher risk of dependency after the age of 75, many now speak of the 65–74 age group as the "young-old," and the 75 and over group as the "old-old."

Population Changes

The extraordinary increase in the numbers and proportions of old people in our society, especially in industrialized countries, is a recent phenomenon. In the U.S. in 1900 the percentage of people 65 and older was 4.0%, in 1980 it was 11.3%; in the year 2030 it is projected to reach 21.1% Of special significance is the increase in the oldest segment of the population. In 1900 people 85 and over comprised 0.2% (123,000), in 1980 0.9% (2,240,000), and in 2030 the percentage projected is 2.9% (8,801,000) (U.S. Senate, Special Committee on Aging, 1983, p. 3).

This increase in the proportion of old people has been due to the reduction of early death in childhood and mid-life; more recently there has been a reduction of mortality rates among the elderly themselves (U.S. Department of Health and Human Services, National Center for Health Statistics, 1982). Much of this progress has been due to public health measures.

Multiple Deficiencies

Old people are extremely heterogeneous in their personal characteristics. As a *group,* however, old people have a greater tendency towards physical, mental, and social defects than younger people, and the proportion with these defects increases with age. With advancing age, the need for assistance and the use of short-stay hospitals and long-stay nursing homes increases (U.S. Department of Health and Human Services, Federal Council on Aging, 1981, pp. 31, 41, 43).

In addition to their losses in bodily capabilities, old people risk economic losses because of inability to work, retirement, or other reasons. Social losses such as bereavement, migration of children, or divorce, aggravate the problem of dependency and may result in a need for outside help.

Share of the National Budget

It is not surprising that the 11 percent of the population which is 65 and over absorbs 30 percent of the national health care budget. Moreover, over a quarter of the entire federal budget goes towards programs which benefit the elderly (White House Conference on Aging *Final Report,* 1981, p. 13). More than half of this money (56%) is paid out as Social Security benefits. However, the Social Security system was designed as social insurance, not welfare, and benefits are related to the amount contributed by workers and their employers. Much of the remainder of federal outlays is for health care (i.e. Medicare and Medicaid).

Although a very substantial amount of public money is being spent on the well-being of the elderly, it is noteworthy that their families and those who provide them with goods and services are also major beneficiaries.

The Rationale for Public Health Interventions in Aging

Public health adopts a holistic view of the dynamics of health. The health of individuals and groups is determined by:

1. their biological background (genetics, stage of life cycle, biochemical status)
2. their environment (physical, social, economic)
3. their life style (health-related behavior)
4. their health and medical services

Moreover, health status today is much influenced by the past, and events today will largely determine health status in the future.

It follows that ensuring an optimal level of well-being depends on both an understanding of the ways in which health status is affected, and a knowledge of how to promote good health. This applies not only to disease prevention, but also to increasing the ability of people to cope with disability when illness does arise. This holistic, dynamic perspective is especially important with regard to the well-being of the elderly, a population group at high risk of disease and disability whose quality of life can be significantly affected by the presence or absence of public health measures.

We can thus summarize a public health perspective on aging as follows:

1. Old people are increasing rapidly both in number and proportion. This trend will continue for some decades.
2. Because of the relationship between old age and ill health, and between old age and poverty (at least for certain groups), old people have a high risk of becoming dependent on their relatives, friends, neighbors, and the community at large.
3. We are now aware of many ways to mitigate, delay, modify, or even prevent some of the disability associated with aging.
4. While older people as a group presently use a disproportionate share of the nation's health resources, many still lack adequate care.
5. The problems of an aging population are currently being addressed, but in a fragmented, inefficient, and uncoordinated fashion.
6. Our culture dictates that we take responsibility, and have compassion, for our elders.

Public health with its broad population approach can serve to provide a holistic, conceptual framework for the application of research, training, and service in the field of aging.

It is fitting to close with the reasons given in the historic Shattuck Report (Sanitary Commission of Massachusetts, 1850, p. 6) for accepting its public health recommendations:

    I. Because it is a practical measure,
   II. Because it is a useful measure,
  III. Because it is an economical measure,
  IV. Because it is a philanthropic and charitable measure,
   V. Because it is a moral measure,
  VI. Because the progress of the age demands it,
 VII. Because it involves an important duty.

Organization of the Book

This book reflects the multidisciplinary nature of the public health perspective. In the first chapter, the health background of the elderly population, the focus of our concern, is outlined in epidemiological terms. In the remaining nine chapters, the holistic model of health determination previously outlined is used to provide a framework for a public health approach to the aging of our population. The following areas are dealt with:

Biology. In two chapters, the biological potential and limits of human health are discussed, and the field of nutrition and aging reviewed.

Environment. In this section, two selected areas of special relevance to the elderly—injury prevention and housing—are surveyed.

Psychosocial factors. The effects of life style and behavior on health, and strategies for changing behavior are discussed in this section.

Health services. In this section, chapters address three topics—organization of community health services, interorganization of health services, and public policies on the health of the aged.

A brief epilogue suggests ways in which the public health perspective on aging in the United States could be promoted.

References

Hanlon, J. J. *Public Health Administration and Practice.* Sixth Edition. Saint Louis, Mo.: Mosby, 1974.

McGavran, E. G. The community as the patient of public health. *Texas State Journal of Medicine,* 1958, *54,* 719–723.

Milbank Memorial Fund Commission *Higher Education for Public Health.* New York, N.Y.: Prodist, 1976.

National Commission on Community Health Services. *Health is a Community Affair.* Cambridge, Ma.: Harvard University Press, 1966.

Sanitary Commission of Massachusetts. *Report.* Boston, Ma.: Dutton and Butterworth, 1850.

U.S. Department of Health and Human Services, National Center for Health Statistics. *Changes in Mortality Among the Elderly: United States, 1940–78.* DHHS Publication No. (PHS) 82-1406. Hyattsville, Md., 1982.

U.S. Department of Health and Human Services, Federal Council on Aging. *The Need for Long Term Care.* DHHS Publication No. (OHDS) 81–10704. Washington, D.C. 1981.

U.S. Senate Special Committee on Aging. *Developments in Aging 1982:* Vol. 1. Washington, D.C.: U.S. Government Printing Office, 1983.

Vickers, G. What sets the goals of public health? *New England Journal of Medicine,* 1964, *258,* 589–596.

White House Conference on Aging, 1981. *Final Report.* Washington, D.C.: U.S. Department of Health and Human Services, 1981.

THE POPULATION AT RISK

An Epidemiologic Profile
of the Elderly

LISA FREDMAN AND SUZANNE G. HAYNES

Introduction

Epidemiology is commonly defined as the science of the distribution and determinants of health and disease in population groups. Thus, the epidemiology of aging is not merely the study of disease conditions in older people, but encompasses the analysis of biological and social factors in younger adults that affect their health in later years. It includes the study of how disease and health conditions vary among the elderly as reflected by demographic data and vital statistics, studies of associations between well-being and life style, and implications for the prevention of disease.

This chapter provides a survey of selected findings from subject areas within the purview of an epidemiology of aging: topics include mortality and morbidity trends, and the influences of retirement, lifestyle, and other important sociopsychological factors on the health of the elderly. This survey is not intended as a thorough review of the epidemiology of aging. Rather, it provides a basis for discussion of public health issues which are raised in later sections. It also provides a profile of the population group which is the focus of attention in this book. For more extensive reviews of the epidemiology of aging the reader is referred to such publications as the *Second Conference on the Epidemiology of Aging* (U.S. Department of Health and Human Services [U.S. DHHS], 1980a), and for a review of demographic data, *Changes in Mortality Among the Elderly, U.S. 1940–1978* (U.S. DHHS, 1982a).

Finally, this chapter emphasizes the causes and consequences of morbidity among the elderly. Extending the life expectancy is a major public health achievement of this century. Yet, new public health challenges result from it. These include accommodating the health care and housing needs of a larger elderly population, managing the provision and costs of long-term care, and assuring that the quality of life is not compromised by increasing the quantity of life. The types of chronic illnesses affecting the elderly influence both the choice of public health interventions and policy decisions.

Unavoidably this chapter reviews some of the same topics that are addressed in ensuing chapters. This applies particularly to so-cial and behavioral factors in epidemiology which have special relevance to aging and which provide scientific bases for public health interventions.

Demographic, Mortality, and Morbidity Trends

An excellent review of this subject is provided by Fingerhut and Rosenberg (1981) from which we have drawn extensively in this section; unless otherwise noted, information is drawn from this source.

Demography

As has been reported in numerous other writings, the United States population aged 65 and over has been increasing rapidly both in numbers and proportion. This is attributable to both the decline in mortality and the fall in fertility.

The numbers and proportions of the elderly (people aged 65 and over) have increased from 9 million (7%) in 1940, to 25 million (11%) in 1979. Moreover, the proportion of very old (aged 80 and over) has been increasing more rapidly than the younger sub-groups of the elderly—13% in 1940 to 21% in 1979. In 1978, 73% of 65 year olds could expect to live to 75; in 1940 only 61% could do so.

Another important demographic trend is the increasing pro-

portion of the elderly who are female. In 1940 there were 95 males
for every 100 females; by 1979 there were only 70 males.

All these demographic changes have far-reaching implications
for the nation's social and health policies and programs.

Mortality

There has been a remarkable decline in mortality among the elderly
from 1940 to 1978. Over this period the death rate decreased by
16.7% for males, and 33.0% for females. If the population aged 65
years and over is adjusted for changes in overall age composition
(i.e., age-specific death rates), then the decline is even more striking: the rates decreased by 24.5% for males, and 46.7% for females.

The major trends in mortality of the elderly can be summarized as follows:

1. Between 1940 and 1978, the mortality rate for persons 65
   and older decreased by 27% (U.S. DHHS, 1982a).
2. The decline in mortality rates was two times greater for
   women than for men: 33% compared to 17% (U.S. DHSS,
   1982a).
3. The 1980 census reported that 11.3% of the United States
   population (25.12 million people) was over 65 (U.S. Senate, Special Committee on Aging, 1982).
4. By the year 2000, the elderly population is expected to
   increase by 30%, while the population under age 65 will
   probably increase by only 15% (U.S. Senate, Special Committee on Aging, 1982).
5. If fertility remains at low levels and mortality rates continue to decline, the proportion of elderly persons in the
   United States could approach 18% by the year 2020 (Siegel, 1980).
6. In the 1980 census, there were 68 men for every 100
   women aged 65 and older. Projections for the year 2000
   estimate a ratio of 65 elderly men for every 100 elderly
   women. The sex differential is greater among persons
   aged 85 years and older: the 1980 census showed a ratio of
   44 men for every 100 women (U.S. Senate, Special Committee on Aging, 1982).
7. Persons aged 85 years and older constitute the fastest

growing group of elderly. Since 1900, this age group has grown seventeenfold, while the population aged 75 years and older has increased 10 times, and the population over 60 has increased by almost seven times. In 1975, persons over age 85 comprised 8% of the elderly population. Projections for the year 2000 predict that they will comprise 11% of the elderly population (U.S. DHEW, 1978).

8. Chronic diseases are the major causes of mortality in the elderly. With the exception of some cancers, the mortality rates are decreasing for all leading chronic diseases (U.S. DHEW, 1978).

9. Death rates from all causes increase with age. In 1977, deaths per 1,000 non-institutionalized population rose from 24.8 deaths among persons aged 65 to 69 years, to 88.1 deaths among those aged 80–84 years, to 147.3 deaths per 1,000 persons aged 85 and older (U.S. DHEW, 1978).

10. Black males show the highest death rates in the 65 to 79 year age category; after age 80, there is a crossover, and white males show higher death rates (U.S. DHEW, 1978).

11. Mortality rates for older females are generally lower than those for males. The black female death rate is higher than the white female death rate until age 80, whereupon the white female death rate exceeds it (U.S. DHEW, 1978). (See Figure A.1.)

Major Causes of Mortality

Heart disease, cancer, and stroke together cause three out of four deaths among the elderly (see Table A.1). Death rates from all causes increase with age.

Heart Disease. The leading cause of death among the elderly for many years has been heart disease. In 1978, 44 percent of deaths in this age group were attributed to this cause. Mortality rates from heart disease increase markedly with this age group. However, over the last 30 years there has been a general decline in mortality rates for females, and a more moderate decline for males, especially in the period 1968–78 (see Figure A.2).

The major trends in mortality from heart disease can be summarized as follows:

FIGURE A.1   Age-adjusted death rates for persons 65 years of age and over, according to sex: United States, 1940–78

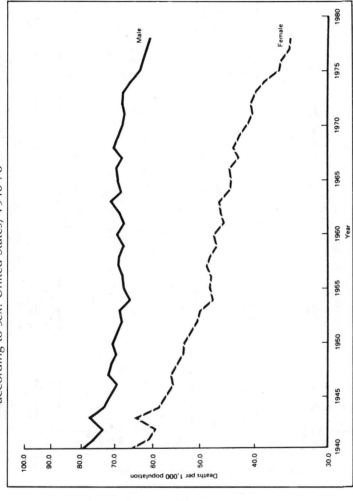

Notes: Age adjusted by the direct method to the population 65 years of age and over in the United States as enumerated in 1940, using 5 age groups. Death rates for the group 85 years of age and over in 1970 used in computation of rates are based on population estimates revised by the U.S. Bureau of the Census to correct for overestimates of the group 100 years of age and over.

Source: National Center for Health Statistics: Computed by the Division of Analysis from data compiled by the Division of Vital Statistics.

FIGURE A.2 Death rates for diseases of heart among persons 65 years of age and over, according to sex and age: United States, 1950–78

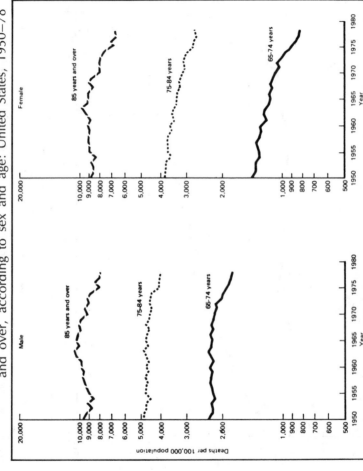

Notes: *Death rates for the group 85 years of age and over in 1970 are based on population estimates revised by the U.S. Bureau of the Census to correct for overestimates of the group 100 years of age and over.*
Sources: *National Center for Health Statistics: Vital Statistics of the United States, Vol. II, 1950-76. Public Health Service. Washington. U.S. Government Printing Office, and 1977–78 to be published, and unpublished data.*

TABLE A.1
Death Rates for the 10 Leading Causes of
Death for Ages 65 and Over, By Age: 1976
[Deaths per 100,000 population]

Cause of death by rank	65 years and over	65 to 74 years	75 to 84 years	85 years and over
All causes	5.428.9	3,127.6	7,331.6	15,486.9
1. Diseases of the heart	2,393.5	1,286.9	3,263.7	7,384.3
2. Malignant neoplasms	979.0	786.3	1,248.6	1,441.5
3. Cerebrovascular diseases	694.6	280.1	1,014.0	2,586.8
4. Influenza & pneumonia	211.1	70.1	289.3	959.2
5. Arteriosclerosis	122.2	25.8	152.5	714.3.
6. Diabetes mellitus	108.1	70.0	155.8	219.2
7. Accidents	104.5	62.2	134.5	306.7
Motor vehicle	25.2	21.7	32.3	26.0
All other	79.3	40.4	102.2	280.7
8. Bronchitis, emphysema and asthma	76.8	60.7	101.4	108.5
9. Cirrhosis of liver	36.5	42.6	29.3	18.0
10. Nephritis and nephrosis	25.0	15.2	34.1	64.6
All other causes	677.5	427.8	908.6	1,638.8

Source: National Center for Health Statistics (U.S. Public Health Service), "Advance Report—Final Mortality Statistics, 1976," Monthly Vital Statistics Report, Vol. 26, No. 12, Supplement (2), March 1978; and unpublished data provided by the National Center for Health Statistics.

1. Heart disease mortality rates increase rapidly with age: in 1977, the death rate from heart disease among those aged 85 and over was almost twice as high as the death rate for those aged 80 to 84 (71 deaths versus 40 deaths per 1,000 persons), and over seven times higher than the death rate for those aged 65 to 69 years (9.92 deaths per 1,000 persons) (U.S. DHHS, 1980b).

2. Males are at higher risk of death from heart disease than females. Among the four race-sex groups, white males have the highest mortality rates (U.S. DHHS, 1980b).

3. Between 1968 and 1977, ischemic heart disease deaths fell most steeply (by 33%) in the 65 to 74 age category: from 12.1 to 8.8 deaths per 1,000 population (U.S. DHHS, 1980b).

4. Whites aged 65 to 74 showed a greater decline in ischemic heart disease than any other age category of elderly whites: females showed a bigger decline than males—27 percent compared to 20 percent (Havlik and Feinleib, 1979).

5. Blacks aged 85 years and older showed the greatest decline

in ischemic heart disease among the minority elderly: ischemic heart disease rates declined by 30 percent for both males and females (Havlik and Feinleib, 1979).

Cancer. Unlike other major causes of death in the elderly, cancer has continued to rise since 1900. In 1978 it accounted for 26% of all deaths in the age group 65–74, 18% in the age group 75–84, and 10% in the 85 and over age group.

Cancer comprises a wide group of malignant neoplasms. Lung, colon, and breast cancers combined cause more than half of the deaths reported in 1978. For most age and sex groups among the elderly the increase in cancer mortality has been mainly due to lung cancer, a largely preventable disease. Since 1968 there has been a rapid upturn in female lung cancer death rates attributed to increasing prevalence of cigarette smoking in this group (see Figure A.3).

Apart from the continued rise in mortality from lung cancer in both sexes, and the slight rise in colon cancer in males, there are only irregular trends in other age, sex, and race groups (U.S. DHHS, 1982b).

The major trends in cancer mortality in the elderly can be summarized as follows:

1. Cancer is the second leading cause of death in the elderly under 85 years of age, and the third leading cause of death in the elderly 85 years and older (U.S. DHHS, 1982a).
2. The death rate from cancer has continued to rise since the 1950s for all elderly age groups (U.S. DHHS, 1980b).
3. Black males are at greatest risk of dying from cancer. In 1977, the death rate for black males 65 and over was 15.2 deaths per 1,000 persons (U.S. DHHS, 1980b).
4. White males show the next highest overall cancer mortality rates, 13.3 deaths per 1,000 persons. Cancer death rates for elderly white males increase consistently with age, so that white males over age 80 have the highest mortality rate from cancer (U.S. DHHS, 1980b).
5. Females 65 years and over show lower mortality rates than males. The overall rate for both white and black females is 7.5 deaths per 1,000 persons. Black females have higher mortality rates than white females in the 65 to 79 year age category. After age 80, white females show a higher cancer mortality rate than black females (U.S. DHHS, 1980b).

FIGURE A.3 Death rates for malignant neoplasms among persons 65 years of age and over, according to sex and age: United States, 1950–78

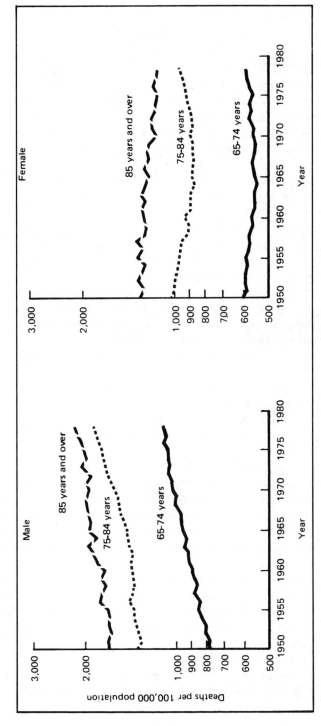

Notes: *Death rates for the group 85 years of age and over in 1970 are based on population estimates revised by the U.S. Bureau of the Census to correct for overestimates of the group 100 years of age and over.*

Sources:*National Center for Health Statistics: Vital Statistics of the United States, Vol. II, 1950–76. Public Health Service. Washington. U.S. Government Printing Office, and 1977–78 to be published, and unpublished data.*

6. Lung cancer is the leading cause of cancer mortality among males aged 65 to 84, while cancer of the genital organs (mainly the prostate) is the leading cause among males older than 85 years (U.S. DHHS, 1982a).

7. Breast cancer accounts for most of the cancer deaths among women aged 65 to 74 years, but among older women, colon cancer causes more cancer deaths. While the annual increase in lung cancer mortality is increasing among older women, it still causes fewer deaths than breast or colon cancer (U.S. DHSS, 1982a).

8. Lung cancer mortality rates increased in every age category of elderly males and females from 1950 to 1978. These increases were greater for males than females in every age group, peaking in an almost six-fold increase in lung cancer mortality rates among males aged 75 to 84 years (U.S. DHHS, 1982a).

9. Elderly black males in every age category, except 80 to 84 years old, are more likely than white males to die from lung cancer. Conversely, lung cancer mortality in elderly white females exceeds that of black females, except in women aged 70 to 79 years (U.S. DHHS, 1982a).

10. Breast cancer mortality rates are higher in elderly white than black females at every age. White females also show a consistent increase with age in breast cancer mortality, from 106 deaths per 100,000 population aged 65 to 69 years to 188 deaths per 100,000 population over 85 years (U.S. DHHS, 1982a).

11. Breast cancer mortality rates in elderly black females are lowest among 65 to 69 year olds (84 deaths per 100,000 population) and highest among 80 to 84 year olds (118 deaths per 100,000 population). Unlike white females, elderly black females exhibit no consistent increase in breast cancer mortality with age; rates rise in the 70 to 74 age category and fall in the 75 to 79 age category.

12. Colon cancer causes more deaths among men than women in every age category over 65 years. Mortality increases greatly with age among blacks and whites of both sexes. Mortality is greater among blacks aged 65 to 74, but after age 75, the death rate in whites exceeds that in blacks (U.S. DHHS, 1982a).

13. Colon cancer mortality rates have increased slightly for elderly males since 1950. This increase rises with age, and

is greatest among males over 85 years old; colon cancer mortality was one and a half times greater in 1978 than in 1950. In contrast, colon cancer mortality rates for females have decreased slightly during the same period (U.S. DHHS, 1982a).

14. The risk of stomach cancer mortality increases with age, and is greater in males than females. Blacks younger than 75 years old show a stomach cancer mortality rate almost twice as high as same-aged whites (U.S. DHHS, 1982a).

15. Pancreatic cancer death rates increase consistently with age in elderly whites. The mortality rate increases in elderly blacks, but not consistently. Elderly males are more likely to die from pancreatic cancer at every age. Black females under age 80 have higher mortality rates than white females. Black males aged 65 to 74, and those older than 85 experience higher pancreatic cancer mortality than white males (U.S. DHHS, 1982a).

16. Prostate cancer mortality data from 1973 to 1977 show a higher death rate among elderly blacks than whites, and increasing mortality with age for both blacks and whites (U.S. DHHS, 1981a).

Stroke. The second most common cause of death for people aged 85 and older is cerebro-vascular disease or stroke. In younger groups of the elderly it ranks third, after heart disease and cancer. However, since 1950 there has been a rapid decline in deaths from this cause, most marked in the 1968–78 period (Figure A.4).

The major trends in stroke mortality in the elderly can be summarized as follows:

1. Stroke is the third leading cause of death among persons 65 years and older, and the second leading cause of death among persons 85 years and older (U.S. DHHS, 1982a).

2. Stroke accounts for 16% of all deaths in elderly persons 85 years and older (U.S. DHHS, 1982a).

3. Death rates due to stroke are steadily decreasing; since 1975, they have decreased by 5 to 7% annually (U.S. DHHS, 1982a).

4. Age is a major risk factor for stroke fatalities. In people younger than 75 years, the case fatality rate remains relatively stable at about 28%, but increases to almost 45% in stroke victims 85 years and older (Weinfeld, 1981).

FIGURE A.4 Death rates for cerebrovascular diseases among persons 65 years of age and over, according to sex and age: United States, 1950–78

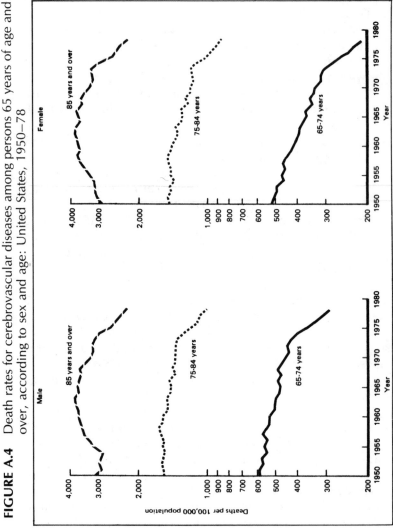

Notes: Death rates for the group 85 years of age and over in 1970 are based on population estimates revised by the U.S. Bureau of the Census to correct for overestimates of the group 100 years of age and over.
Sources: National Center for Health Statistics: Vital Statistics of the United States, Vol. II, 1950–76. Public Health Service. Washington, U.S. Government Printing Office, and 1977–78 to be published, and unpublished data.

Injuries. A major cause of mortality is injury, which is also the second most frequent cause of acute problems and disability in the elderly. In 1977, accidents were the fourth leading cause of death in the United States, following heart disease, cancer, and stroke (U.S. DHHS, 1980b, p. 137). For all injuries combined (i.e., motor vehicle accidents, falls, burns, and others), elderly people had the highest mortality rate (Hogue, 1982). In general, the elderly have a low incidence of injury compared to other age groups, but an extremely high case-fatality rate. People aged 75 to 84 years showed an injury case-fatality rate that was twice as high as those aged 15–24 years, the group with the second leading death rate due to unintentional injury. In 1978, 22.9 percent of all fatal injuries occurred in people 65 years and older.

The major causes of injury in the elderly are falls, burns, and motor vehicle accidents (Hogue, 1982). Women have higher rates of injury due to falls, while men have higher injury rates due to burns and motor vehicle accidents. Yet, men have a higher case fatality rate than women in all injury categories. In addition to sex differences in injury mortality, there is an age effect for the types of fatal injuries. Among persons aged 65–74, over one-third of the injury deaths are caused by motor vehicle accidents, while just under one-fourth are due to falls. After age 75, most of the injury deaths are caused by falls, and fewer than one-fifth are due to motor vehicle accidents. Fire and contact with hot substances cause about 8 percent of the injury deaths in both age groups. The epidemiology of injuries is reviewed more fully in Chapter 3.

Influenza and Pneumonia. Major causes of mortality in the elderly are still influenza and pneumonia. These were the fifth leading cause of death in 1977, after heart disease, cancer, stroke, and accidents (U.S. DHHS, 1980b, p. 137). It is noteworthy that the death rate for influenza and pneumonia declined from 26.2 per 100,000 in 1950 to 14.2 in 1977.

Suicide. A small number of deaths among the elderly are from suicide, especially among white males (U.S. DHHS, 1982b, p. 73). It is included in this section to illustrate one way that quality of life and physical illness and mortality are interconnected. Suicide among the elderly has been related to serious physical illness, depression, organic brain disease, and stressful life events such as widowhood and retirement (Atchley, 1980). Some studies suggest that elderly people with chronic diseases are more likely to commit suicide (Atchley, 1980). Male suicide rates increase steadily with age, but female suicide rates are highest at younger ages when women are most likely to have children at home, and continue to decline among women over 65 years of age.

Since 1950, suicide rates have been highest in the age group 75–84 years and have shown a steady decline among the elderly, in contrast to the trend among young adults. However, suicide rates tend to be highest in the oldest, white, male population groups (U.S. DHHS, 1982b, p. 73).

Morbidity in the Elderly

Morbidity and disability among the elderly are the major considerations of health policymakers because of the enormous increase in long-term care. This section will focus primarily on those conditions related to dependency and long-term care.

Elderly people suffer from relatively few illnesses that are unique to their age group (Estes, 1977). What makes illness more severe in the elderly is the prevalence of multiple chronic pathologies and the possibility that treatment for one disease might exacerbate the problems caused by another disease. With regard to a number of acute illnesses, for instance, elderly persons show a lower yearly incidence than younger persons (U.S. DHHS, 1982b, p. 82). Upper respiratory infections and influenza account for most of the acute illness episodes in the elderly, as in all other age groups (Estes, 1977). Injuries and digestive system conditions follow as the next most frequent cause of acute illness. However, when elderly people become acutely ill, they have more disability and restricted activity days than any other age group except children under five years old (Estes, 1977).

People 65 years and over on the whole enjoy good health. However, in a 1980 nationwide survey, 31 percent of the elderly assessed their health as being fair or poor and 45.2 percent reported some limitation of activity with the following levels of severity:

Limited, but not in major activity	6.2%
Limited in amount or kind of major activity	21.8%
Unable to carry on major activity	17.2%
(U.S. DHHS, 1982b, p. 80).	

It is important to emphasize that the age category, "65 years and over," represents a heterogeneous group, and includes people with a wide variety of physical and other characteristics, ranging from complete independence to severe disability.

Chronic and acute illnesses occur more frequently in elderly persons who are minorities, poor, have little education, live in rural areas or in inadequate housing, or who are older women. While elderly blacks and whites do not differ significantly in the number of chronic conditions, elderly blacks experience more chronic and acute diseases, more bed disability and restricted activity days, and a lower life expectancy (Taylor, 1981). Both male and female nonwhites spend almost twice as many days in bed or in restricted activities as whites; some authors contend that these measures are better indicators of health status than reports of chronic illness (Taylor, 1981). Those groups that are socially and economically vulnerable also run a higher risk of disability.

Chronic disabling conditions, defined as those disorders lasting longer than three months, are the major causes of limited activity in the elderly (Metropolitan Life Insurance Foundation, 1982). Arthritis and rheumatism cause limitations in 11.7 percent of all persons over 65 years old (Metropolitan Life Insurance Foundation, 1982). Heart conditions effect 11 percent of elderly persons. Hypertension disables 5.6 percent, and visual impairments and diabetes each limit the daily activities of 2.9 percent of the elderly. These figures indicate the extent of, and the complications resulting from, the leading forms of morbidity in the elderly.

Hospital discharge data provide indications of the amount of disease among the elderly who seek medical treatment (U.S. DHHS, 1982b, pp. 97, 98). Heart disease, malignant neoplasms, and cerebro-vascular diseases were the most frequent first-listed diagnoses among elderly males and females at hospital discharge in 1980.

Four conditions of special importance to the health and support of the elderly, because they cause dependency and often lead to institutionalization, will now be considered. They are senile dementia, incontinence, injury, and osteoporosis.

Senile dementia. Although some loss of intellectual ability may occur with normal aging, severe global impairment, termed *dementia,* occurs infrequently and reflects disease, rather than the normal aging process. It is estimated that about 10 percent of persons over 65 years old have intellectual impairment of clinical significance (National Institute on Aging [NIA] Task Force, 1980).

Prevalence rates appear consistent across population studies: four percent of those over 65 years old have a "malignant" form of senile dementia. The prevalence rises with age so that about 20 percent of those over age 80 show severe forms of senile dementia (Brody, 1982).

According to the 1977 National Nursing Home Survey, 32 percent of all nursing home residents (not just those over age 65) were chronically impaired with senile dementia, although senility was seldom the primary medical condition at their most recent examination (U.S. DHEW 1979).

The prevalence of senile dementia is greater in women than men, with onset most likely occurring in the late seventies or early eighties (Kral, 1972). Brody (1982) presents reasons why the female excess of senile dementia might be an artifact (i.e., there are more older females, females tend to visit physicians more than males, and tend to be institutionalized more at older ages). There do not seem to be racial or geographical trends (Brody, 1982). Yet, genetic predispositions to senile dementia might exist (Kral, 1972). Since more people are living to older ages, the number of people at risk of developing senile dementia will naturally also increase.

Senile dementia of the Alzheimer's type (SDAT) and multi-infarct dementia together account for about 80 percent of dementia in the elderly (NIA Task Force, 1980). SDAT is characterized by "relentlessly progressive dementia, alertness in the early stages of the disease, and a course leading to death in five to ten years . . ." That Alzheimer's disease, which has both a presenile form (onset before age 65), and a senile form (onset after age 65), is one disease entity cannot be conclusively determined from the available information (Brody, 1982). For both SDAT and Alzheimer's disease, little is known about etiology, risk factors, or epidemiologic trends (Brody, 1982).

It is important to note that SDAT may be confused with other kinds of mental impairment, some of which are presently incurable, others of which are reversible or treatable (NIA Task Force, 1980). Present indications are that 10 to 20 percent of all elderly persons with intellectual impairment actually have reversible conditions (NIA Task Force, 1980).

Senile dementia might be confused with depression, acute brain syndrome, or normal pressure hydrocephalus, since these conditions are associated with intellectual impairment (Eisdorfer and Cohen, 1978). Yet, dementia-like syndromes accompanying these conditions are often reversible. Depression, for example, is a common cause of reversible intellectual impairment (NIA Task Force, 1980). Almost any disorder that alters the internal environment, such as cardiac, pulmonary, renal, or liver failure, or endocrine disorders, might produce dementia. Acute and chronic infections may cause intellectual impairment which will be reversed upon treating the infection (Eisdorfer and Cohen, 1978). In addition, hypoglycemia, thyroid insufficiencies, pernicious anemia, and elevated calcium levels may produce reversible intellectual deterioration. Drugs, particularly sedatives, may cause cognitive dysfunction in the elderly, especially since the elderly often take multiple drugs and are sensitive to their side effects. Structural abnormalities, such as intracranial tumors, pain, sensory deprivation, and metabolic dysfunctions may produce symptoms of dementia. Such symptoms may subside when the disorder is alleviated. Dementing disorders which are clearly not reversible include senile dementia of Alzheimer's type, multi-infarct dementia, Creutzfeldt-Jakob disease, and Huntington's disease. Senile dementia is clearly a disease whose prevalence is greatest among the elderly, yet overdiagnosis, misdiagnosis, and acceptance of senile dementia as an untreatable condition increase its apparent frequency.

Incontinence. It is estimated that 3 million elderly people in the United States are incontinent (Ouslander, 1981). While this condition may result from, or accompany, different underlying problems, its primary importance lies in the fact that incontinence itself is often the main reason for institutionalization. There are currently no reliable data on the prevalence of incontinence in the United States. However, the 1977 National Nursing Home Survey provides information on the prevalence of incontinence among nursing home residents (U.S. DHEW, 1979). About two-thirds of nursing home residents with stroke, paralysis, senility, or chronic brain syndrome were incontinent. Only 54.7 percent of all nursing home residents had no difficulty in bowel or bladder control, or both, or had ostomies (U.S. DHEW, 1979, p. 45).

Factors associated with incontinence include cognitive impairment and acute illness (Ouslander, 1981). The exact correlation of cognitive impairment with incontinence is uncertain, since this observation is based mostly on institutional populations where the prevalence of senile dementia is high.

Urinary incontinence can be caused by anatomical, neurological, or acute medical conditions, which are sometimes reversible (Ouslander, 1981).

As with the symptoms of dementia, it is important from a public health standpoint to recognize that incontinence is only a symptom. The underlying causes often can be prevented, successfully treated, or perhaps controlled if adequate services are available and accessible.

Injury. Only the highlights of the epidemiology of injury will be described here because a more detailed account of this topic is given from an injury-control point of view in Chapter 3.

While injury is a serious cause of mortality in the elderly, it presents a major morbidity problem as well. Elderly people incur almost three times more days of disability in bed (299 days) due to injury each year, as compared to 6–16 year olds who constitute the second highest injury group (Hogue, 1982). In terms of the total number of days in short-stay hospitals for women 65 and older in 1980, "fractures" was the third most important first-listed diagnosis, after heart disease and malignant neoplasms (U.S. DHHS, 1982b, p. 100).

When older people fall, fractures are the most frequently treated injury and are often precipitated by an acute or chronic health problem, including misuse of alcohol (Hogue, 1982). The elderly tend to fall in environments that are new to them and have a disproportionately high hospitalization rate.

Burns also disproportionately affect the elderly (Hogue, 1982). The incidence of new burns requiring hospitalization each year is about 27 per 100,000 people. For people aged 75–79, the incidence is 28 burns per 100,000 persons; for those aged 80–84 it is 37 per 100,000 persons; and for those 85 years and older, it rises to 41 burns per 100,000 persons. Elderly people are at greater risk for infections and complications after burns than younger people with the same injuries. This might be due to the presence of other chronic illnesses or to a diminished recuperative ability. Thus, complications resulting both directly and indirectly from injuries in the elderly represent a major morbidity problem and an overwhelming proportion of health care resources.

Osteoporosis. It is estimated that about 25 percent of all white women have had one or more fractures by age 65 due to osteoporosis (Marx, 1980). Each year about 190,000 people in late middle age or older suffer from broken hips, and it is estimated that one-sixth of them die from ensuing complications. In osteoporosis, the bones lose unusually large amounts of a calcium-containing mineral that helps to give them strength. Elderly women (especially whites and Orientals) are at high risk because they have lighter bones than men, and their bone losses tend to accelerate at menopause due to decreased estrogen production. The high rate of bone loss continues for about twenty years, with an annual peak bone mass loss of between 0.5 and 1.5 percent. It results in vertebral fractures, drop falls, broken hips, pain, and costly secondary complications. This topic is also discussed more fully in Chapter 3.

Disability among the Elderly

The most striking effect of morbidity in older, as compared with younger, adults is the resulting chronic disability. Adults over age 65 in 1980 experienced 50 percent more restricted activity days per year than adults aged 45 to 64 (39.2 versus 26.5 days per year).

In public health practice, assessment of functional status is more useful than the identification of medical diagnosis, since it more clearly indicates areas where providing assistance could promote independent living (Branch, 1980). Assessment of physical functioning status is complicated by the interaction of physical, psychological, and social health, as noted by Kane and Kane (1981) in their comprehensive review of instruments that measure physical functioning in the elderly.

Several studies of functional ability among the noninstitutionalized elderly report a high prevalence of morbidity associated with a low prevalence of disability. In a study of the elderly in Massachusetts, level of dependency was based on an individual's unmet needs in activities of daily living. The presence of someone to provide social support automatically eliminated an unmet need rating. Only three to seven percent of the sample showed needs for intensive health care and social support services that were unmet. Males reporting inability to perform heavy work around the house and lack of independence in personal care showed a 15-month mortality rate that was more than twice as high as that for females at the same functional level (40% mortality compared to 17%) (Branch, 1980).

A study of the overall well-being and service needs of the community elderly in Cleveland revealed that almost all of the persons interviewed had one or more illnesses, but that two-thirds of those persons reported no limitation in their activities (U.S. General Accounting Office, 1979). Even among persons reporting that one or more illnesses interfered with their activities, over one-fifth could complete all activities of daily living without help, and fewer than one in three (among those just reporting one severely limiting illness, the figure was one in five) were completely dependent in activities of daily living

In a 1975 national study of noninstitutionalized people aged 65 and over, 14 percent of the elderly were found to be restricted in physical mobility—i.e., they were bedfast, housebound, and/or able to go outdoors only with difficulty (Shanas, 1980). Seven percent of the elderly were bedfast or housebound, including those that were confined to wheelchairs. Black women were the most restricted in activities. Black men were least restricted; only eight percent reported mobility limitation. (These statistics, like others that group the elderly into a single "aged 65 and over" category, give the overall prevalence of mobility limitations among older people, but fail to show how these limitations differ among age sub-groups.)

Major limitations in capacity for self-care were reported by 12 percent of all elderly Americans (Shanas, 1980). Level of difficulty and amount of assistance needed in three categories of mobility and three categories of personal care determined degree of limitation. Twice as many elderly blacks as whites reported limitations in capacity for self-care; the tasks which caused people the most difficulty were walking up and down stairs, and cutting their toenails. Like the Massachusetts study, this study showed a sharp decline in capacity for personal care with age. Whereas only 7 percent of 65 to 69 year olds reported major limitations, over three times as many people over age 80 were restricted in personal care activities. Women reported more major limitations than men at every age group, but in older age groups, the sex differences in restriction decreased. This trend suggests several occurrences: that women survive longer with disability than men; that diseases causing major limitations in women are not as often fatal as such diseases in men; that men and women reach a maximum level of disability before they either receive help or die.

In 1973 and 1978, the proportions of people 65 years and older reporting limitations of activity were 44.1 and 45 percent respectively (U.S. DHHS, 1980b, p. 159). It appears that there is no evidence of a relative total increase of disability despite the greater life expectancy.

As is to be expected, dependency in personal care increases with advancing age. Consequently, the proportion of people in nursing homes rises from five percent for the 65 and older age group to 10 percent for the 75 and over to 20 percent or more for the 85 and over group (U.S. DHEW, 1979, p. 28). While 14 percent of those residents in nursing homes aged 65 to 74 were independent in personal care activities (bathing, dressing, toileting, mobility, continence, and eating), fewer than five percent of every 100 persons over age 85 were independent in these areas (U.S. DHEW, 1979, Table 23). Dependency in personal care increases with age. Women need more assistance than men, which is consistent with the community survey findings of greater limitations among elderly women, and from the greater proportion of women among very old nursing home residents.

Well-Being and the Quality of Life of the Elderly

Introduction

The well-being of the elderly is dependent upon health status, functional ability, socioeconomic status, housing, and the availability of services. Well-being is also influenced by life events that are particularly common among the elderly—retirement, widowhood, and relocation, to name a few—and by past events and life style. In this section, studies on the role of psychosocial factors in predicting longevity will be reviewed. Then, the effects of life events on life satisfaction, morbidity, and mortality among the elderly will be evaluated. In most of the studies reviewed, both physical and psychosocial factors were found to predict longevity (Palmore, 1969; Bartko and Patterson, 1971; Bartko et al., 1971; Palmore, 1971; Pfeiffer, 1971; Palmore and Stone, 1973; Wingard, 1982). Satariano and Syme (1981) and Kasl and Berkman (1981) provide comprehensive reviews of studies affecting the longevity and quality of life among the elderly.

Health or functional status is consistently the strongest predictor of longevity for men and women, whether it is measured by a physician or by self-report. Yet, sex differences exist in terms of the psychosocial factors affecting longevity. Palmore (1969) found that work satisfaction was the strongest predictor of longevity in men aged 60 to 69, while physical functioning was the strongest predictor of how long women of the same age would live. In another analysis of the same sample (Palmore, 1971), work satisfaction and low levels of tobacco use were the best predictors of longevity in men aged 60 to 69 years; and physical functioning, work satisfaction, and happiness (in that order) best explained longevity in men 70 years and older. Happiness was consistently the strongest predictor of longevity among women in both age groups. This might be due to differences in social norms and work opportunities, for the sample was initially tested between 1955 and 1959 and was composed of self-selected *volunteers* aged 60 to 94.

In another study, self-health rating and intelligence test scores significantly differentiated long-lived from short-lived persons of both sexes. Education, occupation, and marital status were significant predictors of longevity among women, while financial self-evaluation and physical function rating were significant predictors among men only.

Sex differences in factors affecting longevity were also found in a recent longitudinal study that began in Alameda County, California, in 1965 (Wingard, 1982). Unlike the studies discussed above, this sample was not restricted to the elderly but contained community residents aged 30 to 69 years. Factors that significantly predicted nine-year mortality risk for men included age, physical health status, smoking history, alcohol consumption, and marital status. For women, age, physical health status, and smoking history were also important predictors, along with physical activity, contacts with friends and relatives, and life satisfaction. Only three factors—age, physical health status, and life satisfaction—significantly affected mortality in this relatively young sample. Thus, while these results are not exclusively derived from the elderly, they suggest further evidence for the effects of both behavioral and physical risk factors on longevity, and for the differential effects of these factors on women and men.

Several studies note intelligence test scores as important predictors of longevity (Jarvik and Blum, 1971; Palmore, 1971; Pfeiffer, 1971; Riegel, 1971; Cohen and Brody, 1981). Other psychological factors, such as mental status (Bartko and Patterson, 1971) and happiness (Palmore, 1971) are shown to affect longevity. In several studies showing significant effects of psychological variables, health status appears to be the main predictor of longevity and, indeed, might be a major determinant of mental status. The importance of psychological factors should thus be viewed in the context of other study variables and study sample characteristics.

The overall generalizability of these studies is limited. Most used homogeneous, volunteer samples. Minorities, women, and a range of socioeconomic groups were seldom represented. In most cases, these longitudinal studies began in the 1950s and 1960s. Independent variables to predict longevity were measured at that time. Since then, health care and personal health practices have changed; a great emphasis on healthier life styles at all ages has occurred. More studies are needed to evaluate current psychosocial and behavioral factors that might affect longevity in today's elderly, although Cohen and Brody (1981) assert that most cultural, social, and psychological processes affecting survival probably began early in life. Studies assessing further racial and sex differences in longevity, as well as the effects of different psychosocial factors (type A personality, intelligence, and depression) would shed more light on the role of subjective factors in longevity.

Life Satisfaction

Assessing life satisfaction is a global evaluation of how closely one has come to achieving one's goals. With regard to the elderly, life satisfaction is an inherent feature of quality of life, but it is probably influenced less by events that are prevalent among the elderly than by factors determined earlier in life. The link between life satisfaction and longevity, then, might represent the influence of another factor affecting life span. But the central position of life satisfaction in defining the well-being of the elderly provides a route toward explaining the variations in their psychological well-being.

George and Bearon (1980) warn that the concept of life satisfaction is ambiguous, and that methodological problems in selecting measurement tools may compromise the findings and generalizability of studies.

A review of studies on life satisfaction in the elderly shows a consistent impact of certain factors. Income and health are the strongest correlates of life satisfaction (Edwards and Klemmack, 1973; Markides and Martin, 1979; Elwell and Maltbie-Crannell, 1981; Liang, 1982). Others report that health alone is the best predictor (Palmore and Luikart, 1972). Many investigators observe no sex differences in life satisfaction in the elderly (Palmore and Luikart, 1972; Dressler, 1973; Edwards and Klemmack, 1973; Linn et al., 1979; Liang, 1982) although one might expect lower life satisfaction in elderly women due to their increased morbidity and functional disability. Significant race or cultural variation exists in life satisfaction (Linn et al., 1979; Elwell and Maltbie-Crannel, 1981). Linn et al. (1979) attribute the significant race/cultural differences in adjustment partly to cultural integration of the aged and to "transplant shock."

Another culture phenomenon that affects life satisfaction is role loss in the elderly. Elwell and Maltbie-Crannell (1981) found that role loss had a significant negative impact on the life satisfaction of elderly men, and a significant but weaker effect on life satisfaction in elderly women.

These studies of life satisfaction suffer from two major deficiencies. First, they are *cross sectional* and thus have limited predictive value. While the findings may show strong correlations between life satisfaction and other variables, they do not prove causation. Secondly, the data tend to be self-reported and therefore subject to selective recall or selective responses. Linn et al., (1979) suggest that their findings of race differences might result from racial differences in admitting to feelings of depression or low life satisfaction. Palmore and Luikart (1972) note that their measure of self-reported health was conceptually similar to their measure of life satisfaction, and since individuals tend to respond in the same way to a stimulus over time, the high correlation between these two variables might result partially from the measurement tools. Nonetheless, many of these studies include large numbers of subjects representing a range of health and socioeconomic characteristics and provide insight into factors that are highly related to the quality of life in the elderly today.

Retirement

Retirement is, by far, the most common event that exclusively affects the elderly. In essence, it is the *rite-de-passage* from "middle age" to "old age," complete with changes in social and working role, financial power, and social entitlements. It ranks among the ten most stressful events in the Holmes and Rahe Social Readjustment Rating Scale (Holmes and Rahe, 1967). Certain factors predispose people to positive anticipation of retirement, such as better planning for retirement, voluntary retirement, and better adjustment to retirement in terms of health, morale, life satisfaction, and activity level indices. Career experience preceding retirement influences adjustment, although this is partly due to studies evaluating adjustment differences by employment group. Other factors that cause variations in adjustment to retirement include health, income, and the economy at time of retirement.

Major studies on factors affecting adjustment to retirement are largely cross-sectional and focus either on satisfaction with retirement based on occupational status, or on correlates of satisfaction in retirement. Few include women since it has been assumed that retirement from paid jobs had little effect on women due to their deeper involvement in family roles. Studies evaluating adjustment based on occupational prestige and meaning of work are confounded by a variety of factors such as age, income, socioeconomic status, health, and social support networks. Their generalizability to other working populations is questionable. For example, Havighurst et al. (1979) studied retired male social scientists while Holahan (1981) assessed retirement adjustment in older gifted women. Many of these studies are based on volunteer samples, or responses to mailed questionnaires, both of which limit generalizability.

Nevertheless, several trends emerge. Timing of retirement is related to subsequent adjustment (Barfield and Morgan, 1978; Price et al., 1979; Haynes et al., 1980). The fact that health status is a significant predictive factor in each of these studies underscores the influence of health status in the decision to retire and thus in subsequent adjustment. Health status is a strong predictor of retirement adaptation in other studies (Atchley, 1976; Schmitt et al., 1979), as well as a confounder of study results (Back and Guptill, 1966; Simpson et al., 1966a, 1966b; Bengtson et al., 1969; Jaslow, 1976; Fox, 1977; Holahan, 1981; Schnore and Kirkland, 1981).

Work orientation has been found to influence adjustment to retirement by some investigators (Stokes and Maddox, 1967; Schmitt et al., 1979; Holahan, 1981), and to have no impact at all by others (Schnore and Kirkland, 1981). The three studies that reported an influence due to work orientation were based on quite diverse study populations: Stokes and Maddox looked at white-collar, middle status, and semi-skilled male volunteers from Durham, North Carolina; Schmitt sampled male and female retirees from the Michigan Civil Service; Holahan studied gifted older women. The consistency of work orientation predicting retirement adjustment across these samples lends credence to its impact. By contrast, the Schnore and Kirkland sample was small, and their finding of professional/nonprofessional differences in retirement adjustment might have masked underlying work orientation differences.

Activity level is positively related both to morale and life satisfaction in retirement and to career status (Back and Guptill, 1966; Simpson et al., 1966a, 1966b; Bengtson et al., 1969; Holahan, 1981). Bengtson, et al. found differences in the type of activities that retired male school teachers and steelworkers engaged in, but concluded that degree of involvement in activities was what influenced life satisfaction. Similarly, Holahan found that retired female career workers maintained greater involvement in activities than retired job holders, and were more likely to report high life satisfaction. Again, health is an important determinant of activity level, and hence a possible confounder of this effect as well.

Only one study reported sex differences in adjustment to retirement (Atchley, 1976). In comparing adjustment levels in retired male and female teachers and telephone company employees, Atchley found that men tended to adjust more quickly to retirement and tended to show better health and psychological well-being than women. This observation, however, does not account for prior psychological or physical health status in women, nor for sex differences in employment status.

The few studies that looked exclusively at women (Jaslow, 1976; Fox, 1977; Holahan, 1981) basically support the findings of studies done on men. Employment and activity level contribute to higher levels of life satisfaction and morale in older women. Women in higher status careers have higher levels of life satisfaction than do job holders or housewives. Marital status and income tend to confound these results, suggesting that type of job might not be as influential as financial constraints or role overload. Health and age are confounders in two of the studies (Jaslow, 1976; Fox, 1977) that found higher morale in currently working women compared to nonworking women. Since these factors affect life satisfaction and retirement adaptation in men, too, the argument for excluding women from retirement adjustment studies seems unfounded.

In short, few studies have looked at race and sex differences in adjustment to retirement. Perhaps this is unnecessary since the major factors determining adjustment to retirement are health status and income. Since these are the basic determinants of life satisfaction, perhaps retirement is not as stressful or as important as we have assumed. Future studies on career characteristics and psychological traits might shed more light on remediable factors affecting adjustment, and might provide more specific information about the basic effects of career status on retirement adjustment.

Relocation

Relocation is another event that commonly affects the elderly. While relocation of the elderly in general is seen as a detrimental change (Rowland, 1977), comparison of studies indicates that psychological factors, the type of relocation (i.e., voluntary versus involuntary), and the contrast between pre- and post-relocation environments influence responses to relocation. Kasl (1977) points out that relocation brings about changes not simply in one's residential environment but in many other known and unknown factors. Among all age groups, he states, the elderly are most vulnerable to the adverse effects of involuntary relocation. In particular, the move means a disruption of existing social networks, and perhaps a financial hardship due to already precarious economic conditions.

Theories accounting for the increased morbidity, mortality, and dissatisfaction seen in relocated elderly basically rest on the psychological implications of voluntary versus involuntary relocation. Schulz and Brenner (1977) assert that perceived predictability and controllability of the events surrounding a move, and the differences in controllability between the pre- and post-relocation environments affect an elderly person's adjustment. Kasl (1972) suggests that unfavorable consequences of relocation might result from a clustering of life changes, or object loss leading to feelings of hopelessness and helplessness. Many authors view relocation as a stressful life event that should be mediated by factors that typically modify such circumstances (Jasnau, 1967; Rowland, 1977; Schulz and Brenner, 1977).

Studies find both beneficial and unfavorable outcomes of relocation that seem to be due to several factors such as whether the move is voluntary or involuntary; how the relocatee perceived his/her new environment compared to his previous home; the type of preparation involved; and whether the move was from a home to an institution, intrainstitutional, or from a home to a home. Characteristics of the relocatees also influence their adjustment to the move. However, no consistently predictable trends exist for any of these factors.

Several studies comparing the death rates of institutionalized relocatees to those of institutionalized controls show a significantly higher mortality rate among the relocatees (Killian, 1970; Pablo, 1977). Aldrich and Mendkoff (1963) similarly found a higher than expected mortality rate after one year in residents transferred from one nursing home to another. Jasnau (1967) observed a higher death rate in institutional elderly who relocated en masse, but a lower death rate in those who were individually transferred to different nursing homes. Other studies show no differences in mortality due to intrainstitutional relocation (Ogren and Linn, 1971; Zweig and Csank, 1975), or between community residents who moved to housing for the elderly compared to those who remained in their old neighborhoods (Lawton and Yaffe, 1970; Wittels and Botwinick, 1974). Beneficial effects, indicated by lower mortality rates among relocated nursing home residents (Borup et al., 1979), higher stamina and functioning levels in relocated nursing home residents (Borup et al., 1980), and higher morale and satisfaction in relocated community elderly (Lawton and Cohen, 1974) can also result.

Typically, voluntary relocation brings about changes for the better (Carp, 1977; Lawton and Cohen, 1974; and Wittels and Botwinick, 1974), whereas involuntary moves are detrimental (Brand and Smith, 1974). Lawton and Yaffe (1970) found no significant change in community elderly who voluntarily moved to housing for the elderly. The issue of voluntary versus involuntary relocation simultaneously covers the issue of how environmental change affects adjustment. Most of the relocatees in Carp's (1977) eight-year follow-up study had moved from "substandard housing which was also socially isolating" to modern apartments; their consistently better ratings of health, activities, and mortality when compared to controls might be a result of an improved environment. Pino et al. (1978) found that nursing home transferees fared better than community residents who moved to the same nursing homes; this lends support to the theory that environmental congruence promotes better adaptation than environmental change.

Pino et al. (1978) also reported that mortality rates were somewhat (though not to a statistically significant degree) lower in prepared relocatees nine months following the move compared to unprepared transferees. Prepared residents showed slightly (but not significantly) smaller declines in performance of activities of daily living and mental alertness, but no significant difference in life satisfaction following the move. Zweig and Csank (1975) point to a lower mortality rate in prepared relocated nursing home patients compared to the mortality rate in that nursing home for the previous year as support for preparation programs. However, the mortality rate in relocatees does not differ significantly from the nursing home death rate in the second and third year before that. Rather than concluding beneficial effects of a relocation preparation program, the higher than usual death rate in the year prior to the study year should be questioned. Borup et al. (1980) similarly conclude from a review of the literature that preparation programs have no effect on post-relocation mortality rates. However, Bourestom and Pastalan (1981) cite other studies that show beneficial effects of preparation programs.

Besides environmental factors, individual factors affect adjustment to relocation. Physical status, degree of independence in activities of daily living, and mental status were significant predictors of relocation adjustment (Markus et al., 1972), as were personality and psychological traits (Aldrich and Mendkoff, 1963; Turner et al., 1972). Aldrich and Mendkoff found that relocated psychotics had the highest mortality rates during the year following transfer from one nursing home to another. Residents who responded to the news of relocation with denial, depression, or regression fared worse than others. People in poor health had significantly more negative reactions to enforced relocation in the community compared with those in good health (Brand and Smith, 1974). Some investigators find higher mortality in males than females following relocation (Markus et al., 1972; Pablo, 1977), while others find lower life satisfaction among females than males (Brand and Smith, 1974). Likewise, age is an inconsistent predictor; Markus et al. (1972) found that age was not a significant factor in adjustment to relocation, while Killian (1970) disagreed. In one study (Borup et al., 1979), the relocated group was younger than the control group, and in fact experienced fewer deaths; age might have accounted for these results. Unfortunately, other studies did not analyze these demographic factors, thus preventing definite conclusions of their role in relocation of the elderly.

Other deficiencies of these studies to date include a lack of pre-relocation data and lack of comparison groups. The effects of relocation cannot easily be separated from the effects of the environment. Furthermore, selective factors may determine who will or will not move. Kasl (1972) wrote that the "most convincing evidence" of the detrimental effects of relocation were those on institutionalized samples. Studies since that time have opened more areas of doubt. Kasl's recommendations for future research still hold: prospective studies are needed to determine effects of factors at several stages of relocation, from the decision-making process to the stage of anticipation of change to the short-term adaptation stages. More interdisciplinary studies are needed to measure bio-chemical and psychological health variables.

Widowhood

Demographic projections show that more people will be widowed in their later years and that greater numbers of elderly widows will be living to older ages. Whether widowhood has a different effect on the elderly than the young, and whether there are differential effects among the elderly is therefore of interest. While many investigators point to adverse results of widowhood (Helsing and Szklo, 1980; Parkes et al., 1969; Ward, 1976), others suggest that the elderly are not significantly affected by the loss of a spouse (Heyman and Gianturco, 1974; Palmore and Stone, 1973). Studies have tended to focus on the effects of widowhood on young people, in particular on their increased risk of mortality.

Susser (1981) cautions that studies on marital status and health may be confounded by selection bias, for the healthy are more likely than the unhealthy to remarry, and males are more likely than females to remarry due to the sex differential in survivorship. Age can confound the results of these studies. Among older adults, those who are married are generally younger than those who are not married. Few studies contrast the adjustment of elderly and younger spouses, and there is a lack of overall concurrence on sex differences and length of time needed to adjust to widowhood.

In a pilot study on the effects of bereavement on the activities, attitudes, psychiatric, and physical health of older people, Heyman and Gianturco (1974) found very few changes due to widowhood. Their sample of 14 male and 27 female volunteers over 65 years old showed no change in health, activities, or social workers' ratings of happiness and adjustment. Depressive feelings increased in women, as did a feeling of uselessness. Men showed a significant decline in work attitudes. Yet, in general, the subjects adapted "reasonably well" to widowhood. The authors suggest that factors accounting for this easy adjustment might be the stability of the subjects' daily lives, the relatively advanced age at which they became widowed, and minimal family responsibilities (Heyman and Gianturco, 1973).

Studies focusing on mortality trends in the bereaved show a

range of effects. A study of white persons aged 18 years and older in Washington County, Maryland, who became widowed between 1963 and 1974, found significantly higher mortality rates in widowed males than in married males, but no significant differences in mortality between widowed and married females (Helsing and Szklo, 1980). Widowed males aged 55 to 64 and 65 to 74 showed the most significant differences in mortality compared to married males the same age. Another study of age- and sex-matched widowhood and married people found no differences in mortality rates after one year of widowhood (Clayton, 1974). A study of the spouses of cancer victims showed a higher than expected but not statistically significant mortality rate in women (Ward, 1976). In this sample, significantly more widowers died within the first six months of bereavement. This supports other studies (Parkes et al., 1969) that find higher than expected mortality rates among older men during the first six months of widowhood. No conclusive evidence from mortality studies supports the bereavement-stress theory among the elderly.

However, other indications of stress and unhappiness have been found. At one year after widowhood, bereaved subjects reported significantly more depression, crying, psychological symptoms, and auditory and visual hallucinations than married controls (Clayton, 1974). Heyman and Gianturco (1973) found an increase in depression among widowed women. Since few, if any, studies have measured depressive symptoms before and after widowhood, or have compared widowed and matched married controls on physical and mental health variables, these findings can only be interpreted in reference to these samples.

An interesting finding related in the ameliorative effects of factors during bereavement is that widowed males who remarried showed significantly lower mortality rates than married males (Helsing et al., 1981). Change in marital status did not affect the mortality rates of widowed females. For both sexes, a move into a nursing home, retirement home, or chronic care facility following loss of a spouse resulted in higher mortality than other residential change or no change at all (although factors predisposing those widows to mortality might have led to their nursing home placement). Moreover, widows living alone experienced higher death rates than those living with another person in the household. Thus, certain factors appear associated with a better quality of life following widowhood in the elderly.

These studies, nevertheless, present various problems and

leave several questions unanswered. More conclusive information is needed on the pre-mortality effects of widowhood in the elderly as well as the possibility of sex differences in bereavement.

Social Support

The quality and quantity of social relations are recognized as important determinants of well-being, health, and even mortality. This connection is especially strong for the elderly because of the high prevalence of dependency among them. More on this topic will be stated in Chapter 5.

Social support serves as protection against the adverse health effects of stressful events throughout life (Cobb, 1976). It facilitates adaptation to changes and crises ranging from pregnancy to hospitalization to job loss. Since the elderly experience a greater number of stressful life events and losses than other age groups (retirement, widowhood, loss of friends, health problems, to name a few), the existence of social supports should clearly influence their quality of life. Only a few studies will be cited here to illustrate the importance of social support for the elderly.

Berkman and Syme (1979) linked social support to mortality in adults. Evaluation of the nine-year mortality rate of a sample of adults in Alameda County showed significantly fewer deaths among people with large social networks. This inverse relationship between social network and mortality held even when controlling for health status, and health practices known to increase mortality (smoking, obesity, alcohol consumption, and physical activity).

Social support from family members can prevent institutionalization of dependent elderly relatives (Shanas, 1979). Data from the 1975 National Survey of Noninstitutionalized Community Elderly show that an elderly person's spouse and a child living in the household are the major sources of help in time of illness (Shanas, 1979).

Findings from two longitudinal studies that assessed risk factors leading to institutionalization among the elderly also show the protective effects of social support; Vincente et al. (1979) report that married persons are least likely to go into long-term care facilities before they die, whereas persons living alone or in households with just one other member are most likely to be institutionalized. Palmore (1976) found that the risk of institutionalization was greatest among persons who were living alone, who were never married or separated from their spouse, or who had no living children.

Whether the presence of relatives fulfills psychological needs, or fails to meet needs that the elderly person considers important, is not addressed by these studies. Nor is the issue of whether social support and life satisfaction increase with larger numbers of family helpers. Rather, the more basic caretaking aspects of social support are presented.

Recently, investigators have questioned the assumption that social support is a unidimensional entity (Blazer, 1982; Hogue and Gorton, 1981). Blazer (1982) proposed a three-parameter model of social support. Its components include roles and available role attachments, perceived social support, and frequency of social interaction. Hogue and Gorton (1981) differentiate social support from social network, stating that social network is the quantitative characteristic of an individual's social and community ties whereas social support is the psychological characteristic of an individual's social network. A comparison of elderly retired women and elderly women who had not recently worked showed that social support, not social network size, influenced morale. Both of these studies separate the objective and subjective aspects of social support, and suggest that the subjective part is the key health promotive factor. Blazer (1982) hypothesized that social support may influence health in a variety of ways but always through the mechanism of perception of social support.

The studies on social support among the elderly thus show two things: they exemplify the beneficial aspects of social support in terms of lower mortality, lower institutionalization, and higher morale; and they substantiate the new theories of the multidimensional nature of social support.

These studies lack comparative information on the role of social supports among different subpopulations of the elderly, such as different ethnic groups, widowed people, and elderly with varying health care needs. The findings should be cautiously interpreted at present.

The abuse and neglect of the elderly is another aspect of interpersonal relations. Ill treatment of old people has probably been prevalent for a long time but only recently has it become a matter for public concern and study. Much of the current literature is anecdotal and exploratory (Cazenave, 1979; Hickey and Douglass, 1981; Phillips, 1983; Salend et al., 1984). Neglect (such as withholding medication, food, or companionship) is reported more often than abuse (such as psychological, verbal or physical abuse, financial exploitation, or violation of personal rights), but much underreporting is suspected (Salend et al., 1984). Clearly, the prevalence of abuse and neglect in the community is a significant factor in determining the health of the older population.

Conclusion

Although there are many epidemiological questions yet to ask and answer, we are already beginning to benefit from our growing knowledge of the distribution and determinants of health and disease in the older population. For example, a direct outcome of epidemiological findings is the dramatic decline in heart disease and stroke in the last four decades. However, just as there is much more to be learned about the epidemiology of aging, there is much further potential for its application in public health practice. Epidemiology should continue to serve as the scientific basis for effective public interventions in the promotion of health and control of disability in the aging population.

References

Aldrich, C. K. and Mendkoff, E. Relocation of the aged and disabled: a mortality study. *Journal of the American Geriatrics Society*, 1963, *11*, 185–194.

Atchley, R. C. Aging and suicide: reflection of the quality of life? In S. G. Haynes and M. Feinleib (Eds.), *Second Conference on the Epidemiology of Aging*. Bethesda, Md.: U.S. Department of Health and Human Services, 1980, pp. 141–161.

Atchley, R. C. Selected social and psychological differences between men and women in later life. *Journal of Gerontology*, 1976, *31*, 204–211.

Back, K. W. and Guptill, C. S. Retirement and self-ratings. In I. H. Simpson and J. C. McKinney (Eds.), *Social Aspects of Aging*. Durham, N.C.: Duke University Press, 1966, pp. 120–129.

Barfield, R. E. and Morgan, J. N. Trends in satisfaction with retirement. *The Gerontologist*, 1978, *18*, 19–23.

Bartko, J. J. and Patterson, R. D. Survival among healthy old men: a multivariate analysis. In S. Granick and R. D. Patterson (eds.), *Human Aging II, An Eleven-Year Follow-Up Biomedical and Behavioral Study*. Rockville, Md.: U.S. Department of Health, Education and Welfare, 1971, pp. 105–117.

Bartko, J. J., Patterson, R. D., and Butler, R. N. Biomedical and behavioral predictors of survival among normal aged men: a multivariate analysis. In E. Palmore and F. C. Jeffers (Eds.), *Prediction of Life Span*. Lexington, Ma.: D.C. Heath and Co., 1971, pp. 123–137.

Bengtson, V. L., Chiroboga, D. A., and Keller, A. B. Occupational differences in retirement: patterns of role activity and life outlook among Chicago teachers and steelworkers. In R. J. Havighurst, Munichs, J. M. A., Neugarten, B., and Thomae, H. (Eds.), *Adjustment to Retirement, A Cross-National Study*. Assen, The Netherlands: Konin-klijke Van Gorwin and Company, 1969, pp. 53–70.

Berkman, L. F. and Syme, S. L. Social networks, host resistance, and mortality: a nine-year follow-up study of Alameda County residents. *American Journal of Epidemiology*, 1979, *109*, 186–204.

Blazer, D. G. Social support and mortality in an elderly community population. *American Journal of Epidemiology*, 1982, *115*, 684–694.

Borup, J. L. H., Gallego, D. T., and Heffernan, P. G. Relocation and its effect on mortality. *The Gerontologist*, 1979, *19*, 135–140.

Borup, J. L. H., Gallego, D. T., and Heffernan, P. G. Relocation: its effect on health, functioning, and mortality. *The Gerontologist*, 1980, *20*, 468–479.

Bourestom, N. and Pastalan, L. The effects of relocation on the elderly: a reply to Borup, J. H., Gallego, D. T., and Heffernan, P. G. *The Gerontologist*, 1981, *21*, 4–7.

Branch, L. G. Functional abilities of the elderly: an update on the Massachusetts health care panel study. In S. G. Haynes and M. Feinleib (Eds.), *Second Conference on the Epidemiology of Aging*. Bethesda, Md.: U.S. Department of Health and Human Services, 1980, pp. 237–285.

Brand, F. N. and Smith, R. T. Life adjustment and relocation of the elderly. *Journal of Gerontology*, 1974, *29*, 336–340.

Brody, J. A. An epidemiologist views senile dementia—facts and fragments. *American Journal of Epidemiology*, 1982, *115*, 155–162.

Carp, F. M. Impact of improved living environment on health and life expectancy. *The Gerontologist*, 1977, *17*, 242–249.

Cazenave N. A. Family violence and aging blacks: theoretical perspectives and research possibilities. *Journal of Minority Aging*, 1979, *4*, 99–108.

Clayton, P. J. Mortality and morbidity in the first year of widowhood. *Archives of General Psychiatry*, 1974, *30*, 747–750.

Cobb, S. Presidential Address—1976: social support as a moderator of life stress. *Psychosomatic Medicine*, 1976, *38*, 300–314.

Cohen, J. B. and Brody, J. A. The epidemiologic importance of psychosocial factors in longevity. *American Journal of Epidemiology*, 1981, *114*, 451–461.

Dressler, D. M. Life adjustment of retired couples. *International Journal of Aging and Human Development*, 1973, *4*, 335–349.

Edwards, J. N. and Klemmack, D. Z. Correlates of life satisfaction: a re-examination. *Journal of Gerontology,* 1973, *28,* 497–502.

Eisdorfer, C. and Cohen, D. The cognitively impaired elderly: differential diagnosis. In M. Storandt, I. C. Siegler, and M. F. Elias (Eds.), *The Clinical Psychology of Aging.* New York, N.Y.: Plenum Press, 1978, pp. 7–42.

Elwell, F. and Maltbie-Crannell, A. D. The impact of role loss upon coping resources and life satisfaction of the elderly. *Journal of Gerontology,* 1981, *36,* 223–232.

Estes, Jr., E. H. Health experience in the elderly. In E. W. Busse and E. Pfeiffer (Eds.), *Behavior and Adaption in Late Life.* Boston: Little, Brown and Company, 1977, pp. 115–128.

Fingerhut, L. A. and Rosenberg, H. M. Mortality among the elderly. In Health, United States, 1981. DHHS Publication No. (PHS) 82–1232. Washington, D.C.: U.S. Government Printing Office, December, 1981.

Fox, J. H. Effects of retirement and former work life on women's adaptation in old age. *Journal of Gerontology,* 1977, *32,* 196–202.

George, L. K. and Bearon, L. B. *Quality of life in older persons, meaning and measurement.* New York, N.Y.: Human Sciences Press, Inc., 1980.

Havighurst, R. J., McDonald, W. J., Maevlen, L., and Mazel, J. Male social scientists: lives after sixty. *The Gerontologist,* 1979, *19,* 55–60.

Havlik, Richard J. and Feinleib, M. *Proceedings of the Conferences on the Decline in Coronary Heart Disease Mortality.* Bethesda, Md.: National Institutes of Health, 1979.

Haynes, S. G., McMichael, A. J., and Tyroler, H. A. Survival after early and normal retirement. In S. G. Haynes and M. Feinleib (Eds.), *Second Conference on the Epidemiology of Aging.* Bethesda, Md.: U.S. Department of Health and Human Services, 1980, pp. 187–209.

Helsing, K. J. and Szklo, M. Mortality after bereavement. *American Journal of Epidemiology,* 1980, *114,* 41–52.

Helsing, K. J., Szklo, M., and Comstock, G. W. Factors associated with mortality after widowhood. *American Journal of Public Health,* 1981, *71,* 802–809.

Heyman, D. K. and Gianturco, D. T. Long-term adaptation by the elderly to bereavement. *Journal of Gerontology,* 1973, *28,* 359–362.

Heyman, D. K. and Gianturco, D. T. Long-term adaptation by the elderly to bereavement. In E. Palmore (Ed.), *Normal Aging II.* Durham, N.C.: Duke University Press, 1974, pp. 180–185.

Hickey, T. and Douglass R. L. Neglect and abuse of older family members: professionals' perspectives and case experiences. *The Gerontologist,* 1981, *21,* 171–176.

Hogue, C. C. Injury in late life: epidemiology. *Journal of the American Geriatrics Society,* 1982, *30,* 183–190.

Hogue, C. C. and Gorton, T. A. Social support and morale of older women.

Paper prepared for presentation at the XII International Congress of Gerontology, Hamburg, Federal Republic of Germany, July, 1981.

Holahan, C. K. Lifetime achievement patterns, retirement, and life satisfaction of gifted aged women. *Journal of Gerontology*, 1981, *36*, 741–749.

Holmes, T. H. and Rahe, R. H. The social readjustment rating scale. *Journal of Psychosomatic Research*, 1967, *11*, 213–218.

Jarvik, L. F. and Blum, J. E. Cognitive declines as predictors of mortality in twin pairs: a twenty-year longitudinal study of aging. In E. Palmore and F. C. Jeffers (Eds.), *Prediction of Life Span*. Lexington, Ma.: D.C. Heath and Co., 1971, pp. 199–211.

Jaslow, P. Employment, retirement, and morale among older women. *Journal of Gerontology*, 1976, *31*, 212–218.

Jasnau, K. F. Individual versus mass tranfer of nonpsychotic geriatric patients from mental hospitals to nursing homes, with special reference to the death rate. *Journal of the American Geriatrics Society*, 1967, *15*, 280–284.

Kane, R. A. and Kane, R. L. *Assessing the Elderly. A Practical Guide to Measurement*. Lexington, Ma.: Lexington Books, 1981.

Kasl, S. V. Physical and mental health effects of involuntary relocation and institutionalization on the elderly: a review. *American Journal of Public Health*, 1972, *3*, 377–383.

Kasl, S. V. The effects of the residential environment on health and behavior: a review. In L. E. Hinkle, Jr. and W. C. Loring (Eds.), *The Effect of the Man-made Environment on Health and Behavior*. Atlanta, Ga.: U.S. Department of Health, Education, and Welfare, 1977, pp. 65–127.

Kasl, S. V. and Berkman, L. F. Some psychosocial influences on the health status of the elderly: The perspective of social epidemiology. In J. L. McGaugh and S. B. Kiesler (Eds.), *Aging, Biology and Behavior*. New York, N.Y.: Academic Press, Inc., 1981, pp. 345–385.

Killian, E. Effect of geriatric transfers on mortality rates. *Social Work*, 1970, *15*, 19–26.

Kral, V. A. Senile dementia and normal aging. *Canadian Psychiatric Association Journal*, 1972, *17*, SS25–SS30.

Lawton, M. P. and Cohen, J. The generality of housing impact on the well-being of older people. *Journal of Gerontology*, 1974, *29*, 194–204.

Lawton, M. P. and Yaffe, S. Mortality, morbidity, and voluntary change of residence by older people. *Journal of the American Geriatrics Society*, 1970, *18*, 823–831.

Liang, J. Sex differences in life satisfaction among the elderly. *Journal of Gerontology*, 1982, *37*, 100–108.

Linn, M. W., Hunter, K. I., and Perry, P. R. Differences by sex and ethnicity in the psychosocial adjustment in the elderly. *Journal of Health and Social Behavior*, 1979, *20*, 273–281.

Markides, K. S. and Martin, H. W. A causal model of life satisfaction among the elderly. *Journal of Gerontology,* 1979, *34,* 86–93.

Markus, E., Blenkner, M., and Downs, T. Some factors and their association with post-relocation mortality among institutionalized aged persons. *Journal of Gerontology,* 1972, *27,* 376–382.

Marx, J. L. Osteoporosis: new help for thinning bones. *Science,* 1980, *207,* 628–630.

Metropolitan Life Insurance Foundation, *Statistical Bulletin,* Jan.–Mar., 1982.

National Institute on Aging Task Force. Senility reconsidered. Treatment possibilities for mental impairment of the elderly. *Journal of the American Medical Association,* 1980, *244,* 259–263.

Ogren, E. H. and Linn, M. W. Male nursing home patients: relocation and mortality. *Journal of the American Geriatrics Society,* 1971, *19,* 229–239.

Ouslander, J. G. Urinary incontinence in the elderly. *The Western Journal of Medicine,* 1981, *135,* 482–491.

Pablo, R. Y. Intra-institutional relocation: its impact on long-term care patients. *The Gerontologist,* 1977, *17,* 426–435.

Palmore, E. B. Physical, mental, and social factors in predicting longevity. *The Gerontologist,* 1969, *9,* 103–108.

Palmore, E. The relative importance of social factors in predicting longevity. In E. Palmore and F. C. Jeffers (Eds.), *Prediction of Life Span.* Lexington, Ma.: D. C. Heath and Co., 1971, pp. 237–247.

Palmore, E. Total chance of institutionalization among the aged. *The Gerontologist,* 1976, *16,* 504–507.

Palmore, E. and Luikart, C. Health and social factors related to life satisfaction. *Journal of Health and Social Behavior,* 1972, *13,* 68–80.

Palmore, E. and Stone, V. Predictors of longevity: a follow-up of the aged in Chapel Hill. *The Gerontologist,* 1973, *13,* 88–90.

Parkes, C. M., Benjamin, B., and Fitzgerald, R. G. Broken heart: a statistical study of increased mortality among widowers. *British Medical Journal,* 1969, *1,* 740–743.

Pfeiffer, E. Physical, psychological, and social correlates of survival in old age. In E. Palmore and F. C. Jeffers (Eds.), *Prediction of Life Span.* Lexington, Ma.: D. C. Heath and Co., 1971, pp. 223–236.

Phillips, L. R. Abuse and neglect of the frail elderly at home—an exploration of theoretical relationships. *Journal of Advanced Nursing,* 1983, *8,* 379–392.

Pino, C. J., Rosica, L. M., and Carter, J. J. The differential effects of relocation on nursing home patients. *The Gerontologist,* 1978, *18,* 167–172.

Price, K., Walker, J. W., and Kimmel, D. C. Retirement timing and retirement satisfaction. *Aging and Work,* 1979, *2,* 235–245.

Riegel, K. F. The prediction of death and longevity in longitudinal research. In E. Palmore and F. C. Jeffers (Eds.), *Prediction of Life Span.* Lexington, Ma.: D. C. Heath and Co., 1971, pp. 139–152.

Rowland, K. F. Environmental events predicting death for the elderly. *Psychological Bulletin,* 1977, *84,* 349–372.

Salend, E., Kane, R. A., Satz, M., and Pynoos J. Elder abuse reporting: limitations of statutes. *The Gerontologist,* 1984, *24,* 61–69.

Satariano, W. A. and Syme, S. L. Life changes and diseases in elderly populations: coping with change. In J. L. McGaugh and S. B. Kiesler (Eds.), *Aging, Biology and Behavior.* New York, N.Y.: Academic Press, 1981, pp. 311–327.

Schmitt, N., White, J. K., Coyle, B. W., and Rauschenberger, J. Retirement and life satisfaction. *Academy for Management Journal,* 1979, *22,* 282–291.

Schnore, M. M. and Kirkland, J. B. Sex differences in adjustment to retirement. Paper presented at the joint meetings of the Canadian Association on Gerontology and the Gerontological Society of America. Toronto, Canada, Nov., 1981.

Schulz, R. and Brenner, G. Relocation of the aged: a review and theoretical analysis. *Journal of Gerontology,* 1977, *32,* 323–333.

Shanas, E. The family as a social support system in old age. *The Gerontologist,* 1979, *19,* 169–174.

Shanas, E. Self-assessment of physical function: white and black elderly in the United States. In S. G. Haynes and M. Feinleib (Eds.), *Second Conference on the Epidemiology of Aging.* Bethesda, Md.: U.S. Department of Health and Human Services, 1980, pp. 269–285.

Siegel, J. Recent and prospective demographic trends for the elderly population and some implications for health care. In S. G. Haynes and M. Feinleib (Eds.), *Second Conference on the Epidemiology of Aging.* Bethesda, Md.: U.S. Department of Health and Human Services, 1980, pp. 289–315.

Simpson, I. H., Back, K. W., and McKinney, J. C. Attributes of work, involvement in society, and self-evaluation in retirement. In I. H. Simpson and J. C. McKinney (Eds.), *Social Aspects of Aging.* Durham, N.C.: Duke University Press, 1966a, pp. 55–75.

Simpson, I. H., Back, K. W., And McKinney, J. C. Orientations toward work and retirement, and self-evaluation in retirement. In I. H. Simpson and J. C. McKinney (Eds.), *Social Aspects of Aging.* Durham, N.C.: Duke University Press, 1966b, pp. 75–89.

Stokes, R. G. and Maddox, G. L. Some social factors on retirement adaptation. *Journal of Gerontology,* 1967, *22,* 329–333.

Susser, M. Widowhood: a situational life stress or a stressful life event? *American Journal of Public Health,* 1981, *71,* 793–795.

Taylor, R. J. The impact of federal health care policy on the elderly poor:

the special case of the black elderly. In *Policy Issues for the Elderly Poor*. Community Services Administration Office of Policy, Planning, and Evaluation. CSA Pamphlet 6172-8, 1981, pp. 65–73.

Turner, B., Tobin, S., and Lieberman, M. A. Personality traits as predictors of institutional adaptation among the aged. *Journal of Gerontology*, 1972, *27*, 61–68.

U.S. Department of Health, Education, and Welfare. *A Staff Report, Public Policy and the Frail Elderly*. Washington, D.C.: Office of Human Development Services, Federal Council on Aging, 1978.

U.S. Department of Health, Education, and Welfare. *The National Nursing Home Survey: 1977 Summary for the United States*. DHEW Publication No. (PHS) 79-1794. Washington, D.C.: U.S. Government Printing Office, July 1979.

U.S. Department of Health and Human Services, National Center for Health Statistics. *Changes in Mortality Among the Elderly: United States. 1940-1978*. DHHS Publication No. (PHS) 82-1406. Washington, D.C.: U.S. Government Printing Office, March 1982a.

U.S. Department of Health and Human Services. *Health, United States, 1980*. DHHS Publication No. (PHS) 81-1232. Washington, D.C.: U.S. Government Printing Office, 1980b.

U.S. Department of Health and Human Services, National Center for Health Statistics. *Health, United States, 1981*. DHHS Publication No. (PHS) 82-1232. Washington, D.C.: U.S. Government Printing Office, December, 1981b.

U.S. Department of Health and Human Services, National Center for Health Statistics. *Health. United States, 1982*. DHHS Publication No. (PHS), 83-1232. Washington, D.C.: U.S. Government Printing Office, December, 1982b.

U.S. Department of Health and Human Services, National Institute of Health. S.G. Haynes and M. Feinleib (Eds.), *Second Conference on the Epidemiology of Aging*. NIH Publication No. 80-969. Washington, D.C.: U.S. Government Printing Office, July, 1980a.

U.S. Department of Health and Human Services. *Surveillance, Epidemiology, and End Results: Incidence and Mortality Data, 1973–1977*. Washington, D.C.: U.S. Government Printing Office, 1981a.

U.S. Government Accounting Office, Comptroller General's Report to the Congress of the United States. *Conditions of Older People: National Information System Needed*. HRD 79–95, September, 1979.

U.S. Senate, Special Committee on Aging. *Volume I, Developments in Aging: 1981*. Washington, D.C.: U.S. Government Printing Office, 1982.

Vincente, L., Wiley, J. A., and Carrington, R. A. The risk of institutionalization before death. *The Gerontologist*, 1979, *19*, 361–367.

Ward, A. W. M. Mortality of bereavement. *British Medical Journal*, 1976, *1*, 700–702.

Weinfeld, F. D. (Ed.). The national survey of stroke, *Stroke* (Supplement Number 1), 1981, *12*.

Wingard, D. L. The sex differential in mortality rates. *American Journal of Epidemiology*, 1982, *115*, 205–216.

Wittels, I. and Botwinick, J. Survival in relocation. *Journal of Gerontology*, 1974, *29*, 440–443.

Zweig, J. P. and Csank, J. Z. Effects of relocation on chronically ill geriatric patients of a medical unit: mortality rates. *Journal of the American Geriatrics Society*, 1975, *23*, 132–136.

PART I

BIOLOGICAL ASPECTS OF AGING AND PUBLIC HEALTH

The biology of aging, as it relates to public health, defines the limitations and potentials of human beings as protoplasmic organisms. As living beings, humans experience birth, growth, senescence, and dying as natural processes. Public health, in its role of actualizing collective human potential, seeks not to eliminate aging, but to prevent or delay the ill health which often accompanies aging, and to promote well-being in the later years of life.

At birth, some characteristics of an individual are genetically more or less predetermined; others are somewhat malleable, and subject to environmental influences. It is important to know which health-related characteristics are subject to manipulation, how and when they can be influenced, and with what consequences. Moreover, it is the role of public health to apply such information to the making of policies, programs, and services which fulfill the goals of preventing ill health and promoting well-being.

Chapter 1 is an overview of the current knowledge and understanding of the biology of aging, as it pertains to public health. Although whole volumes could have been written on any one of the subtopics so briefly covered, this overview should serve as an introduction for some, and a review for others, of the range of knowledge on the biological basis of aging.

Chapter 2 focuses on one topic which is basic to public health and to healthy aging—nutrition. Historically, the application of nutritional knowledge has been one of the fundamental strategies in the prevention of disease. For example, the observation that consumption of limes prevented the development of scurvy in sailors led to subsequent use of this knowledge on a mass scale by the

British Navy. That nutritional deficiencies can manifest themselves as epidemics, just as communicable diseases do, is illustrated by the case of pellagra, prevalent among the poor of the Southern United States some decades ago. In a classic example of the use of epidemiological methods, it was discovered that pellagra, previously assumed to be an infectious disease, was actually due to inadequate diet. Some prevalent diseases of the elderly, such as atherosclerosis, could be regarded as epidemics of malnutrition.

Public health nutrition is an example of a biological science which has been successfully translated into a public health program. Effective application of nutritional knowledge to the aging population requires the combined efforts of medical professionals, government, industry, business, and educators, as well as scientists.

1

Biological Aging: Public Health Implications

SUSAN A. GAYLORD

Introduction

Biology is concerned with the organic infrastructure and functioning of living systems at the molecular, cellular, organ, and individual levels. It sheds scientific light on reproduction, growth, nutrition, and the developmental phases of the life cycle. Biological aging is sometimes defined as a developmental process beginning at birth and encompassing the life span of the organism; however, for purposes of this chapter the term will refer only to those post-maturational changes within an organism which correlate over time with an increasing probability of functional losses and death. Such a process is inevitable, but the rate of change varies greatly among different organs, different individuals, and different species.

For public health workers, knowledge of biological aging provides a necessary basis for research and policy formulation, in that it defines the limits of and potentials for physical health and longevity inherent in the human species. In dealing with an aging population, the following questions become increasingly important:

- Which aspects of the aging process are normal and inescapable, and which aspects are preventable, deleterious effects of personal habits and environmental influences?
- How malleable are effects of the aging process?
- How do various populations age, and are differences among populations genetically or environmentally determined?

- What is the normal life span for humans, and what is the potential, and the motivation, for increasing the human life span?

This chapter provides an overview of rapidly accumulating information which is beginning to provide some answers to such questions.

Mechanisms and Manifestations of Aging

Within an organism, aging proceeds at various levels of organization: the molecular, cellular, tissue, organ, and whole-organism levels. In the following pages, these levels of organization will be used as a framework for describing aging research. Several theories of aging which have emerged from such research will be mentioned below. Although none of them can account for all the facts, and no one theory can be said to completely explain aging, they are useful in organizing facts and testing hypotheses. For more complete reviews of these theories, such texts as Finch and Hayflick (1977), Strehler (1977), and Behnke et al. (1978) should be consulted.

Broadly speaking, two main lines of thought as to determinants of aging may be discerned in the research literature: aging results either from genetically programmed changes, or from an accumulation of errors due to environmental hazards. Programmed cell death is seen as a regular feature of embryogenesis, and some researchers have attempted to apply this developmental model to the aging process. Others see aging as a phase in which the organism, having served its reproductive function, has essentially "run out of program," and in which increasing vulnerability is a result of random error. Unequivocal evidence for one or the other of these approaches does not yet exist.

Aging at the Molecular Level

Any attempt to summarize briefly the complexity of experimental findings in this area fails to do them justice. The discussion which follows may be supplemented by excellent reviews provided by Sinex (1977), Schneider (1978), and Rothstein (1982).

Alterations in the Genetic Materials, Proteins, or Enzymes. One group of theories focuses on the possibility that aging is a result of changes in information provided by the cell nucleus for normal cell function. Such changes could be due to (1) alterations in DNA (deoxyribonucleic acid), through either coding errors during replication or mutation; (2) errors in the synthesis of RNA (ribonucleic acid) or protein; (3) alterations in chromatin structure that would alter gene expression; or (4) a positive genetic program (Sinex, 1977).

If coding errors in DNA were found to accumulate during succeeding replications of somatic cells, theoretically such errors could alter messages to RNA, which in turn could cause incorrect protein synthesis. In resting cells, which do not replicate (e.g., nerve and muscle cells), point mutations in DNA could accumulate with the passage of time, and cause errors in protein synthesis. It has been hypothesized that such faulty proteins could produce further faulty proteins and enzymes, possibly leading to an "error catastrophe" (Orgel, 1963; 1970). However, no conclusive evidence yet exists for increase of such errors as a result of the aging process. Altered proteins have been observed in older animals, but the evidence so far suggests that these errors result from post-translational alterations rather than from errors in biosynthesis (U.S. DHHS, 1982, p. 41).

Evidence for programmatic changes in DNA or chromatin structure with age is conflicting, with positive or negative findings often dependent on differences in technique or tissue studied. A possible explanation for such discrepancies is that certain genes in a small number of key tissues trigger an aging-related change that in turn causes changes in other tissues. Alternatively, programmed changes may proceed in most or all tissues, although at different rates (Rothstein, 1982, pp. 138–139).

Free-Radical Damage. Free radicals are chemically reactive entities produced in the body as part of normal metabolism, as well as from radiation and from the breakdown of rancid fats in the body. When produced as part of normal metabolism, free radicals are controlled by enzymes. Damage by free radicals can take place when the body receives large doses of high energy radiation, causing tissue damage, or when the breakdown of hydrogen peroxide, or oxidation and breakdown of fats takes place. In such situations, uncontrolled free radicals can do damage to proteins, fats, and the genetic materials–DNA and RNA. Free radicals have been implicated in a number of aging-related phenomena, including cancers, arthritis, cross-linking of tissues, and age-pigment accumulation (Harman, 1981).

DNA Error and DNA-Repair Capability. For long-lived cells, it is important that damage to DNA caused by free radicals and other mechanisms be repaired without translating the error on to RNA and protein synthesis. At least four types of DNA repair have been uncovered: strand-breakage rejoining, excision repair, post-replication repair, and photoreactivation. In general, studies have shown no decline of DNA-repair capability with age of the individual, although conflicting evidence exists (Tice, 1978).

Some research has found a positive correlation between length of life span of species and ability of DNA to repair itself (Hart and Setlow, 1974), although another study casts doubt on the strength of this relationship (Woodhead et al., 1980). In any case, it may be that short-lived strains do not need as much repair, since significant environmental damage from radiation and free radicals occurs over longer periods of time.

Aging at the Cellular Level

In mammals, at least, three classes of cells can be distinguished on the basis of division-potential: some divide continuously (e.g., epithelial cells of the small intestine); some do not divide except when stimulated to do so (e.g., hepatocytes, kidney cells, and many others); and others do not divide at all after differentiation (e.g., keratinizing epithelial cells of the skin, neurons) (Baserga, 1977). In vivo studies have shown that in dividing cells, the time length of the cell cycle is longer in old than in young mice (Lesher, 1961). Also, in resting cells that are stimulated to divide (e.g., liver cells after partial hepatectomy), the time between stimulation and the beginning of DNA synthesis is longer in older animals than in younger ones (Bucher, 1963). A decrease in the percentage of cells that respond to stimulation has also been noted (Oh and Conard, 1972).

Limitations on Cell Replication. Hayflick and Moorhead (1961) demonstrated in a now classic study that human fibroblast cells cultivated in vitro could replicate only a limited number of times before entering a phase in which cell chromosomes mutated and no longer faithfully replicated themselves. The number of population doublings prior to this phase ranged from 35 to 63, averaging about 50. Fibroblast cells from the skin and lungs of older individuals, and cells derived from liver, have been shown to replicate fewer times, on the average, than cells from younger people (Hayflick, 1977).

Further evidence for the correlation of cell doubling potential and life span comes from comparisons of doubling capacity of shorter and longer lived species, where a correlation exists between mean maximum life span and doubling potential (Hayflick, 1977). In the genetic, life-shortening condition of progeria, a rare disorder which manifests many symptoms of premature aging, only two to four cell doublings were found to occur. Limits on cell doubling capacity in vitro have been interpreted as evidence of cellular senescence, leading to the hypothesis that doubling capacity imposes limits on an organism's life span. However, there is some question as to the correspondence and relevance of such findings to cell division potential in the whole organism.

Aging at the Tissue and Organ Level

The Immune System and Aging. With age, there are changes in both the structure and function of the immune system (Weksler, 1980). After puberty, the thymus gland begins a rapid involution so that by about age 45, only 10 to 20 percent of its former cellular mass is retained. The thymus gland serves as a site of T-cell differentiation, and its hormones instruct T-cell precursors as to what to attack and when. The level of thymic hormone in serum begins to decrease after age 30, until after age 60 it can no longer be detected. T-cell dependent immune function becomes progressively impaired after about 45 years of age.

The rise in chronic diseases of aging may be related to the decline in the immune system. T-cells may fail to recognize bacteria, viruses, and cancer cells, or mistakenly attack the body's own cells, as in autoimmune disorders. Weksler et al. (1978) found that the administration of thymic hormone could reverse age-associated deficits in immune function of lymphocytes in aged mice. B-cells (bone marrow lymphocytes usually programmed by T cells) make antibodies necessary to resist disease. With age, B-cells may make errors with increasing frequency, creating increased numbers of "autoantibodies" (possibly under faulty instructions from T-cells) which attack the body's own tissues (Hallgren et al., 1973). Such autoantibodies may be the cause of conditions believed to be auto-immune diseases such as multiple sclerosis, and some forms of arthritis.

Growth Hormone. The pituitary releases a substance called growth hormone during sleep and in response to exercise, fasting, hypogly-cemia, trauma, and dopaminergic stimulants. Growth hormone helps maintain the immune system, stimulates the growth of muscle, and performs other functions. After about age 30, growth hormone is no longer stimulated by exercise, though it is still se-creted in response to other stimuli.

Diminishing Organ Function. Changes in the structure and func-tion of various tissues and organs have been well documented. For the most part these changes consist of a decline in the bulk of the tissues comprising the organs, often with a replacement by fatty deposits (Rossman, 1977). The rate of change varies greatly among individuals and among individual organs. Most organs have been found to lose some functional ability, and measures of functional ability of the heart, lungs, kidneys, skeletal muscles, and other organs show various rates of decline (Finch and Hayflick, 1977).

Of particular importance to the ability of old people to cope with the necessities of daily life is the decline in sensory capacity (Corso, 1981). Vision, hearing, and balance are especially of inter-est, and will be discussed below in detail. Changes in motor coordi-nation, bone strength, and memory are also discussed.

It should be noted that a brief description of age-related modi-fications must deal in statistical generalities and cannot properly address the wide range of variation present in the elderly. In fact, for most functions the range of individual differences is greater for the elderly than for any other age group. Nevertheless when per-formances are averaged there are age-related differences that are readily apparent.

1. *Vision.* Perhaps the most obvious and easily measured of these changes is vision. One of the most common visual problems associated with aging is presbyopia, impaired ability to focus on near objects. In addition there is a gradual decrease in visual acuity that usually becomes evident about age 40 or shortly there-after. Both of these problems are likely to progress as age in-creases. It should be noted, however, that for many people the impairment can be remedied through the use of corrective lenses.

The process of dark adaptation, that is, the length of time it takes to adjust visually from a lighted condition to one of darkness (switching from the use of cones to the use of rods) is strongly correlated with age. The elderly take much longer to complete the shift. McFarland (1968) reports that the relationship to age is so consistent that a person's chronological age may be predicted to within three years on the basis of his dark adaptation performance. Furthermore, the differences between young and old are striking. In McFarland's study, at the second minute the young were almost five times more sensitive than most of the aged subjects, and by the fortieth minute the young were 240 times more sensitive than the old. Many routine tasks of daily living involve abrupt changes in lighting and hence present special problems for the elderly person.

Normal aging is accompanied by an increased lens thickening and increased light scatter that result in decreased light transmission through the lens. In addition, the pupil becomes less responsive to changes in illumination (Hughes and Neer, 1981). The ability to see in the presence of glare decreases gradually with age, but the decrease accelerates abruptly at about age 40. This increase in sensitivity to glare decreases the ability to recognize targets in the vicinity of a glare source. When individuals in the age range between 5 and 15 years are compared with those between 75 and 85 years, the latter group requires a 50- to 70-fold increase in target screen luminance to match the performance of the younger group (Wolf, 1960; see also Wolbarsht, 1977).

It has been found further that older persons require greater contrast between target and background in order to identify the target accurately. Although both young and old subjects experience problems at levels of illumination requiring shifts between rod and cone vision, such as would be experienced at twilight, older subjects experience much greater difficulty and benefit more from increases in contrast (Sekuler, Hutman, and Owsley, 1980; Fozard, 1981; Hughes and Neer, 1981).

Peripheral vision also shows age-related changes. With increasing age the field of vision tends to decrease, thus reducing the amount of visual information available (Cole, 1979; McFarland, (1968). To what extent older persons can learn to compensate for these changes is not clear.

2. *Hearing.* Although hearing loss may occur at any age, the probability of its occurrence increases with increasing age. After about age 32 for men and age 37 for women there is almost always some degree of hearing loss present (Corso, 1981). Pitch discrimi-

nation begins to deteriorate in the 30s but after age 55 there is a marked increase in the rate of deterioration (Botwinick, 1978). The ability to process auditory information also shows impairment with increasing age.

The loudness of the signal to be heard is not the only factor of concern in the ability to hear and comprehend, and may not even be the most important one. A high signal-to-noise ratio is found to be especially helpful to older subjects. Older subjects show great improvement in performance when the context is made more plausible. Fozard (1981) concludes that hearing aids can provide relief for only some of the auditory problems experienced by the elderly.

3. *Balance and Gait.* Another difficulty often observed in the elderly concerns balance. Older people are more likely to experience degenerative changes in balancing mechanisms. The difficulty may be exacerbated by increased problems in the perception of one's body in space. To compensate, older people are more likely than younger people to rely on more than one modality to conduct a task. For example, in picking up objects they may monitor their performance visually in addition to using kinesthetic cues.

Closely related to changes in balance is change in gait. This may occur in response to changes in vision and in the awareness of one's body in space as well as problems in balance. As a result, some elderly move with a shuffling gait with feet lifted only a short distance above the surface. Consequently, even small irregularities in the ground or the floor or carpet may cause the person to trip or fall. Perhaps in response to the possibility of loss of balance, some elderly people move with the body leaning forward so as to be able to watch their feet and to protect themselves in case of a fall.

4. *Motor Skills.* Most old people cannot compete successfully with the young on tests of physical strength or tests involving large movements at maximum speeds. Many older people are characterized by slower movements (Botwinick, 1984). However, the slower movement seen in the elderly may not be entirely attributable to limitations in physical capacity. Rather it appears that limitations in speed of decisions may play a part. There is some evidence that older people deliberately take longer to arrive at a decision in order to compensate for loss of speed by increased accuracy (Salthouse, 1979). The retardation of motor performance is also accompanied by an increase in caution, that is, older people are less likely to respond at all if they are unsure of the accuracy of their response. When tasks become more complex and responses

are no longer simple and straightforward, the performance of older people becomes both slower and less accurate (Welford, 1977).

Careful in-depth examination of a group of older men found a slowing of psychomotor responses associated with age. Mental as well as physical behaviors were slowed, indicating a general phenomenon that cannot be attributed solely to specific physical or personality factors (Birren et al., 1971).

5. *Bone Strength.* Calcium is essential to bone strength, but beginning around age 40, people absorb less of the calcium they consume than do younger people. As a result, they are more likely to develop osteoporosis, a condition in which the bones lose abnormally large quantities of calcium. The loss reduces bone density and hence bone strength. The bones become thinner or more brittle and thus more vulnerable to fracture (Marx, 1980).

Women are at higher risk of developing osteoporosis. In postmenopausal women there is a rapid increase in the proportion showing signs of osteoporosis, and in older women the incidence of fractures of the femur doubles every five years (Steinbach, 1965). Furthermore, the probability of fracture is much more related to the degree of osteoporosis than it is to the severity of the trauma.

White and oriental women are more likely to develop osteoporosis, presumably because on the whole their bones are less heavy than those of black women. This difference in bone weight may explain in part the sex differences that are observed, although it is clear that after menopause the rate of bone resorption accelerates in women. No comparable acceleration is observed in men.

The process of decalcification may be slowed by such measures as calcium supplements in the diet, increased exercise, and hormone therapy. Chapter 3 discusses some of these measures in greater detail.

6. *Memory.* Although brain cells diminish in number with increasing age, a decline in intelligence has not been substantiated, although responses to tests reveal slowing of response (Botwinick, 1984).

It is frequently observed that older people can recall in great detail early memories while they may not be able to recall as well what they had for breakfast that morning. While many if not most people experience some impairment of memory with increasing age, it is not clearly understood what mechanisms are operating.

One of the most important observations concerning memory is the well established fact that it is easier to recognize learned information than it is to recall it. While this relationship holds true at all ages, the disparity is greatest in the elderly, who show very little, if any, loss of recognition memory. Thus it appears that the aging process interferes more with the ability to retrieve information than to store it (Botwinick, 1984). However, the greater difficulty experienced by the elderly in learning and memory can be overcome through better learning of the materials to be recalled or recognized (Schonfield and Stones, 1979).

Because the elderly have more difficulty with the acquisition of new information and skills than they do with retaining and using already learned information and skills, the effects of memory difficulties associated with aging can often be minimized by maintaining a familiar environment. In addition, props for aiding memory can be used, such as lists of things to do that are prominently displayed in appropriate places (Miller, 1979).

Aging at the Whole Organism Level

Homeostasis. Homeostasis is the ability of living organisms, in varying degrees, to maintain the relatively constant internal environment which is necessary to carry on biological processes in the face of widely varying external environmental conditions. With advancing age, homeostatic regulatory mechanisms tend to become less efficient, resulting in slower reactions to external stimuli, wider variations in internal functioning, and slower return to resting states. Decline in homeostasis is exhibited in a number of systems; e.g., in increase in length of time necessary for dark and light adaptation, and in reduced ability of the liver to metabolize various drugs. A serious and often fatal example of failure to maintain a balance is accidental hypothermia, in which core or deep body temperature drops to 35 degrees centigrade or below in a cold environment. This results from a failure of the homeostatic mechanism of temperature regulation. In a field survey of elderly people in England, Exton-Smith (1981) found that 10 percent had some impairment of thermoregulatory function. (Hypothermia is discussed in more detail in Chapter 3.)

Compensatory Mechanisms. Compensation for the losses and declines associated with the aging process occurs at all levels of organization, from the cell, through tissue and organ systems, to psychological and social levels. These adaptive changes may be able to mask an initial shift in performance. Such second-order mechanisms may remain virtually intact during the available life span, or they may themselves weaken in turn. "It is this peculiarity of senescent deterioration, that it is in expression a multievent failure in a very well-buffered system, with several layers of precautionary response, which explains the rapid and diverse eventual collapse of homeostasis of many old subjects" (Comfort, 1979, p. 256).

Heterogeneity (or Variability) and Aging Processes. It is important to emphasize the potential for wide variance in individual response. Variation among individuals in measures of senescence is great, and often increases with increase in chronological age. Our knowledge about the factors responsible for such individual differences and the relation of such measures to health and disease in later years is limited.

Nature and Nurture

Biological aging seems to be the result of an accumulation of decrements from a variety of causes, both genetic and environmental. Realistic steps to postpone the process or mitigate its effects must necessarily involve multiple strategies.

A recent report from the National Institute on Aging emphasized the importance of distinguishing genetic and environmental factors in aging:

> Determination of the relative contribution of genetic factors and environmental factors to individuality among the elderly is a critical first step toward differential diagnosis of individual problems related to aging as well as to individually tailored interventions. Furthermore, the identification of individual differences, their causes, and their correlates has powerful implications for a range of considerations from retirement policy to health care delivery systems (U.S. Department of Health and Human Services [U.S. DHHS], 1982, p. 52).

Early studies addressing the nature-nurture issue attempted to determine inheritance patterns associated with longevity. For example, Pearl and Pearl (1934), in a classic study, demonstrated that long-lived individuals tend to have long-lived parents and grandparents. However, since influences other than genes are inherited (e.g., social status, educational advantage, and wealth) the influence of genetic or environmental factors in the Pearls' study is indeterminate.

Genetic Influences

That aging has a genetic basis is seen most obviously in the fact that various species mature, grow old, and die at vastly different rates, even under optimal environmental circumstances. For example, the life span of mice is at best only a few years; elephants, on the other hand, may live up to 40 or 50 years. Genetically determined life span differences occur even within orders and within species: the white-footed field mouse (Peromyscus leucopus) lives more than twice as long (1400 days) as his distant cousin, Mus musculus, the common house mouse (600 days) (Sacher and Hart, 1978); the Oregon R strain of D. melanogaster, the common fruit fly, lives twice as long (60 days) as the Swedish C strain (30 days), under similar environmental circumstances (Clark and Gould, 1970).

Confirmation of the genetic influence on human life span comes from findings of greater correlation in longevity in monozygotic than in dizygotic twins (Kallmann and Sander, 1948 and 1949; Bank and Jarvik, 1978). Physical aging characteristics of monozygotic twins are often remarkably similar, including "the degree of general enfeeblement or its absence, the graying and thinning of the hair, the configuration of baldness and senile wrinkle formation, and the type and extent of eye, ear and tooth deficiencies" (Kallmann and Sander, 1948, p. 353). Psychological tests (Wechsler-Bellevue) performed in a longitudinal study of aged monozygotic and dizygotic twins found greater similarity in cognitive performance in the one-egg twin pairs (Bank and Jarvik, 1978). Using the same sample of aged twins, Jarvik and Falek (1961; 1962) found hereditary influences in the propensity for cancer.

Another strong indication of aging's genetic basis is found in those rare progeroid disorders, mentioned above, that exhibit in some respects the characteristics of premature or accelerated aging. Several syndromes have been described and seem to be transmitted as autosomal recessive traits (Epstein et al., 1966).

Within limits, short and long life spans within species can be obtained by selective breeding. Inbred lines often exhibit harmful life-shortening genetic traits that would be masked by greater heterogeneity. Heterosis, or hybrid vigor, is most likely the result of an avoidance of this inbreeding effect (Comfort, 1979, p. 155).

Male-female differences in longevity. For most species, from spiders to man, females outlive males (Comfort, 1979, p. 163). This biological superiority is seen even in the prenatal phases of human survival. As humans age, the male-female survival rates become even more diverse (see the initial chapter). Opinions vary, but the prevailing view is that the differences are due to a combination of genetic and social factors.

The greater longevity of women has important implications for public health practice. In combination with the social custom of men generally marrying women younger than themselves, greater female longevity contributes to the marked preponderance of aged women who are dependent and in need of support.

Environmental Factors Affecting Aging and Death

In comparison with the great interspecies differences in aging and death, variations due to environmental factors play a much smaller role. Nevertheless, within the limits imposed by genetic mechanisms, there is a range of environmental factors influencing both the length of life and its quality. Some of these factors are covered in depth in the chapters on injury prevention, nutrition, and life styles, and so will be mentioned here only briefly.

Sacher posits that an increase in an organism's longevity is due to one of two factors: "either to decrease of a parameter governing the rate of aging, or to decrease of another parameter governing the age-dependent vulnerability to disease and death" (Sacher, 1977, p. 628). These two parameters are useful in describing the effects of various experimental manipulations of the aging process.

Ionizing Radiation. Doses of ionizing radiation in large quantities have been shown to greatly shorten the life of experimental animals and humans, producing permanent injury in the organism's molecular structure (Sacher, 1977). There is no evidence to suggest that the mechanism responsible for aging is the same as that responsible for the deleterious effects of radiation; rather, decrease in life expectation is most likely due to increased vulnerability of the organism to subsequent microenvironmental influences.

Temperature and Metabolic Rate. In poikilotherms (cold-blooded animals), the mean life span varies inversely with the ambient temperature. Loeb and Northrop (1917) first made this discovery with fruit flies. In reviewing evidence from a number of studies, Sacher (1977) concludes that for poikilotherms, changes in temperature, which correlate with changes in metabolic rate, modify the rate of aging.

Surveys of homeotherms (warm-blooded animals) have found a general inverse correlation between life span and metabolic rate among species (Sacher, 1959; 1977). (Increased cephalization also tends to correlate with increased life span.) Increase in metabolic rate can account for the finding that reduction of ambient temperature in rats (5 degrees centigrade vs. 26 degrees centigrade) actually shortened median survival time (Carlson et al., 1957). For the 5° C group, body weight was 16% less, and food intake per kg body weight was 2.3 times greater than in the 26° C control group. The shortened life expectancies with lower ambient temperatures are attributable to increased "energy dissipation" per unit time and to increased rate of aging (Sacher, 1977).

Diet. McCay et al. (1935), in a classic study of rats, found that dietary restriction increased the length of life. Incidence of respiratory diseases and tumors was reduced. However, in their study, the drastic underfeeding to which the rats were subjected stunted their growth and kept them sexually immature. Berg and Simms (1960) placed less extreme restrictions on rats, and found that with restricted feeding, life was extended by 200 days for male rats (from 800 to 1,000 days), and by 300 days for female rats (from 1,000 to 1,300 days). Cardiac, vascular, and renal lesions were delayed in onset, and their cumulative lifetime incidence was lower. Tumors were delayed in onset, but their incidence over the lifetime was not significantly different from that found in the unrestricted group. Increased longevity was attributable to later onset of disease in the thinner animals. Studies which have placed food restrictions on *adult* rats have tended to find moderate increases in life span. However, in some reports, severe dietary restriction shortened life (Ross, 1966; Rothstein, 1982).

In humans, there are indications that diets low in saturated fats and meat act to lower serum cholesterol, which correlates with low incidence of cardiovascular diseases. Coronary heart disease has been found to be less prevalent in populations that eat no meat and little fat (Nutrition Reviews, 1980).

Chemical agents. The chemical antioxidants known as free-radical inhibitors have been found in some cases to increase survival time. The mechanism of such chemical effects involves a decrease in vulnerability of the organism to disease, rather than a prolongation of the life span by slowing the rate of aging (Sacher, 1977).

Life style factors. Not smoking, moderation in drinking, adequate exercise, rest, diet high in fiber content, and lack of stress have all been found to correlate with better health and living longer. The life prolonging mechanisms of such factors most likely involve a reduction in the organism's vulnerability. An in-depth discussion of life style factors is left to Chapter 5.

Normal Aging and Disease

Aging per se does not necessarily imply disease or disability, and "natural death" in old age may occur without the individual's succumbing to a major illness (Kohn, 1982). "Minor illnesses" may become life threatening when physiological reserves are limited.

There are several major classes of disease that tend to increase in probability of occurrence in the population with age: these include most cancers, atherosclerosis, arthritis, circulatory ailments, and liver and pulmonary disorders. Such diseases were reviewed in the initial chapter and will not be discussed here.

Two important points may be made here about these chronic disorders: (1) the first symptoms of the disease may not emerge until many years after the disease process has begun, and (2) these diseases, although by definition not curable, are in many cases preventable through maintaining a healthy life style or by changes in the environment. As Fries and Crapo (1981, p. 5) point out, if the progression of a particular age-related disease can be slowed enough, although the disease process itself will not have been halted, from the individual's standpoint, the disease will have been prevented. Other treatable conditions such as depression or drug intoxication may be mistaken for irreversible disease such as senility. Careful diagnoses must therefore be made to avoid such errors.

Death certificates, which require a statement of cause of death, may give a false impression of the relation in the very old between disease and death. In autopsies of persons dying at age 85 or older, 30 percent of persons were found to have no disease that could be labelled as cause of death. Death could be attributed only to "complications of the aging syndrome" (Kohn, 1982). The conclusion is that senescence itself should therefore be labelled as a cause of death.

Statisticians and epidemiologists as a whole do not accept "senility" as a cause of death. However, it seems that in extreme old age, where there is a general decline in the physiological reserves of important organs, it might be scientifically justifiable to attribute death to "old age."

Life Span, Life Expectancy, and Public Health Goals

For centuries people have regretted, resisted, or philosophically accepted the aging process as an intimation of their own mortality, but it is only more recently, in economically advanced societies, that large numbers and proportions of the population have reached old age and experienced its effects. This demographic shift was due to several main factors. The Industrial Revolution brought about a dramatic increase in the standard of living for large segments of society. Improvements in nutrition were responsible for the decline of endemic diseases that hasten death, such as tuberculosis, scurvy, and rickets. Although initially industrialization and the concomitant move to the cities brought on degraded environmental conditions, by the mid-nineteenth century sanitation had improved so that communicable diseases, such as gastroenteritis, typhoid fever, and cholera were receding (McKeown, 1976, Chapter 1). The growth of knowledge and practice in preventive medicine in the early twentieth century reduced the incidence of morbidity and mortality of infancy, childhood, and childbirth. In the last forty years, antibiotics and other efficacious drugs have reduced mortality in large numbers from acute infections. Such successes have allowed millions of people, including those with chronic diseases, to live years longer. Advances in the high technology of diagnosis, surgery, and anesthesiology have enabled many with previously fatal diseases to continue living more or less full lives. The result of all these influences—some fortuitous like industrialization, others deliberate like the development of diptheria vaccine—has been the striking growth in the number and proportions of older people in populations in industrialized nations.

Public health is concerned with this phenomenon for several reasons. The negative concomitants of biological aging may range from mildly distressing to seriously deleterious, and may have not only physical, but psychological and social consequences. Although people adapt, in varying degrees, to the aging process, aging in many instances means increased suffering due to increased disease and disability. For both the individual and those who care for him/her, the quality of life may decrease. When multiplied, such effects may have negative societal consequences.

Obviously, the aim of public health, with regard to the aging population, is not merely to extend life further, nor only to cure or prevent diseases and disorders which increase with age. Its primary goal is the improvement of the quality of life, both for the elderly and the future elderly. In this regard, several important questions face public health. In this demographic change, have we merely increased the number of chronically ill and aged people rather than increasing the years of worthwhile living? How can we enhance the quality of life as well as increase longevity? Will this demographic trend continue, and if so with what consequences? These issues are discussed below.

Maximum life span is the theoretical species-specific, biological limit to length of life, excluding premature, "unnatural" death. In most species, individuals rarely live out their biological life span—disease, accident, starvation, or predation take their toll. A measure of *life expectancy,* then, is a better predictor of actual longevity: it is a measure of the average number of additional years of life expected for a member of a population, based on probability of death from all causes.

Survival curves are a way of illustrating actual rate of death in a population. For those populations in which risk of death is independent of age (deaths occur randomly), the survival curve (percentage of population remaining alive over time) will show a logarithmic decline (see Figure 1.1a). Certain invertebrates and classes of fishes (as well as some inanimate objects, such as glassware), exhibit this type of survival curve (Comfort, 1979, pp. 21–43). In a population exhibiting senescence, or age-related deterioration, death occurs with greater probability with advancing age, due to increased susceptibility of the individual to accident, injury, or disease, events which might not have killed the individual at an earlier time. Such increased susceptibility occurs in inanimate as well as animate objects, in the form of accumulated environmentally induced deterioration. In organisms subject to biological laws, there is in addition the intrinsic aging process, discussed above, manifested at molecular, cellular, tissue, and organ levels. For the theoretical population in which aging-related death is the only factor, the survival curve would assume an almost rectangular form (Figure 1.1b). The slope of the rectangle would then be limited only by genetically determined intra-species differences in life span.

Human beings are subject to both age-related and random death. Benjamin Gompertz, an English insurance actuary, demonstrated that for human populations the probability of dying doubles about every seven or eight years (Gompertz, 1825). Thus the chance of dying is about 1,000 times greater for a person of 100 than for a person of 25 years (Strehler, 1973). As random deaths have become less frequent in industrialized societies, human population survival curves have become increasingly retangular. The reduction in mortality from infectious disease, especially in infants and small children, was particularly dramatic in its effect, and is reflected in the significant increase in average life expectancy at birth: from 1900 to 1980 in the U.S., life expectancy at birth increased from 47 to 74 years. In that same time period, life expectancy at age 65 increased from 77 to 81 years (U.S. DHHS, 1982, p. 53).

In spite of the continual increments in life expectancy, there is no evidence that the species maximum life span has increased. There is no verifiable record of any human being living past age 116 (McWhirter, 1982), and the percentage of centenarians in the U.S. population remains low, at about 14 per 100,000.

Fries and others (Fries, 1980; Hayflick, 1980) have interpreted the dovetailing life expectancy curves as an indication that life expectancy is fast approaching the theoretical life span limit, which they estimate to be about 85 to 100 years of age. Other researchers have produced evidence that human populations have not yet reached the bounds imposed by genetic make-up (Manton, 1982; Schatzkin, 1980).

A closely related issue is whether or not chronic disease in later life is increasing as a result of increased life expectancy. Gruenberg (1977) maintains that, overall, life with disability is being prolonged through science's achievements in preventing death of patients with disabling diseases such as diabetes and cystic fibrosis. Fries (1980), on the other hand, suggests that disease and disability in later life are in the process of being compressed into fewer and later years, due to the fixed upper limit on life imposed by the maximum species life span, combined with better health habits. According to Manton (1982) there is evidence suggesting that although life expectancy for older people increased in the 1960s and 1970s, there was no marked deterioration in their health status.

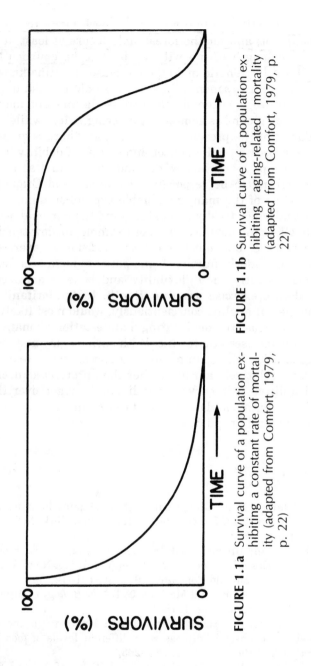

SURVIVORS (%)

TIME ⟶

FIGURE 1.1a Survival curve of a population exhibiting a constant rate of mortality (adapted from Comfort, 1979, p. 22)

SURVIVORS (%)

TIME ⟶

FIGURE 1.1b Survival curve of a population exhibiting aging-related mortality (adapted from Comfort, 1979, p. 22)

That death will eventually overtake each being that is born, there is no doubt; and for the foreseeable future at least, it would seem that the length of life will continue to be bounded by the upper limit set by genetic makeup. (Because scientific knowledge is increasing in an exponential fashion it would be rash to predict permanent failure of attempts to surpass the present maximum lifespan by such means as genetic engineering.) Meanwhile, within the boundaries of the present human lifespan, there is great flexibility in the process of aging, onset and degree of debility, and age of death—perhaps more than we as individuals and as a society have been willing to be responsible for. Fries and Crapo (1981, p. 125) list some of the many modifiable aspects of aging—modifiable, but usually not totally avoidable—and the personal decisions required to effect the modification. For example, to slow the decline of cardiac reserve, one must make the decision to exercise and avoid smoking. Elderly nursing home patients have been found to increase significantly their flexibility and bone mineral content with a moderate exercise program (Smith, 1973; Moritani, 1981). Such strategies, if applied conscientiously, would most likely delay the onset, or at least the debilitating manifestation of, many of the major chronic diseases of later life. With such a delay and with the prolonging of a healthy span of life, the end of one's life might be preceded by a relatively abrupt, rather than protracted, decline in functional ability. This curve for individual's vigor over the life span, if plotted for a population, would represent the ideal of public health for its elderly population.

References

Bank, L. and Jarvik, L. F. A longitudinal study of aging human twins. In E. L. Schneider (Ed.), *The Genetics of Aging.* New York, N.Y.: Plenum Press, 1978, pp. 303–333.

Baserga, R. L. Cell division and the cell cycle. In C. E. Finch and L. Hayflick (Eds.), *Handbook of the Biology of Aging.* New York, N.Y.: Van Nostrand Reinhold Company, 1977, pp. 101–121.

Behnke, J. A., Finch, C. E., and Moment, G. B. *The Biology of Aging.* New York, N.Y.: Plenum Press, 1978.

Berg, B. N. and Simms, H. S. Nutrition and longevity in the rat. II. Longevity and onset of disease with different levels of food intake. *Journal of Nutrition,* 1960, *71,* 255–263.

Birren, J. E., Butler, R. N., Greenhouse, S. W., Sokoloff. L., and Yarrow,

M. R. *Human Aging I. A Biological and Behavioral Study.* (Publication No. (ADM) 77-122). Washington, D.C.: U.S. Government Printing Office, 1971.

Botwinick, J. *Aging and Behavior.* Third Edition. New York, N.Y.: Springer Publishing Company, 1984.

Bucher, N. L. R. Regeneration of mammalian liver. *Internal Review of Cytology,* 1963, *15,* 245–300.

Carlson, L. D., Scheyer, W. J., and Jackson, B. H. The combined effects of ionizing radiation and low temperature on the metabolism, longevity, and soft tissues of the white rat. I. Metabolism and longevity. *Radiation Research,* 1957, *7,* 190–197.

Clark, A. M. and Gould, A. B. Genetic control of adult lifespan in Drosophila melanogaster. *Experimental Gerontology,* 1970, *5,* 157–164.

Cole, D. G. *A Follow-Up Investigation of the Visual Fields and Accident Experience Among North Carolina Drivers.* Chapel Hill, N.C.: University of North Carolina Highway Safety Research Center, 1979.

Comfort, A. *The Biology of Senescence.* Third Edition. New York, N.Y.: Elsevier, 1979.

Corso, J. F. *Aging Sensory Systems and Perception.* New York, N.Y.: Praeger Publishers, 1981.

Czlonkowska, A. and Korlak, J. The immune response during aging. *Journal of Gerontology,* 1979, *34,* 9–14.

Epstein, C. J., Martin, G. M., Schultz, A. L., and Motulsky, A. G. Werner's syndrome: A review of its symptomatology, natural history, pathologic features, genetics and relation to the natural aging process. *Medicine,* 1966, *45,* 177–221.

Exton-Smith, A. N. The elderly in a cold environment. In Tom Arie (Ed.), *Health Care of the Elderly.* London, England: Croom Helm, 1981, pp. 42–56.

Finch, C. E. and Hayflick, L. (Eds.). *Handbook of the Biology of Aging.* New York, N.Y.: Van Nostrand Reinhold Company, 1977.

Fozard, James L. Person-environment relationships in adulthood: implications for human factors engineering. *Human Factors, 1981, 13,* 7–27.

Fries, J. F. Aging, natural death, and the compression of morbidity. *The New England Journal of Medicine,* 1980, *303,* 130–135.

Fries, J. F. and Crapo, L. M. *Vitality and Aging. Implications of the Rectangular Curve.* San Francisco, Ca.: W. H. Freeman and Company, 1981.

Gompertz, B. On the nature of the function expressive of the law of human mortality. *Philosophical Transactions of the Royal Society of London,* 1825, *1,* 513–585.

Gruenberg, E. M. The failures of success. *Milbank Memorial Fund Quarterly/Health and Society,* 1977, *55,* 3–24.

Hallgren, H. M., Buckley, C. E., Gilbertsen, V. A., and Yunis, E. J. Lymphocyte phytohemagglutinin responsiveness, immunoglobulins and auto antibodies in aging humans. *Journal of Immunology,* 1973, *111,* 1101–1107.

Harman, D. The aging process. *Proceedings of the National Academy of Science,* 1981, *78,* 7124–7128.

Hart, R. W. and Setlow, R. B. Correlation between deoxyribonucleic acid excision repair and life-span in a number of mammaliam species. *Proceedings of the National Academy of Sciences,* 1974, *71,* 2169–2173.

Hayflick, L. The cellular basis for biological aging. In C. E. Finch and L. Hayflick (Eds.), *Handbook of the Biology of Aging.* New York, N.Y.: Van Nostrand Reinhold Company, 1977, pp. 159–186.

Hayflick, L. Future directions in aging research. *Proceedings of the Society for Experimental Biology and Medicine,* 1980, *165,* 206–214.

Hayflick, L. and Moorhead, P. A. The serial cultivation of human diploid cell strains. *Experimental Cell Research,* 1961, *25,* 585–621.

Hughes, P. C. and Neer, R. M. Lighting for the elderly: a psychological approach to lighting. *Human Factors,* 1981, *12,* 65–85.

Jarvik, L. F. and Falek, A. Cancer rates in aging twins. *American Journal of Human Genetics,* 1961, *13,* 413–422.

Jarvik, L. F. and Falek, A. Comparative data on cancer in aging twins. *Cancer,* 1962, *15,* 1009–1018.

Kallmann, F. J. and Sander, G. Twin studies on aging and longevity. *Journal of Heredity,* 1948, *39,* 349–357.

Kallmann, F. J. and Sander, G. Twin studies in senescence. *American Journal of Psychiatry,* 1949, *106,* 29–36.

Kohn, R. R. Cause of death in very old people. *Journal of the American Medical Association,* 1982, *247,* 2793–2797.

Lesher, S., Fry, R. J. M., and Kohn, H. I. Influence of age on the transit time of cells of the mouse intestinal epithelium. I. Duodenum. *Laboratory Investigation,* 1961, *10,* 291–300.

Loeb, J. and Northrop, J. H. On the influence of food and temperature upon the duration of life. *Journal of Biological Chemistry,* 1917, *32,* 103–121.

Manton, K. G. Changing concepts of morbidity and mortality in the elderly population. *Milbank Memorial Fund Quarterly/Health and Society,* 1982, *60,* 183–244.

Marx, J. L. Osteoporosis: new help for thinning bones. *Science,* 1980, *207*(4431), 628–630.

McCay, C. M., Crowell, M. F., and Maynard, L. A. The effect of retarded growth upon the length of life span and upon the ultimate body size. *Journal of Nutrition,* 1935, *10,* 63–79.

McFarland, R. A. The sensory and perceptual processes in aging. In K. Warner Schaie (Ed.), *Theory and Methods of Research on Aging.* Morgantown, W.V.: West Virginia University, 1968, 9–52.

McKeown, T. *The Role of Medicine. Dream, Mirage, or Nemesis?* London, England: Nuffield Provincial Hospitals Trust, 1976.

McWhirter, N. (Ed.) *Guinness Book of World Records.* New York, N.Y.: Bantam Books, 1982.

Miller, E. Memory and aging. In M. M. Gruneberg and P. E. Morris (Eds.), *Applied Problems in Memory.* New York, N.Y.: Academic Press, 1979, pp. 127–149.

Moritani, T. Training adaptations in the muscles of older men. In E. L. Smith and R. C. Serfass, (Eds.) *Exercise and Aging: The Scientific Basis.* Hillside, N.J.: Enslow Publishers, 1981, pp. 149–166.

Nutrition Reviews. Dietary fiber, exercise and selected blood lipid constituents. *Nutrition Reviews,* 1980, *38,* 207–209.

Oh, Y. H. and Conard, R. A. Effect of aging on thymidine incorporation in nuclei of lymphocytes stimulated with phytohemagglutinin. *Life Sciences,* 1972, *11,* 677–684.

Orgel, L. E. The maintenance of the accuracy of protein synthesis and its relevance to ageing. *Proceedings of the National Academy of Sciences,* 1963, *49,* 517–521.

Orgel, L. E. The maintenance of the accuracy of protein synthesis and its relevance to ageing: a correction. *Proceedings of the National Academy of Sciences,* 1970, *67,* 1476.

Pearl, R. and Pearl, R. de W. *The Ancestry of the Long-Lived.* Baltimore, Md.: Johns Hopkins University Press, 1934.

Plemons, J. K., Willis, S. L., and Baltes, P. B. Modifiability of fluid intelligence in aging: a short-term longitudinal training approach. *Journal of Gerontology,* 1978, *33,* 224–231.

Ross, M. H. Life expectancy modification by change in dietary regimen of the mature rat. *Proceedings of the Seventh International Congress of Nutrition,* 1966, *5,* 35–38.

Rossman, I. Anatomical and body composition changes with aging. In C. E. Finch and L. Hayflick (Eds.), *Handbook of the Biology of Aging.* New York, N.Y.: Van Nostrand Reinhold Company, 1977, pp. 189–221.

Rothstein, M. *Biochemical Approaches to Aging.* New York, N.Y.: Academic Press, 1982.

Sacher, G. A. Life table modification and life prolongation. In C. E. Finch and L. Hayflick, (Eds.), *Handbook of the Biology of Aging,* New York, N.Y.: Van Nostrand Reinhold Company, 1977.

Sacher, G. A. Relation of lifespan to brain weight and body weight in mammals. In G. E. W. Wolstenholme and M. O'Connor (Eds.), *CIBA Foundation Colloquia on Ageing, Vol. 5, The Lifespan of Animals,* pp. 115–133. London, England: Churchill Publishing Co., 1959.

Sacher, G. A. and Hart, R. W. Longevity, aging, and comparative cellular and molecular biology of the house mouse, Mus musculus, and the white-footed mouse, Peromyscus leucopus. In D. Bergsma and D. E.

Harrison (Eds.) *Genetic Effects on Aging. Birth Defects: Original Article Services,* 1978, *14*(1), 71–96.

Salthouse, T. A. Adult age and the speed-accuracy trade-off. *Ergonomics,* 1979, *22,* 811–820.

Schatzkin, A. How long can we live? A more optimistic view of potential gains in life expectancy. *American Journal of Public Health,* 1980, *70,* 119–1200.

Schneider, E. L. (Ed.). *The Genetics of Aging.* New York, N.Y.: Plenum Press, 1978.

Schonfield, D. and Stones, M. J. Remembering and aging. In J. F. Kihlstrom and F. J. Evans (Eds.), *Functional Disorders of Memory.* Hillsdale, N.J.: Erlbaum, 1979.

Sekuler, R., Hutman, L. P. and Owsley, C. J. Human aging and spatial vision. *Science,* 1980, *109*(4462), 1255–1256.

Sinex, F. M. The molecular genetics of aging. In C. E. Finch and L. Hayflick (Eds.), *Handbook of the Biology of Aging.* New York, N.Y.: Van Nostrand Reinhold Co., 1977. pp. 37–62.

Smith, E. L. The effects of physical activity on bone in the aged. In *International Conference on Bone Mineral Measurements.* R. B. Mazess (Ed.), Washington, D.C.: U.S. DHEW Publication No. NIH 75-683, 1973.

Steinbach, H. A. L. Symposium on problems in geriatric radiology: roentgenology of the skeleton on the aged. *Radiology Clinics of North America,* 1965, *3,* 227.

Strehler, B. L. A new age for aging. *Natural History, 82* (Feb. 1973), 9–18, 82–85.

Strehler, B. L. Implications of aging research for society. *Proceedings of the 58th Annual Meeting of Federation of American Societies for Experimental Biology,* 1975, *34,* 5–8.

Strehler, B. L. *Times, Cells, and Aging.* New York, N.Y.: Academic Press, 1977.

Tice, R. R. Aging and DNA-repair capability. In E. L. Schneider (Ed.), *The Genetics of Aging.* New York, N.Y.: Plenum Press, 1978, pp. 53–89.

U.S. Department of Health and Human Services, National Center for Health Statistics. *Health. United States. 1982.* DHHS Publication No. (PHS) 83-12332. Washington, D.C.: U.S. Government Printing Office, December, 1982.

U.S. Department of Health and Human Services, National Institute on Aging. *A National Plan for Research on Aging.* NIH Publication No. 82-2453. Bethesda, Md.: National Institutes of Health, National Institute on Aging, September, 1982.

Weksler, M. E. The immune system and the aging process in man. *Proceedings of the Society for Experimental Biology and Medicine,* 1980, *165,* 200–205.

Weksler, M. E., Innes, J. B., and Goldstein, G. Immunological studies of aging. *Journal of Experimental Medicine,* 1978, *148,* 996–1006.

Welford, A. T. Motor performance. In J. E. Birren and K. W. Schaie (Eds.), *Handbook of the Psychology of Aging.* New York, N.Y.: Van Nostrand Reinhold Co., 1977, pp. 450–496.

Wolbarsht, M. L. Tests for glare sensitivity and peripheral vision in driver applicants. *Journal of Safety Research,* 1977, *9,* 128–139.

Wolf, E. Glare and age. *Archives of Ophthalmology,* 1960, 64, 502–514.

Woodhead, A. D., Setlow, R. B., and Grist, E. DNA repair and longevity in three species of cold-blooded vertebrates. *Experimental Gerontology,* 1980, *15,* 301–304.

2

Nutrition and Older Adults

MARIE T. FANELLI AND MILDRED KAUFMAN

Introduction

Human nutrition is defined as the processes by which food is obtained, ingested, absorbed, and metabolized by the body so that reproduction, growth, and physical and mental development may occur. Adequate nutrition is the biochemical basis for an active, productive, and satisfying life, and has a direct relationship to maintaining the health of people of all ages, including the elderly.

Public health nutrition is the science and art of applying current knowledge of nutrition science to achieve and to maintain the highest possible levels of health for the population. Public health nutrition is a complex field which utilizes knowledge of physiology, biochemistry, medicine, and the behavioral, social, and political sciences. It applies the methods of public health practice in accomplishing the objectives of health promotion and disease prevention in the community throughout the lifespan. For the current generation of older adults, major public health nutrition efforts focus on secondary disease prevention, rehabilitation, and maintenance of independent function. As health promotion efforts directed to the young increasingly promote lifestyles which include lifelong healthful diets and regular exercise, future cohorts of older adults can look forward to more productive years of life and wellness.

Dietary recommendations for older Americans, the results of national nutritional surveys with respect to nutritional problems among older adults, various factors influencing nutritional status, descriptions of community nutrition services available to older

70

adults, and future goals for public health professionals are discussed in this chapter. The terms *older adults* and *elderly* are arbitrarily defined in this discussion as individuals 65 years of age and older.

Food and Nutrient Recommendations

Dietary Guidelines

The dietary recommendations offered to the people of the United States have changed over the years with the shift in the major public health problems. During the past century, infectious diseases, nutritional deficiency diseases, and much of maternal and infant mortality have been largely brought under control and life expectancy has thus lengthened. At the same time, chronic and degenerative diseases have become the major causes of disability and death. For the promotion of wellness and prevention of chronic and degenerative diseases, current dietary recommendations advocate "moderation" in eating practices and the use of a wide variety of foods (see Table 2.1).

Dietary prudence, combined with an adequate intake of essential nutrients, is a means of promoting health, maintaining vigor, and controlling weight. Such a regimen is recommended throughout life. It is especially important for the elderly population, who are vulnerable to both malnutrition and the degenerative diseases. Guidelines for a rational diet for all older adults are similar to

Table 2.1
Dietary Guidelines for Americans

Consume a variety of foods from among the major food groups—fruits; vegetables; whole grains, cereals and enriched breads; dairy products; meats and meat alternatives; to ensure that essential nutrient needs will be met.

Consume food sources of energy in amounts that will maintain appropriate body weight.

Avoid the consumption of too much fat, saturated fat and cholesterol.

Avoid the consumption of too much sugar.

Avoid the consumption of too much sodium.

Drink alcohol in moderation.

Increase the consumption of fiber and complex carbohydrate.

Source: U.S. Department of Agriculture and U.S. Department of Health, Education and Welfare. Nutrition and Your Health. Washington, D.C.: U.S. Government Printing Office, 1980.

those presented in Table 2.1 (Kohrs, 1982). It is strongly advised that they consume a wide variety of foods from the major food groups—dairy products, protein-rich foods, fruits and vegetables, and breads and cereals. Increased use of relatively rich sources of dietary fiber, such as whole grain cereals, bran, fruits, and vegetables, is recommended to prevent or alleviate constipation. For those who need to restrict their energy (kilocalorie) intake, the consumption of foods which provide kilocalories but few other essential nutrients (for example, pastries, candy, fats and oils, and alcoholic beverages) should be controlled. In all diets, the recommended percentage of total calories from protein is about 12, from carbohydrate, 48 to 53, and from fat, 35 to 40 (Kohrs, 1982).

About 80 percent of the elderly population have one or more chronic diseases (U.S. DHEW, 1977). The four most prevalent are arthritis, heart disease, hypertension, and diabetes. Dietary modification is an essential element of treatment of three of these: heart disease, hypertension, and diabetes.

For older adults who suffer from chronic and/or disabling disease(s), the goal is to achieve and maintain improved function and independence. The quality of life and the degree of functional independence may be markedly enhanced through dietary management, even when the disease process cannot be reversed.

Severe dietary modifications, however, may not always be recommended. For example, a diet which restricts salt to a level of 2 to 3 grams per day, the level found in unsalted and unprocessed foods, limits food choices and may tend to be unpalatable to the older person. Adherence to such a diet may diminish appetite and food intake. Hence, severe dietary modifications in combination with a depressed appetite in the older adult may result in malnutrition. This effect may be more detrimental to health than the effect of a less restrictive diet. Those persons who require therapeutic diets (such as sodium-restricted, calorie-restricted, or fat-controlled) should receive individualized diet counseling from qualified nutritionists and registered dietitians (RD) to guide them in planning acceptable, nutritionally balanced diets (Green, 1979).

Recommended Dietary Allowances (RDA)

The Recommended Dietary Allowances of the National Research Council (Table 2.2) are the most commonly used guidelines for estimating the energy and nutrient needs of groups of *healthy* older

TABLE 2.2
Recommended Dietary Allowances for Individuals
23 Years of Age and Older, Revised 1980

Energy and Nutrients	Men		Women	
Energy (kcal):				
23-50 years	2,700 ± 400		2,000 ± 400	
51-75 years	2,400 ± 400		1,800 ± 400	
76 + years	2,050 ± 400		1,600 ± 400	
Nutrients:	23-50 yrs.	51 + yrs.	23-50 yrs.	51 + yrs.
Protein (g)	56	56	44	44
Vitamin A (mcg RE)	1,000	1,000	800	800
Vitamin D (mcg)	5	5	5	5
Vitamin E (mg α TE)	10	10	8	8
Vitamin C (mg)	60	60	60	60
Thiamine (mg)	1.4	1.2	1.0	1.0
Riboflavin (mg)	1.6	1.4	1.2	1.2
Niacin (mg NE)	18	16	13	13
Vitamin B-6 (mg)	2.2	2.2	2.0	2.0
Folacin (ug)	400	400	400	400
Vitamin B-12 (mcg RE)	3.0	3.0	3.0	3.0
Calcium (mg)	800	800	800	800
Phosphorus (mg)	800	800	800	800
Magnesium (mg)	350	350	300	300
Iron (mg)	10	10	18	10
Zinc (mg)	15	15	15	15
Iodine (mcg RE)	150	150	150	150

Source: Committee on Dietary Allowances, Food and Nutrition Board, National Research Council. Recommended Dietary Allowances, 9th ed. Washington, D.C.: National Academy of Sciences, 1980.

adults (National Research Council, 1980). The RDA are revised every five years in accordance with currently published scientific findings. Regrettably, little experimental and clinical data are available with which to formulate nutrient recommendations specifically for the elderly. There is a great need for research to expand the data base used to determine the nutritional requirements of older adults, especially the very old (over 75 years).

The Recommended Dietary Allowances are used as the basis for suggesting the amounts of energy and essential nutrients that should be planned for daily diets. These allowances also are used for estimating food requirements and developing meal patterns for population groups, i.e., the congregate meal program and home-delivered meal program; for licensing and certification standards for menus of nursing homes and other group care facilities; and for evaluating the nutrient intakes of older adult populations.

The 1980 Recommended Dietary Allowances for energy are delineated by age increments for persons 23–50, 51–75, and beyond 75 years of age (Table 2.2). Since energy needs vary with individual body size and physical activity, a range of kilocalories is given. On the assumption that basal metabolism and activity decline progressively, the recommended range for energy intake for adults over 75 years of age is lower than that of adults 51–75 years, whose range is less than that of persons younger than 51 years old.

The Recommended Dietary Allowances are intended to be met by a diet selected from a variety of widely available foods, not by nutrient supplements or extensive fortification of individual foods. The lower energy needs of older adults require reduced total food intake if weight is to be controlled. With the observed consumption of smaller quantities of food by frail old people, it is important to ensure that the food selected provide the needed amounts of essential nutrients.

While the nutrients considered esseential are the same for adults of all ages, physiological changes accompanying aging most likely alter the amounts needed of some nutrients. Due to greater differences in physiological status, variations in nutrient requirements may be greater among individual older adults than among individuals in a younger adult population. Even though it is widely recognized that the older age group is particularly heterogenous and becomes even more heterogenous as age increases, the recommendations for protein, vitamins, and minerals, listed in the 1980 RDA, unfortunately have not been delineated by age increments for persons over 51 years of age (Table 2.2). Thus, the nutrients recommended by the 1980 RDA for a healthy independent individual of 70 are the same as those for a healthy independent individual of 55.

With the exception of the iron allowance for women, and thiamine, riboflavin, and niacin allowances for men, the nutrient allowances listed for persons over 51 years of age are identical to those adults between the ages of 23 and 51 (Table 2.2). Nutrient requirements and alterations in nutrient needs with aging have received relatively little study. However, evidence suggests that while folacin, thiamine, and iron requirements for the elderly population are the same as those of younger adults (Rosenberg et al., 1982; Iber et al., 1982; Lynch et al., 1982), the 1980 RDA for protein, calcium, and Vitamin D may not be sufficient (Heaney et al., 1982; Spencer et al., 1982; Gersovitz et al., 1982; Parfitt et al., 1982).

In addition to the study of the nutritional requirements of healthy older adults, the needs of those having chronic diseases also require investigation. The elderly frequently use over-the-counter drugs and prescribed drugs for many of their chronic conditions. They are more likely to be taking more than one medication over a long time period. Chronic conditions associated with the aging process may influence nutrient needs of older adults more than chronological age, per se.

Community Nutritional Assessments

Several community surveys reflect the dietary intakes of Americans. These include the 1969–70 Ten State Nutrition Survey, the 1976–80 and 1971–74 Health and Nutrition Examination Surveys (HANES), and the 1977–78 and 1965 Nationwide Food Consumption Surveys (NFCS) (U.S. DHEW 1972; U.S. DHEW, 1974; USDA, 1980b; Carroll et al., 1982). These surveys provide nutritionists and other health professionals with a general picture of the diets of older Americans. The data can be used to determine whether older adults are consuming adequate diets by comparison with nutrient intake standards, such as the 1980 Recommended Dietary Allowances. When interpreting the data from these surveys, it is important to recognize that the findings are based on individuals reporting their food intake during limited time periods. Conclusions can only be provisional when relating them to individuals whose nutrient needs may vary from the population studied.

The Ten State Nutrition Survey

This survey, conducted by the U.S. Department of Health, Education and Welfare, was designed to assess the nutritional status of population groups considered to be at risk for undernutrition, with emphasis on low income groups, inner city residents, and Spanish-speaking people in the southwest United States. These population groups were selected from districts with median incomes in the lowest quartile according to the 1960 census. The ten states selected were categorized by the poverty-income ratio (PIR, with a PIR of 1.0 meaning that the income was exactly at the poverty level). The low income ratio states (PIR<1.75) included Kentucky, Louisiana, South Carolina, Texas, and West Virginia. The high income ratio states (PIR>1.75) included California, Massachusetts, Michigan, Washington, and New York plus New York City. The survey included a sample of 2,076 individuals over 60 years of age.

The Ten State Nutrition Survey concluded that the studied persons 60 years of age and older did not consume enough food to meet the Recommended Dietary Allowances (U.S. DHEW, 1972). Significant percentages of the older adults examined, particularly blacks and Spanish Americans, consumed less than 70 percent of the recommended amounts of one or more nutrients (Figure 2.1).

Health and Nutrition Examination Survey I, 1971–1974

Preliminary findings reflect the nutritional status of civilian, non-institutionalized individuals from 1 to 74 years of age. The survey included a representative sample of the total U.S. population, as well as groups considered to be at high risk for malnutrition. The national probability sample included 1,938 older adults (60 years and over). Results indicated that approximately half (56.2%) of the persons 60 years of age and older were consuming diets inadequate in one or more of the nutrients examined (U.S. DHEW, 1974). As in the Ten State Nutrition Survey, calcium, iron, vitamin A, ascorbic acid, and protein were the nutrients most frequently found to be inadequate in the diets of older adults (Figure 2.1).

Health and Examination Survey II, 1976–1980

The objectives were to measure the prevalence of certain health and nutrition indicators in civilian, non-institutionalized Americans, ages 6 months through 74 years, and to assess met and unmet health care needs. The results suggest that the diets of older Americans, especially those with incomes below the poverty level, have improved since HANES I. The nutrients which show the greatest percentage of improvement for both sexes are iron and ascorbic acid, and for men only, vitamin A. Even though the intakes of older individuals with income below the poverty line are less than those of persons with incomes above the poverty line, the mean values of all the nutrients except calcium meet the recommended dietary allowances. In agreement with other national data sources, calcium intake appears to be inadequate for most of the older Americans studied.

The Nationwide Food Consumption Survey

This survey, conducted by the U.S. Department of Agriculture approximately every 10 years, provides a basis for comparing the dietary intakes of non-institutionalized people of various ages and incomes. Stratified area probability sampling was use to designate the households to be surveyed in 1977–78. The preliminary report of this survey contains dietary information obtained from 4,991 individuals 65 years of age and older. This report also shows improvement in the dietary intakes of older Americans. Yet, their diets still appear to be marginal for selected nutrients, namely calcium, magnesium, and vitamin B-6 (USDA, 1980b).

The national surveys reveal that older Americans with incomes below the poverty level are more likely to be at a nutritional risk. Dietary intakes and associated nutritional and health status appear to be more directly related to poverty than to age.

Physiological and Psychological Influences on the Nutritional Status of Older Adults

Chapter 1 described some of the normal changes in physiology which occur with age. Such changes, and accompanying modifications in lifestyle can increase the risk of inadequate nutritional status. The interaction of the physiological, psychological, socioeconomic and enviromental factors which affect nutritional status are depicted in Figure 2.2.

Dentition

Half of the population over age 65 and two thirds of those over age 75 are edentulous (Greene, 1979; Busse, 1978). Among these individuals, one fourth do not have satisfactory dentures (Filner and Williams, 1979). To compensate for biting and chewing difficulties, many elderly persons avoid hard, tough or chewy foods, and consume soft foods which are high in carbohydrate and low in protein,

FIGURE 2.1 Percentage of subjects with dietary intakes below 70% of 1980 RDA for selected nutrients

This graphic presentation represents those nutritional problems identi-fied by two national Nutrition Surveys. It involves some generalizations that do not reflect all the finer differences among various subgroups of the older American population.

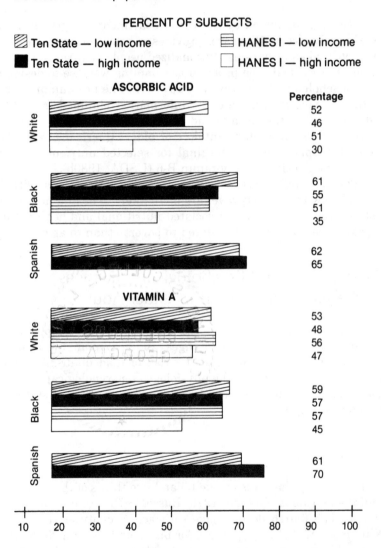

PERCENT OF SUBJECTS

◨ Ten State — low income   ☰ HANES I — low income
■ Ten State — high income   ☐ HANES I — high income

ASCORBIC ACID

	Percentage
White	52
	46
	51
	30
Black	61
	55
	51
	35
Spanish	62
	65

VITAMIN A

White	53
	48
	56
	47
Black	59
	57
	57
	45
Spanish	61
	70

10   20   30   40   50   60   70   80   90   100

FIGURE 2.1, continued

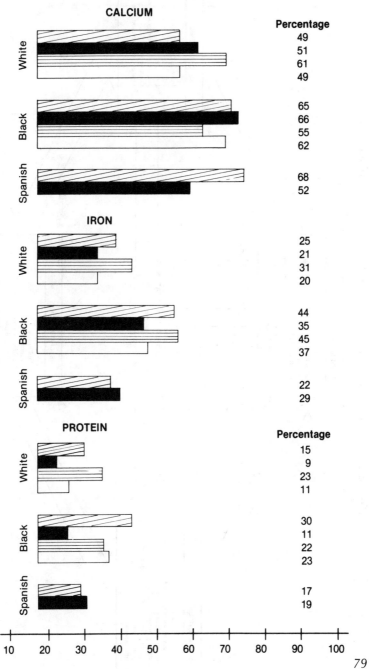

FIGURE 2.2 Factors influencing the nutritional status of older adults

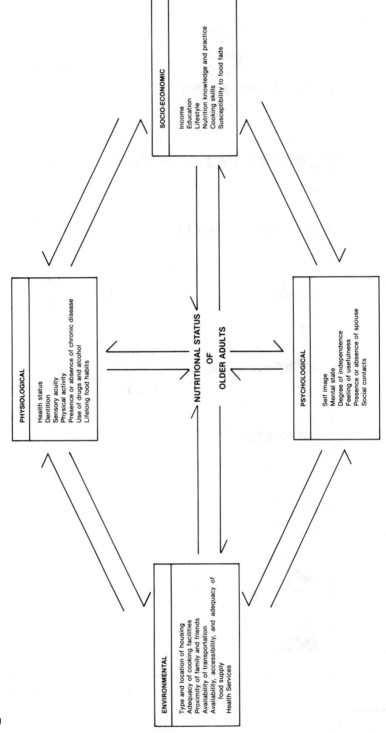

such as cakes, pastries, cereals and desserts (Davidson et al., 1962; Anderson, 1971; Nizel, 1976; Lewis, 1978). Institutions caring for older persons may serve pureed foods. Even though older adults eat these foods, reports indicate that they prefer the consistency of foods enjoyed in youth (Lewis, 1978).

Because of the benefits of preventive dental services, such as fluoridation of water supplies and better dental hygiene, future cohorts of older Americans will probably have better dentition.

Senses of Taste and Smell

It is still debatable as to whether or not the decline in taste sensitivity reported among many elderly is a normal process of aging. Some researchers believe that the changes in taste acuity experienced by older adults are due to disease conditions, such as diabetes and renal failure, drugs, poor oral hygiene, and zinc deficiency (Kamath, 1982).

However, some studies have shown that elderly persons are less sensitive to all basic tastes (Cooper et al., 1959; Kamath 1982). With age, there is a steady decline in the number of frontal taste buds, sensitivity olfactory receptor cells, and secretion of saliva. As a result of these changes, older persons commonly complain that foods taste bitter, sour, and dry (Schiffman, 1977; Busse, 1978).

The use of drugs with anti-cholinergic properties seriously decreases saliva secretion (Lamy, 1981). The diminished flow of saliva makes swallowing difficult and eating less enjoyable.

Vision and Hearing

Impaired vision and hearing are among the five most frequently reported chronic conditions by the elderly (Filner and Williams, 1979); some of these sensory losses have been described in Chapter 1. Uncorrected visual problems can result in difficulty in reading food labels, prices, package directions, and recipes. This may cause a loss of interest in food shopping and preparation and problems in seeing food on a plate. Because of their increased need for illumination, many older persons object to eating in dimly lit rooms or areas lit by flickering candlelight.

Hearing impairments common in old age cause some older persons to be reluctant to eat in public places or at large social gatherings (Busse, 1978). Because of difficulty in communicating, they feel isolated even when surrounded by people.

Digestion and Absorption

With advancing years, there is a reduction in enzymatic activity which adversely affects digestion (Cape, 1978, pp. 23–24). The decreased pancreatic lipase concentration, along with the impairment of gallbladder function, reduces the efficiency of fat digestion and can lead to flatulence, about which so many older persons complain.

Nutrient absorption may be depressed due to reduced gastric acidity, atrophy of the intestinal mucosa and decreased vascularity (Bhanthumnavin, 1977). For example, the reduced gastric acidity may lead to impaired absorption of iron from plant sources (Jacobs, and Owen, 1969).

Many over-the-counter and prescribed medications impair nutrient utilization and change the digestive and absorptive capacities of the gastrointestinal tract (Lamy, 1980; Roe, 1978). Many older adults are overly anxious about constipation. It has been reported that 27% of men and women 45 years of age or older use laxatives more than three times a week (Albanese, 1980). Excessive use of mineral oil may cause deficiencies of the fat soluble vitamins, A, D, E and K (Roe, 1978, p. 130). Cathartic agents may result in increased intestinal loss of potassium and calcium (March, 1976, p. 67; Roe, 1978, p. 130).

Circulation

With age, there is reduced blood flow from the intestinal mucosa to the liver, where food is metabolized. The hepatic blood flow of individuals 65 years or older is approximately 40 to 50% of that of persons 25 years of age (Bhanthumnavin, 1977). The hepatic enzyme concentrations and enzyme response to external stimuli also decrease. Therefore, the absorbed nutrients may not be converted into usable forms. In addition, the absorbed nutrients may not be efficiently transported to tissues because of cardiac insufficiency, arteriosclerotic or other age-related changes in the circulatory system.

Neuromuscular Coordination

In later years, the ability to maintain fine discriminating hand movements may decline, reaction times become slower, and balance may be poorer (Masoro, 1976; Posner, 1979, pp. 3,8). Arthritis and rheumatism may affect mobility and dexterity. Problems in coordination may make food shopping, preparation, and eating both difficult and painful. Accidents associated with food shopping and preparation may increase. Many older adults dislike cooking because of a fear of burning themselves, spilling foods, and dropping containers. Those having difficulty in hand-to-mouth motion of eating may be assisted by self-help eating devices.

Body Composition and Weight

As the human body ages, there is a loss of lean body mass, reflected by a decrease in total body water. This tissue loss is due to death of cells which are replaced by connective tissue and fat. Consequently, the connective tissue and fat proportions of the body increase with age (Watkin, 1982). The loss of tissue also results in a lower basal metabolic rate; on the average, the basal metabolic rate decreases approximately 20 percent between the ages of 30 and 90.

The reductions in voluntary physical activities which occur with age are much greater than the reductions in basal energy expenditures (McGandy et al., 1966), but the combination of factors leads to a significantly lower need for energy in older adults.

Even though investigations have shown energy intake to decrease with advancing years and to be less than the recommended dietary allowances (Table 2.3), many elderly are overweight and some are obese (Weg, 1978, pp. 30,31; Kohrs et al., 1978). (Obesity is defined as an excessive accumulation of fat, where body weight exceeds 20% of "ideal" weight.) Some explanations for this discrepancy may be that the persons surveyed incorrectly reported portions of foods consumed, or forgot to report all foods eaten, or that the adjustment factors for the decrease in basal metabloic rate and reduction in physical activity have been underestimated. There is evidence that older persons tend to underestimate the portions of foods eaten, especially foods high in calories and low in other essential nutrients (Madden et al., 1976; Gersovitz et al., 1978). Also, once a sedentary person becomes overweight, this body weight can be maintained on a very marginal diet.

Jeffay states that in many persons there is a natural tendency to increase both body weight and the percentage of fat with age (Jeffay, 1981). Excessive accumulation of fat is believed to be related to decreased life span. Some health problems—hypertension,

TABLE 2.3
Mean Energy Intakes Studied in HANES II Compared
with the 1980 RDA (persons ≥ 55 years of age)

	N	Mean Energy Intake (Kcal)	Energy–1980 RDA 51–75 years
Males			
55–64 years	1,227	2071	2400 ± 400
65–74 years	1,199	1829	
Females			
55–64 years	1,329	1401	1800 ± 400
65–74 years	1,416	1295	

Source: Carroll, M.D., Abraham, S., and Dresser, C.M. *National Center for Health Statistics: Dietary intake source data, United States 1976–1980.* Hyattsville, Md.: U.S. Government Printing Office, 1982.

cardiovascular disease, diabetes, and renal disease—may be caused or exacerbated by obesity. Reduction in body weight can reduce the harmful effects of these diseases. Recent reevaluation of data examining the effect of obesity on mortality suggests that the best weight for disease prevention and longevity appears to be approximately 10 percent above the "ideal" body weight (Andres, 1980; Keys, 1980; Jeffay, 1982).

Chronic Diseases

The physiological changes described previously tend to complicate chronic degenerative diseases, and in some instances they are directly related to the course of the disease. Among older Americans, heart disease, cancer, and stroke are responsible for 75 percent of all deaths (U.S. DHEW, 1978). Diet appears to play an important role in the etiology, prevention, and treatment of these diseases (National Research Council [NRC] 1982, p. 1.14; Glueck and Connor, 1978; Rifkind et al., 1979).

Both epidemiological evidence and experiments in animals suggest that high fat diets tend to increase the risk of breast and colon cancers and coronary heart disease (NRC, 1982 p. 1.3; Rifkind et al., 1979). Frequent consumption of salt-cured, salt-pickled, and smoked foods has been associated with a greater risk for stomach and esophageal cancers (NRC, 1982 p. 13); whereas low-fat diets or frequent consumption of citrus fruits, carotene-rich and cruciferous vegetables are associated with a reduction in the incidence of cancer at specific sites. For example, investigators have found an inverse relationship between the risk of lung, urinary bladder and larynx cancers and the consumption of foods that are Vitamin A or carotene-rich; and between the risk of stomach and esophageal cancers and the consumption of Vitamin C-rich foods (NRC, 1982 pp. 9.6–9.10).

Osteoporosis contributes greatly to the high incidence of fractures in the elderly. Calcium and vitamin D play important roles in bone integrity and in the development of osteoporosis. Many older Americans are in negative calcium balance due to inadequate calcium intake, decreased intestinal absorption and reduced physical activity. Long-term negative balance results in decreased bone mass (Heaney et al., 1982). Vitamin D deficiency is associated with calcium malabsorption (Bullamore et al., 1970; Parfitt et al., 1982). The principal cause of inadequate vitamin D nutriture in elderly persons is diminished exposure to sunlight.

Psychological Conditions

Loneliness, grief, apathy, and stress due to loss of spouse, relatives, or friends; financial concerns; fear of illness and death; or a change in familiar environment can all contribute to a loss of appetite and possibly to malnutrition (Rao, 1973; Sherwood, 1973; Grotkowski and Sims, 1978; Krondl et al., 1982).

Socioeconomic and Environmental Influences on the Nutritional Status of Older Adults

In applying a public health approach to the development of nutritional intervention programs for the elderly, it is important to consider how their socioeconomic and environmental characteristics may contribute to their nutritional status. The goal of organized efforts is to apply nutrition intervention stategies that will prolong and support independent living in the community for as many older persons as possible. However, it is essential first to identify the sub-groups at risk and to assess their needs.

Incomes

Poor older adults have been found to eat less nutritionally adequate foods and to suffer from more nutrition-related health problems (USDA, 1980b). As food prices rise, older adults on low incomes often reduce the amount of money they spend for food to compensate for increasing costs of medical care, medications, housing, heat, utilities, and transportation (Learner and Kivett, 1981). Older persons living in one- or two-person households have been found to spend a larger proportion of their income for food, yet buy less meat and fewer prepared foods, beverages, and dairy products than younger persons (Gallo et al., 1979 pp. 4,41). Many do not purchase the larger, economy-sized food packages, because they cannot carry these items home, or store or use them (Food Advisory Board, 1981).

Housing

Many older persons live in housing without adequate equipment for storing and preparing foods. Living in housing with inadequate food preparation facilities makes it difficult to obtain a varied nutritious diet. Other barriers to obtaining an appropriate diet are walk-up apartments requiring the older person to carry heavy bundles of food up steps, and, housing in high crime areas, which deters older persons from going out to shop for food (Sherwood, 1973). Another obstacle is living in an urban or rural area without easy access to food markets offering a variety of foods at competitive prices (Howell and Loeb, 1969; Learner and Kivett, 1981).

Transportation

Lack of convenient affordable transportation directly affects access to food for many older adults, especially for women living in rural areas (Learner and Kivett, 1981; Rawson et al., 1978; Kivett, 1978). Even those persons close to transportation may be reluctant to use it if physically handicapped or needing to move at a slower pace than the rushing crowd. Older adults often feel uncomfortable or ashamed to ask relatives or friends repeatedly to transport them to grocery stores or to congregate meal sites (Timmreck, 1977).

Education and Literacy

Nutrition knowledge is found to be associated with general educational attainment (Clancy, 1975; Brown, 1976; Todhunter, 1976; Templeton, 1978; Fanelli, 1984). Fifty percent of persons over 65 years of age have not completed the first year of high school (USDA, 1976). This suggests that many older adults have not had access to current nutrition information, and are unable to read and apply information available in print.

Advertising and Quackery

Because of the increasing prevalance of chronic and crippling disorders among older adults, many are vulnerable to promoters of quick cures. Large numbers of older persons purchase fad diet books, nutrient supplements, and special "health foods" promoted to cure chronic conditions (Grotkowski and Sims, 1978; Harrill and Bowski, 1981). Older persons spend millions of dollars on these expensive and falsely promoted products, often using money which could be more wisely spent on nutritious food, medical care, and more comfortable housing.

The federal government has taken steps through the establishment of the Food and Drug Administration (FDA) to protect the public against false claims and other hazards inherent in the production and distribution of foodstuffs. The FDA administers laws which, among other functions, regulate the safety of foods, the use of additives, and the labeling of food products. It also develops and publishes guidelines on convenience foods and other matters relating to food. Frequently the efforts of the FDA are resisted by manufacturers, or even consumers on the grounds of preserving freedom of choice.

An important responsibility of nutritionists and other health professionals is to educate the elderly so that they can make wise nutritional choices about foods and supplements.

Community Nutrition Services for Older Adults

With an increasing older population, community services must be expanded to help persons to prolong their years of independence with supportive and life-enriching programs. Since adequate nutrition is an essential life support, community food, nutrition, and dietetic services must be elements within the system of organized community efforts.

Goals of community nutrition services for older adults are:

- To assure maximum health and vitality through a nutritionally adequate diet that considers individual physical, social, and emotional needs.
- To provide older persons and their caretakers with current, scientifically sound, understandable nutrition education and diet counseling.
- To provide supportive community food and nutrition services to those older adults who require them because of health needs, physical disabilities, needs for social contacts, or inadequate income.
- To provide consumer protection in relation to safety, cost, quality, packaging, and labeling of nutritious foods.
- To assure standards of nutritional care and quality of food services for all community and group care/health care programs serving the older population.
- To provide education, training, and technical assistance in nutrition, dietetics, and food service management to personnel caring for older persons in institutions, in community programs, or in their own homes.
- To conduct continuing research to advance knowledge regarding the unique nutritional requirements of the aging, and development of cost-effective programs to meet these needs.

The continuum of food and nutrition programs for older adults is displayed in Figure 2.3. These services are designed to meet the needs of people with varying levels of independence.

Public health professionals concerned about the elderly should know about desirable food and nutrition services, and encourage their use in their communities. They should encourage the establishment of needed services not currently available. For the promotion of health, prevention of disease, and maintenance of independent living of the elderly, the following food and nutrition services should be available in every community.

FIGURE 2.3 Overview of community food/nutrition programs for older adults

FROM INDEPENDENCE ————————— SEMI DEPENDENCE ————————— DEPENDENCE

— Well Elderly — to — Mid-level need for support — Fragile Elderly

| Support Self Care In Own Home | Maintain Ability to Live at Home With Help or at Relative's Home | Institutional Care |

Food Stamps
Dining Out Programs
Congregate Meal Programs
Expanded Food & Nutrition Education Program

Nutrition Education
  Mass media
  Senior Centers
  Cooperative Extension
  Dial-a-Dietitian

Diet Counseling Services
Public Health Nutritionists
Dietitians in Private Practice

Home health services with diet counseling
Homemaker Services (Assistance with meal preparation)
Home delivered meal programs

Food Shopping Assistance
Chore Services
Adult Day Care

Food service and Nutritional care in:
  Retirement Homes
  Personal Care Homes
  Nursing Homes
    Intermediate Care Facilities
    Skilled Nursing Care Facilities
  Hospice

State licensure and federal Medicare/Medicaid conditions of participate establish standards for food service meeting nutritional needs and food sanitation.

Consideration in identifying and evaluating community food and/or nutrition programs:

1. Areas of dependency identified among elderly
   a. Economic—e.g., Food Stamps
   b. Social/Emotional—e.g., Congregate Meals, Adult Day Care
   c. Physical disability and mobility—e.g., Food shopping assistance, home delivered meals
   d. Nutritional—all food assistance and food service should address
2. Program availability and accessibility, adequacy to meet total needs
3. Program sponsorship—official (legislation) vs voluntary agencies; use of volunteers
4. Standards—Professional, Licensure/Certification
   a. Food service
   b. Nutrition care
5. Program cost effectiveness, cost benefits, consumer satisfaction

89

Food and Nutrition Services for the Well Elderly

Food Stamps

The U.S. Department of Agriculture funds and administers Food Stamps through the state welfare agencies and county social services. This program provides low-income persons with bonus food purchasing power. Older persons can use Food Stamps to purchase food at the grocery store, or to pay for congregate meals or "Dining Out Programs" in participating restaurants. The Food Stamp Program has been sponsored by the Federal Government since the mid-1960s. The bonus purchasing power provided to participants is based on the current cost of the U.S. Department of Agriculture's Thrifty Food Plan, the applicant's income, and essential expenses. Many elderly persons depend on the Food Stamp Program to enable them to purchase a minimally adequate diet. It has been estimated that in 1981 at least 2.026 million persons over 60 years of age participated in the Food Stamp Program, while some 3.2 million older persons were eligible to receive food stamps (U.S. Senate, 1982, pp. 10–11). Regretfully, no formalized nutrition education program has been funded as a component of this program.

The Expanded Food and Nutrition Education Program of the cooperative Extension Service, also funded by the U.S. Department of Agriculture, has provided limited guidance to low-income elderly in use of Food Stamps.

Congregate Meal Programs

These programs are currently funded by the federal Administration on Aging, as authorized by the Older Americans Act, Title III. Programs are administered by state agencies on aging through the area agencies on aging or service providers on aging. Local service providers in the communities, such as churches, senior centers, schools, and recreation centers, provide one nutritious hot meal a day, five or more days a week, to eligible persons over 60 years of age and their spouses. These meal programs provide both meals and socialization. The meal is designed to meet the nutritional standards of one-third of the current Recommended Dietary Allowances of the Food and Nutrition Board of the National Research

Council. Meals are free of charge, so no one is turned away from a meal for inability to pay. However, participants can make voluntary contributions. Nutrition education, recreation, health screening, supportive services, transportation, and outreach are recommended as adjunct services. In many communities, the limited level of funding and outreach restricts the program size and only a small proportion of eligible older persons enjoy the benefits. In 1981, three million elderly were served by this program (U.S. Senate, 1982, p. 13).

Dining Out Programs

In some areas, state and local agencies concerned about helping older adults to obtain low-cost nutritious meals have negotiated with family type restaurants or cafeterias in residential areas having a concentrated older population. These resturants serve a lower cost, nutritious meal plate to older customers, perhaps with smaller portions of a variety of foods. Participants may be asked to eat at an earlier meal hour to avoid the usual customer rush. Some programs accept Food Stamps from the senior customers.

Nutrition Education

Nutrition education for older adults can be provided through mass media such as radio, television, and local newspapers. If readily accessible in their communities, senior citizens enjoy participating in well-conceived group nutrition education programs presented by public health departments, adult education programs, county cooperative extension services, or congregate meal programs. Potential benefits to older persons participating in nutrition education are the promotion of health and stamina through maintaining optimal nutrition; making better use of their food dollars and/or Food Stamps by selecting more nutrient-dense foods; resisting food and diet fads which might delay seeking necessary medical treatment; better understanding of physician-prescribed therapeutic diets; and enhancing self-esteem and pride by exercising some self-control over food choices for health. Senior citizens enjoy and learn from nutrition education programs in which they actively participate and where the leader respects their experience. Group nutrition education can be enhanced by cooking demonstrations, nutrition games, and group discussions.

Diet Counseling Services

Many older adults have some diet modification prescribed by their physicians, and need guidance in planning meals and purchasing and preparing suitable food. Professional diet counseling that is effective in modifying food choices and patient management, particularly for diets prescribed for weight reduction, diabetes, hypertension, cardiovascular disease, and digestive problems, can be cost beneficial by reducing needs for medical and hospital care. With increasing age and physical and/or mental disability, many elderly people can remain in their own homes or homes of relatives if they have additional supportive services. These services may be provided by qualified nutritionists in public health departments on a sliding fee scale or by registered dietitians (RDs) in private practice. Although many of these services have demonstrated their effectiveness over a period of years, such services are not consistently available and accessible in communities throughout the U.S.

Food and Nutrition Services to Maintain Dependent Elderly Persons at Home

Food Shopping Assistance

This service provides the older person with transportation and help to go to the food market, or home delivery of groceries to the client. Such assistance is frequently organized by area agencies on aging, nutrition service providers, or as a volunteer service by clubs, churches, or women's groups. Those helping with food shopping should have knowledge of basic nutritional needs and individual dietary requirements to help guide food choices. Assistance at the store may include physical help, guidance in finding needed food items, reading package labels or prices, help with checkout, carrying food to the kitchen, and helping with proper food storage.

Homemaker/Home Health Aide Services

Home health agencies may provide these services. If homemakers and home health aides have responsibilities for planning and preparing meals and food shopping, they should be trained in geriatric nutrition and the commonly prescribed therapeutic diets by a qualified nutritionist or registered dietitian. Diet counseling should also be an available service. To date, Medicare will reimburse nutritionists or registered dietitians only as consultants and educators to the nursing staff and not for direct services; however, studies are underway and legislation is being considered for making diet counseling by a registered dietitian available as a reimbursible service under Medicare.

Home Delivered Meals

In many communities, Meals-on-Wheels are sponsored by volunteer church groups, community service groups, or by local caterers or restaurants. Home-delivered meals may be provided for homebound people as a component of the local Congregate Meal Program funded under Title III of the Older Americans Act. These programs deliver one ready-to-eat meal a day and sometimes an additional snack to the client at home. Food may be provided as a hot or cold meal or in a frozen, dried, or canned form. Programs usually provide meals for five or more days of the week. Meals should meet one-third to one-half of RDA standards. For many older persons, the meal and the personal contact of the deliverer are highlights of the day. These programs are particularly useful to the older person isolated at home during a temporary illness, convalescence, or bad weather, as well as those who are permanently home-bound.

Adult Day Care

These programs provide supervised care during the day while a relative is at work. Day care programs for older persons with physical and/or mental disability generally serve one or more nutritious meals and snacks. Programs may be offered by a social service agency, senior center, or as an auxillary service of a home for the elderly.

Food and Nutrition Services for Older Adults in Group Care/Health Care Facilities

Institutional Food Services

About five percent of elderly persons in the United States live in long-term care facilities. Institutional care for the elderly has grown since World War II, partly as a result of the increase in the number and proportion of frail old people. Greater dispersal and geographical separation of families often leaves older relatives separated from their children. Since 1966 increased funds have also been available for institutional care through Medicaid and Medicare which stimulated the growth of nursing homes.

Institutional care for the elderly is provided in retirement homes, boarding homes, personal care homes, homes providing intermediate and skilled nursing care, and hospices providing terminal care. Sponsorship includes proprietary, denominational, non-profit, and government-sponsored facilities.

Assurance of the quality of personal, health, nursing, and nutritional care and safety has evolved through development of state licensure regulations and federal conditions of participation for facilities receiving funds through Medicaid and Medicare. State licensure regulations generally have evolved since the late 1950s. Standards for nutritional care usually require that written menus be planned to meet the current Recommended Dietary Allowances for older adults through three daily meals and snacks served at appropriate times; that therapeutic diets be served as prescribed by physicians; that there be dining rooms to serve those persons able to use them; that help be provided with feeding as needed; and that food sanitation codes be met. Federal conditions of participation for Medicare and Medicaid have additionally required employment of a registered dietitian as a consultant to a designated qualified food service supervisor. Individual patient nutrition assessments, much needed by many of the fragile elderly, and nutrition care planning, are required.

Nutrition Services for Older Adults as a Public Health Concern

Food is important to the older adult not only to meet nutritional needs, but frequently also to manage a medically diagnosed condition. Satisfying meals meet emotional needs and provide satisfying social contacts. Food service and nutrition care programs in the community and in institutions are important to maintain maximum independence and a positive self-image. Access to and/or availability of food and nutrition programs are not consistent over the United States. Unfortunately, except for the Food Stamp Program and Congregate Meal Programs, no data are available for the total funding or numbers participating in the various programs described, despite their importance in maintaining the well being of older people in the community. As the number of older people increases, the need increases for community programs. Food and nutrition services are essential services for the elderly, whether supported by official or voluntary efforts. If appropriate, sliding scale fees for services may be used to help meet the costs.

Expert consultation in nutrition, diet, and in nutrition program development should be utilized by those planning and administering services for the elderly at the local, state, or federal levels. At the state level, consultation is available from the nutrition unit of the state health agency. The nutrition consultant employed in the state aging agency has in-depth knowledge regarding the congregate and home-delivered meal programs funded through Title III of the Older Americans Act. Dietary consultants or institutional nutrition consultants in health facilities service units responsible for licensure and certification are up to date on nutrition care and food service regulations and conditions of participation for Title XVIII (Medicare) and Title XIX (Medicaid). Other sources of nutrition consultation are the departments of nutrition in universities and nutritionists in cooperative extension services. At the local level, resource persons include the public health nutritionist in the county health department, the extension service home economist, and the registered dietitian consulting with area nursing homes or employed in the community hospital. These professionals could be resources to use in planning, implementing, or advocating for needed nutrition services to help older adults in the community.

Professional services of nutritionists and registered dietitians can be expanded by mobilizing retired or homemaker nutrition professionals in the community. Through the state or district dietetic association, these volunteers can be identified and mobilized. They can be used to train care providers or peer counselors or to conduct nutrition education programs.

References

Albanese, A. A. and Wein, E. H. Nutritional problems of the elderly. *Aging*, 1980, Sept.–Oct., 7–16.

Albanese, A. A. *Nutrition for the Elderly*. New York, N.Y.: Alan R. Liss, Inc., 1980.

Anderson, E. L. Eating patterns before and after dentures. *Journal of the American Dietetic Association*, 1971, *58*, 421–426.

Andres, R. Effect of obesity on total mortality. *International Journal of Obesity*, 1980, *4*, 318–386.

Bhanthumnavin, K. and Schuster, M. M. Aging in gastrointestinal function. In C. E. Finch and L. Hayflick (Eds.), *Handbook of the Biology of Aging*. New York, N.Y.: Van Nostrand Reinhold, 1977.

Bullamore, J. R., Gallagher, J. C., Wilkinson, R., Nordin, B. E. C., and Marshall, D. H. Effect of age on calcium absorption. *Lancet*, Sept. 2, 1970, 535–537.

Brown, E. L. Factors influencing food choices and intake. *Geriatrics*, 1976, *31*, 89–92.

Busse, E. W. How mind, body, and environment influence nutrition in the elderly. *Postgraduate Medicine*, 1978, *63*, 118–125.

Cape, R. *Aging: Its Complex Management*. Hagerstown, Md.: Harper and Row Publishers, 1978.

Carroll, M. D., Abraham, S., and Dresser, C. M. *National Center for Health Statistics: Dietary Intake Source Data, United States 1976–1980*. Hyattsville, Md.: U.S. Government Printing Office, 1982.

Cooper, R. M. Bilash, I., and Zubek, J. P. The effect of age on taste sensitivity. *Journal of Gerontology*, 1959, *14*, 56–58.

Clancy, K. L. Preliminary observations on media use and food habits of the elderly. *The Gerontologist*, 1975, *15*, 529–532.

Davidson, C. S., Livermore, J., Anderson, P., and Kaufman, S. The nutrition of a group of apparently healthy aging persons. *American Journal of Clinical Nutrition*, 1962, *10*, 181–199.

Fanelli, M. T. Nutrition knowledge of older Americans. In J. J. B. Anderson, (Ed.), *Nutrition, Aging and the Aged*. Carrboro, N.C.: Health Sciences Consortium, 1984 (in press).

Filner, B. and Williams, T. F. Health promotion for the elderly: reducing functional dependency. In *Healthy People, The Surgeon General's Report on Health Promotion and Disease Prevention. Background Papers*.

Washington, D.C.: U.S. Department of Health, Education and Welfare, 1979, pp. 365–386.

Food Advisory Board. *Profile of Older Americans,* Third edition. Rye, N.Y.: ITT Continental Baking Company, 1981.

Gallo, A. E., Salathe, L. E., and Boehm, W. T. *Senior Citizens: Food Expenditure Patterns and Assistance.* Washington, D.C.: U.S. Department of Agriculture, 1979.

Gersovitz, M., Madden, J. P., and Smiciklas-Wright, H. Validity of the 24-hour dietary recall and the seven-day record for group comparisons. *Journal of the American Dietetic Association,* 1978, *73,* 48–55.

Gersovitz, M., Motil, K., Munro, H. N., Scrimshaw, N. S., and Young, V. R. Human protein requirements: assessment of the adequacy of the current Recommended Dietary Allowance for dietary protein in elderly men and women. *American Journal of Clinical Nutrition,* 1982, *35,* 6–14.

Glueck, C. J. and Connor, W. E. Diet-coronary heart disease relationships reconnoitered. *American Journal of Clinical Nutrition,* 1978, *31,* 727–737.

Green, J. Nutritional care considerations of older Americans. *Journal of the National Medical Association,* 1979, *71,* 791–793.

Grotkowski, M. L. and Sims, L. S. Nutritional knowledge, attitudes, and dietary practices of the elderly. *Journal of The American Dietetic Association,* 1978, *72,* 499–506.

Harrill, I. and Bowski, M. M. Relation of age and sex to nutrient supplement usage in a group of adults in Colorado. *Journal of Nutrition for the Elderly,* 1981, *1,* 51–64.

Heaney, R. P., Gallagher, J. C., Johnston, C. C., Neer, R., Parfitt, A. M., Chir, B., and Whedon, G. D. Calcium nutrition and bone health in the elderly. *American Journal of Clinical Nutrition,* 1982, *36,* 986–1013.

Howell, S. C. and Loeb, M. B. Nutrition and aging: a monograph for practitioners. *The Gerontologist,* 1969, *9,* 1–122.

Iber, F. L., Blass, J. P., Brin, M., and Leevy, C. M. Thiamine in the elderly—relation to alcholism and to neurological degenerative disease. *American Journal of Clinical Nutrition,* 1982, *36,* 1067–1082.

Jacobs, A. M. and Owen, G. M. The effect of age on iron absorption. *Journal of Gerontology,* 1969, *24,* 95–96.

Jansen, C. and Harrill, I. Intakes and serum levels of protein and iron for 70 elderly women. *American Journal of Clinical Nutrition,* 1977, *30,* 1414–1422.

Jeffay, H. Obesity and aging. *American Journal of Clinical Nutrition,* 1982, *36,* 809–811.

Kamath, S. K. Taste acuity and aging. *American Journal of Clinical Nutrition,* 1982, *36,* 766–775.

Keys, A. Overweight, obesity, coronary heart disease and mortality. *Nutrition Reviews,* 1980, *38,* 297–307.

Kivett, V. R. Loneliness and the rural widow. *Family Coordinator,* 1978, *27,* 387–391.

Kohrs, M. B., O'Neal, R., Preston, A., Eklund, D., and Abrahams, O. Nutritional status of elderly residents in Missouri, *American Journal of Clinical Nutrition,* 1978, *31,* 2186–2197.

Kohrs, M. B. A rational diet for the elderly. *American Journal of Clinical Nutrition,* 1982, *36,* 796–802.

Krondl, M., Lau, D., Yurkiw, M. A., and Coleman, P. H. Food use and perceived food meanings of the elderly. *Journal of the American Dietetic Association,* 1982, *80,* 523–529.

Lamy, P. P. Nutrition and the elderly. *The Journal of Practical Nursing,* 1980, *30,* 13–14, 41.

Lamy, P. P. Nutrition, drugs and the elderly. *Occasional Report Series.* Chapel Hill, N.C.: Institute of Nutrition, 1981.

Learner, R. M. and Kivett, V. R. Discriminators of perceived dietary adequacy among the rural elderly. *Journal of the American Dietetic Association,* 1981, *78,* 330–337.

Lewis, C. M. *Nutritional Considerations for the Elderly.* Philadelphia, Penn.: F. A. Davis Company, 1978.

Lynch, S. R., Finch, C. A., Monsen, E. R., and Cook, J. D. Iron status of elderly Americans. *American Journal of Clinical Nutrition,* 1982, *36,* 1032–1045.

Madden, J. P., Goodman, S. J., and Guthrie, H. A. Validity of the 24-hour recall. Analysis of data obtained from elderly subjects. *Journal of The American Dietetic Association,* 1976, *68,* 143–147.

March, D. C. *Handbook: Interactions of Selected Drugs with Nutritional Status in Man.* Chicago, Il.: American Dietetic Association, 1976.

Masoro, E. J. Physiologic changes with aging. In M. Winick (Ed.), *Nutrition and Aging.* New York, N.Y.: John Wiley and Sons, 1976, pp. 61–76.

McGandy, R. B., Barrows, C. H. Spanias, A., Meredith, A., Stone, J. L., and Norris, A. H. Nutrient intake and energy expenditure in man of different ages. *Journal of Gerontology,* 1966, *21,* 581–587.

National Research Council (NRC), Food and Nutrition Board, Committee on Dietary Allowances. *Recommended Dietary Allowances,* Ninth Edition. Washington, D.C.: National Academy of Sciences, 1980.

National Research Council (NRC). *Diet, Nutrition and Cancer.* Washington, D.C.: National Academy Press, 1982.

Nizel, A. E. Role of nutrition in the oral health of the aging patient. *Dental Clinics of North America,* 1976, *20,* 569–584.

Nordstrom, J. W. Trace mineral nutrition in the elderly. *American Journal of Clinical Nutrition,* 1982, *36,* 788–795.

O'Hanlon, P. and Kohrs, M. B. Dietary studies of older Americans. *American Journal of Clinical Nutrition,* 1978, *31,* 1257–1269.

Parfitt, A. M., Chir, B., Gallagher, J. C., Heaney, R. P., Johnston, C. C.,

Neer, R., and Whedon, G. D. Vitamin D and bone health in the elderly. *American Journal of Clinical Nutrition,* 1982, *36,* 1014–1031.

Posner, B. *Nutrition and the Elderly.* Lexington, Ma.: D. C. Heath and Company, 1979.

Rao, D. B. Problems of nutrition in the aged. *Journal of American Geriatrics Society,* 1973, *21,* 362–367.

Rawson, I. G., Weinberg, E. I., Herold, J., and Holtz, J. Nutrition of rural elderly in southwestern Pennsylvania. *The Gerontologist,* 1978, *18,* 24–29.

Rifkind, B. M., Goor, R. S., and Levy, R. I. Current status of the role of dietary treatment in the prevention and management of coronary heart disease. *Medical Clinics of North America,* 1979, *63,* 911–925.

Roe, D. A. *Drug-Induced Nutritional Deficiencies.* Westport, Ct.: The AVI Publishing Co., Inc., 1978.

Rosenberg, I. H., Bowman, B. B., Cooper, B. A., Halsted, C. H., and Lindenbaum, J. Folate nutrition in the elderly. *American Journal of Clinical Nutrition,* 1982, *36,* 1060–1066.

Schiffman, S. Food recognition by the elderly. *Journal of Gerontology,* 1977, *32,* 586–592.

Sherwood, S. Sociology of food and eating: implications for action for the elderly. *American Journal of Clinical Nutrition,* 1973, *26,* 1108–1110.

Spencer, H., Kramer, L., and Osis, D. Factors contributing to calcium loss in aging. *American Journal of Clinical Nutrition,* 1982, *36,* 776–787.

Templeton, C. L. Nutrition counseling needs in a geriatric population. *Geriatrics,* 1978, *33,* 59–66.

Timmreck, T. C. Nutrition problems: A survey of the rural elderly. *Geriatrics,* 1977, *32,* 137–140.

Todhunter, E. N. Lifestyle and nutrient intake in the elderly. In M. Winick (Ed.), *Nutrition and Aging.* New York, N.Y.: John Wiley and Sons, 1976, pp. 119–127.

U.S. Department of Agriculture. Consumer concerns affect food purchases. In *The Farm Index,* Washington, D.C.: U.S. Government Printing Office, 1976.

U.S. Department of Agriculture and U.S. Department of Health, Education and Welfare. *Nutrition and Your Health.* Washington, D.C.: U.S. Government Printing Office, 1980a.

U.S. Department of Agriculture. *Food and Nutrient Intakes of Individuals in 1 Day in the United States, Spring 1977.* Washington, D.C.: Science and Education Administration, 1980b.

U.S. Department of Commerce, Bureau of the Census. *Social Indicators.* Washington, D.C.: U.S. Government Printing Office, 1976.

U.S. Department of Health, Education, and Welfare and Health Services Mental Health Administration. *Ten-State Nutrition Survey 1968–1970.* Atlanta, Ga.: Center for Disease Control, 1972.

U.S. Department of Health, Education and Welfare, Public Health Service, Health Resources Administration: *Preliminary Findings of the First Health and Nutrition Examination Survey, U.S. 1971–72*. Rockville, Md.: National Center for Health Statistics, 1974.

U.S. Department of Health, Education and Welfare, Public Health Service, Health Resources Administration. *Health, United States, 1976–77*. Washington, D.C.: U.S. Government Printing Office, 1977.

U.S. Department of Health, Education and Welfare, Division of Vital Statistics. *Monthly Vital Statistics Report*, Vol. 26, No. 2, Supplement 2. Rockville, Md.: National Center for Health Statistics, 1978.

U.S. Senate, Special Committee on Aging. *Developments in Aging: 1981. Volume 2, Appendix*. Washington, D.C.: U.S. Government Printing Office, 1982.

Watkin, D. M. The physiology of aging. *American Journal of Clinical Nutrition*, 1982, *36*, 750–758.

Weg, R. B. *Nutrition and the Later Years*. Los Angeles, Ca.: Ethel Percy Andrus Gerontology Center, University of Southern California Press, 1978.

Williams, E. J. Meeting the nutritional needs of the elderly. *Nursing*, Sept., 1980, 60–63.

PART II

ENVIRONMENTAL ASPECTS OF AGING AND PUBLIC HEALTH

All living organisms are in continual interaction with their environments. The interaction may be as simple as a physical exchange of oxygen and carbon dioxide, or as complex as the building of a community. The relationship of the environment to health was acknowledged in ancient times by Hippocrates, the patron saint of medicine, when he observed that the air, water, and geographical setting of a community told much about the diseases in its inhabitants.

The effect of the environment on the health of the elderly is cause for special public health concern. Older people are often more vulnerable to smog, very hot or cold weather, unsanitary conditions, poor housing, bad lighting, and a range of other disease or injury-inducing situations.

The modern era of public health was initiated by the scientific study of the influences of environment on well-being, and the strategy of modifying the environment to protect the health of the community. A classic case is that of the "Broad Street pump," in which it was observed that cholera was infecting those persons inhabiting a geographical area in London who derived their water supply from a particular pump. According to legend, upon removing the pump handle, making it inoperable, the epidemic receded. The observation that water carried the epidemic disease, and the use of a successful strategy for its control, predated the identification of the cholera vibrio by a number of years. Yet the cholera vibrio, although the last link in the chain of causation, was not the only cause of an outbreak of cholera. The social and physical factors which led to the presence of the organism in the water supply were also parts of the etiology of the medical condition.

Similarly an inadequate housing situation can be a part of the causal chain leading to dependency. By designing and establishing a benign environment, society can do much to prevent injury and disability among the elderly population, and compensate for some of the losses of physical and social function to which old people are exposed.

In the following two chapters, selected aspects of the physical environment especially germane to the well-being of older people are reviewed. Chapter Three addresses the issue of injury control, describing the physiological and psychological factors which make the elderly especially vulnerable to environmental hazards, and discussing strategies for reduction of risk of injury. Chapter Four provides a look at the outcome of public concern with adequate housing for older people—the range of housing policies in the United States.

A number of other environmental factors which could be dealt with are not covered in this section. Especially important, though not highlighted, is the influence of the non-physical environment on both physical and mental health. Such topics as the role of social support in health are discussed mainly in Chapter Five.

3

Preventing Injury to the Elderly[1]

PATRICIA F. WALLER

Introduction

It is generally accepted that most preventable diseases have now been conquered, but there remains one preventable epidemic of alarming proportions: "accidental" injuries. Although this epidemic is a major cause of injury and death in the young, it is particularly serious for elderly persons because of their slower healing and recuperative powers and because of possible complications arising from pre-existing health problems.

Epidemiology of Injuries Among the Elderly

Extent of the Problem

There were 99,000 deaths and 9,400,000 disabling injuries reported in 1981 in the U.S., according to the National Safety Council (1982). Of these, 50,800 deaths and 1,900,000 disabling injuries resulted from motor vehicle crashes, and 21,000 deaths and 3,200,000 injuries occurred in home accidents. The direct cost of these two classes of accidents is estimated to be $49.8 billion, $15.9

[1]The author wishes to express her sincere appreciation to Margaret H. Jones, who reviewed an early draft of this chapter and made many important and valuable suggestions.

billion of which is incurred by medical costs and insurance administration[2]

These 71,800 motor vehicle and home deaths involve large numbers of elderly people, as do the 5,100,000 injuries. Eight-thousand-six-hundred people age 65–74 died from accidental causes; more than 14,600 people age 75 and over died from accidental injuries. Many more are incapacitated, often permanently.

Health care costs are rising dramatically and in the case of the elderly they have become a major personal, social, and political concern. Since most accidents are preventable, usually through a system change, serious attention to this epidemic should be a top priority for public health professionals.

Mortality and Morbidity

Accidental deaths of older persons are predominantly the result of motor vehicle crashes (including pedestrians) and falls, the former being the major cause of fatal injuries from age 65 through 74 years and the latter above age 74. On a population basis males experience a higher mortality rate at all ages, but, in absolute numbers, above age 74 there are more females accidentally injured because of the greater number of females at the higher ages.

Morbidity rates are especially difficult to obtain since accidents are generally underreported. However, on the basis of available data there are some differences between mortality and morbidity rates in that older persons are much more likely to succumb once an injury occurs. Thus injuries among the elderly appear to pose a much greater threat to life.

Even when injury is not fatal, in the case of the elderly the cost of treatment may be much greater because of slower and less complete recuperation. On the whole fractures take much longer to heal in an older person than in a younger one, and wounds resulting from burns or other injury do not heal as rapidly. When injury results in permanent disability, many older persons prefer death to

---

[2]It should be noted that for motor vehicle deaths and injuries, the National Safety Council relies on state reports that are often underestimates. Data from the National Center for Health Statistics, based on extensive home health surveys, indicate that there are almost twice as many motor vehicle injuries as are reported to the National Safety Council.

total incapacitation with no hope for improvement. Thus treatment is even further complicated because the patient is not always working toward the same goal as the health practitioner.

Physiological Changes Affecting Injury Probability

Clearly there are many physiological changes that occur with increasing age, and many of these changes contribute to the probability of accidental injury. Vision, hearing, memory, motor skill, balance and gait, bone strength, and temperature regulation all tend to show some deterioration with increasing age. These changes are described more fully in Chapter 1. It should be noted, however, that any discussion of such age-related modifications must deal in generalities and cannot address the wide range of variation present in the elderly. In fact, for most functions the range of individual differences is greater for the elderly than for any other age group. Nevertheless when performances are averaged there are age-related differences that are readily apparent.

Strategies for Reducing Injuries

An effective approach to injury reduction must be systems-oriented, that is, it must consider the total person-equipment-environment complex to identify where errors are occurring and under what circumstances. Once such information is available, a judgment must be made as to the most cost-effective modifications that will reduce the probability of injury. The history of public health has shown that modifying the human component is usually not the most cost-effective approach, in part because human behavior is often difficult to change and in part because of the inherent limitations of human behavior. For example, although legally drivers may be held responsible for maintaining a high level of constant vigilance over extended periods of time, it is well established that such behavior is beyond human capabilities. Countermeasures that take into account such inherent limitations have a higher probability of success than legal sanctions imposed when errors occur.

From a public health standpoint it is preferable to redesign the tools people work with or the environment in which they operate or both. Cars can be modified to provide more protection in a crash; stairs can have optimal tread and riser dimensions as well as permanent lighting, or dwellings can be designed without stairs: controls on stoves can be designed and arranged to indicate clearly when burners are on.

Strategies for reducing injuries will be considered from the standpoint of modifying the individual; modifying the environment, including modifying equipment such as tools or machines; and modifying the services and support systems.

Modifying the Individual

Usually it is more difficult, more expensive, and less effective or even impossible to modify the individual. Nevertheless, there are times when we have little choice. Education and training are the major approaches to modifying human behavior. Safety education is more likely to succeed to the extent that there is control over the individual such as in the work place. If an industrial plant requires that all workers wear hard hats in the construction area and that failure to do so leads to job suspension, it is highly likely that most workers will conform. However, if the task to be conducted is in the home, it is much more difficult to achieve widespread observance of safety guidelines. Because the elderly usually do not function in a highly-controlled environment in which failure to abide by rules carries significant consequences, modifying the individual through education and training may not always be a highly desirable approach to injury control in this group.

Individual behavior may also be modified through the provision of information such as instructions or warning signs. Such information transfer is more likely to be effective the closer it occurs in time and space to the point of need. Thus warning signs should be placed in close proximity to the hazard. Instructions for medications including any special precautions should be included with the medicine. In this regard, written materials should be expressed in clear and simple language and in type that is large enough to be readily legible. Elderly people, as well as many younger ones, cannot be expected to read the fine print that appears on some packages and inserts accompanying medicines.

Another approach to modifying the individual is through exercise and nutrition. Dietary supplements such as calcium can increase bone strength under certain circumstances. Artificial lighting that includes ultraviolet radiation is associated with reduced incidence of fracture (Hughes and Neer, 1981). Regular exercise helps astronauts reduce bone loss during prolonged weightlessness and appears to reduce such loss in the elderly. In addition, regular exercise improves muscle development and tone which may in turn provide protection to bones in case of impact.

In recent years there have been major changes in the adoption of healthier life styles that include regular exercise and improved diet. To the extent that these practices can be extended to the elderly, they may improve the overall strength and well-being of these people and thus reduce their injury potential. As the younger cohorts grow older, if the modified life styles are maintained there should be a corresponding reduction in certain types of injury.

Modifying the Environment

In our society all too frequently we think of injury as the result of failure on the part of the individual. Thus, people who experience automobile crashes are considered problem drivers. People who are injured on the job are considered careless and inattentive. Yet some of the major advances in injury control have come through environmental modification. A well-designed guardrail can redirect a vehicle into the line of traffic so that it can proceed without delay, whereas without the guardrail the vehicle may catapult into a chasm, a river, or a highway below. A well-designed dwelling for the elderly can include good lighting for the medicine cabinet, storage space that does not require excessive reaching, elimination of stairs, lighting fixtures that enable bulb replacement without the use of a ladder or stepstool, and perhaps full spectrum lighting that includes ultraviolet radiation. Such design would reduce the probability of a variety of home accidents and injuries.

Modifications in the tools and equipment used by the elderly can simplify tasks and thus reduce the probability of error and resulting injury. The arrangement of controls on a stove can greatly simplify the cooking task and reduce the incidence of burns occurring from errors in turning on the wrong burner. Feedback in the form of a bright light situated next to the burner can indicate when a burner is on and reduce the likelihood that it will be left on through forgetfulness. Microwave ovens may prove especially beneficial to the elderly. Well-designed bannisters on both sides of a stairway can provide guidance to the user and aid in case of a slip or stumble.

Modifying Services and Support Systems

Because it may be difficult for some elderly people to continue to care for themselves as they have been able to do in the past, it can be especially useful if there are services available to assist them in some of the more hazardous activities. Hot meals that are made available on a routine basis can reduce the exposure to heat and flame and thus reduce the probability of burns and scalds. Daily assistance in personal hygiene such as bathing can reduce the probability of injuries resulting from falls getting in and out of bathtubs and showers. Door-to-door bus service for the elderly can reduce exposure to traffic hazards as a pedestrian. Regular contact to determine condition and needs of the elderly can enable older people to remain in their own homes beyond what would be possible otherwise. In some cities, police departments or other public agencies make daily telephone calls to check on the status of elderly people living alone. Likewise, mail delivery personnel may note when mail is not being collected and alert help.

Availability and quality of services also make a difference once injury has occurred. Emergency medical services, appropriate medical treatment, and adequate after-care affect the degree of recovery and disability resulting from injury.

Haddon's Strategies

A somewhat different approach to injury control is described by William Haddon (1970, 1972), who considers injury as an uncontrolled exchange of energy that results in damage to animate or inanimate objects (Gibson, 1961). Haddon describes ten different stategies for preventing such exchange of energy, ranging from preventing the energy from being marshalled in the first place (e.g., do not allow the manufacture of chemicals known to be harmful to life) to reducing long-term disability through reparative and rehabilitative measures. His strategies consider how intervention may occur at any stage of the uncontrolled exchange of energy.

Haddon's strategies are not entirely independent. Some measures do not fall clearly into one rather than another category but instead appear to qualify for more than one. Nevertheless, the range of strategies outlined by Haddon encourages the examination of a broader range of potential countermeasures than are usually included in consideration of injury control.

Although the elderly, like other age groups, may suffer from unintentional injury from a wide variety of sources, this chapter will focus primarily on the three major causes of such injury, namely, falls, motor vehicle crashes, and burns. In addition, some attention is given to hypothermia, although there is little research information available.

Falls

It is well known that as people become older many are not only more likely to experience loss of balance and fall, but also more likely to suffer injury when a fall occurs. For many, a fall is the beginning of the end, and it was not uncommon even twenty years ago for orthopedic wards to be filled with elderly patients wasting away in heavy casts. The development of improved surgical procedures, including the use of metal pins to repair broken bones, has led to profound advances in the convalescence and recovery of victims of fractures from falls. Even so, the elderly continue to live with the haunting threat of loss of balance and the often ensuing inability to care for themselves and then loss of independence and quality of life.

Extent of the Problem

Falls are the leading cause of death due to unintentional injury in persons age 75 and over. The death rate from falls is so high in older people that those aged 65 and older account for over 70 percent of all deaths attributed to falls. Studies of populations aged 65 and older suggest that as many as one-third experience falls in a year's time (Campbell, et al. 1981; Prudham and Evans, 1981). While data on nonfatal injuries from falls are not routinely reported, Planek (1982) extrapolates data from the National Health Survey and estimates that approximately 8.5 million persons were injured in home falls in the U.S. in 1977.

While reliable cost figures are not available, Riggs (in Marx, 1980) of the Mayo Clinic estimates that it costs more than one billion dollars each year for acute medical care for elderly persons suffering from broken hips, usually the result of falls. This figure does not include the cost of long-term care.

Age and Sex Differences

The probability of fatal injury resulting from a fall increases with increasing age. Indeed, the progressive vulnerablility of the aged is reflected in the change in death rates between the 65 through 74 age group and the 75 and older group. The population death rate jumps from 13 per 100,000 to 86 per 100,000 (National Safety Council, 1982).

In contrast to some other types of unintentional injury in the elderly, injury-producing falls are much more likely to occur to women. This sex difference may be related to the fact that women are more likely to develop osteoporosis and hence are more susceptible to fracture should a fall occur. As indicated earlier, osteoporosis increases with increasing age, although usually at a higher rate in women than in men. Another possible reason for higher fall rates for women concerns differences in design of shoes. Templer, Mullet, Archea, and Margulis (1978) found that shoes with flat soles and no heels were over represented in stair mishaps.

Although earlier reports indicated higher population death rates for older females than males (Iskrant and Joliet, 1968, reporting data for 1959 through 1961), 1978 data from the National Center for Health Statistics (quoted in National Safety Council, 1982) show that older males (75+) now experience a higher death rate from falls than females. It now appears that women may experience more falls but men are more likely to succumb to the effects of a fall.

In contrast to other types of injuries, death rates from falls are higher among whites than nonwhites (Planek, 1982; Hogue, 1982a).

Major Sources of Hazard

Falls can result from many factors and almost always are the result of complex causes. As has been noted, the elderly are likely to suffer from a variety of sensory and motor deficiencies and hence are less able to cope with the environment effectively. Other possible contributing factors are poor muscle tone from lack of exercise and the use of shoes that interfere with balance. It is only rarely that design of the environment has considered some of the limitations of function that characterize the elderly. As a result, it is no wonder that this group is more likely to experience unintentional injury from falls.

Acute or Chronic Health Conditions. Although alcohol is not widely misused by the elderly, they are not immune to this problem. J. Waller (1978) studied falls experienced by 150 people aged 60 and older and found that 19 of them (13%) had used alcohol prior to the fall. For 12 of them (8%) the alcohol was believed to have contributed to the fall, while for five the role of alcohol was considered to be negligible. In the remaining two cases it could not be determined whether the use of alcohol was a significant factor. Although alcohol affects the performance of the elderly in much the same way as it does that of younger users, they reach a higher blood alcohol concentration at the same dosage level because they have relatively less body water. Waller's study included one man, impaired by alcohol, who fell off a bicycle that he was using because he had lost his driver's license for drunk driving!

It is more characteristic of the elderly to suffer from health problems other than the misuse of alcohol. Sheldon (1960) conducted what is still considered the classic study of falls. He carefully investigated 500 falls involving 202 people aged 50 and older who were treated in Wolverhampton, England. Fully one-fourth of the falls (125 occurring to 58 individuals) were the result of drop attacks, that is, attacks in which the person falls to the ground without any warning. The victims usually reported that they had been feeling well and functioning normally but suddenly found themselves on the ground or on the floor. Furthermore, they experienced immense difficulty in getting back up. Persons who came to their aid reported that the fallen person felt like dead weight, that is, they had no muscle tone. Neither leg nor trunk muscles were functioning, although arms apparently were not affected. In such episodes, victims cannot even turn over, but in some instances they can drag themselves with their arms. The duration of the attack may be only momentary or last for hours. Surprisingly, once the victim is righted to his feet all symptoms immediately disappear and function is fully recovered. Sheldon concludes that something interferes with the normal functioning of the anti-gravity muscles and reports that pressure to the soles of the feet triggers the return of normal functioning.

Some of the falls studied by Sheldon were attributed to vertigo, that is, an attack of giddiness. However, these attacks usually were preceded by enough warning that the victim could take precautionary measures. A smaller proportion of the falls resulted from movement that included throwing the head back. In most of these instances the person was working with hands over the head, e.g., reaching for something from a high shelf or hanging curtains. Apparently the movement interferes with the flow of blood through the vertebral arteries, a condition that is exacerbated by osteoarthritis. It is also possible that the behavior involved interferes with the visual control of balance, and older people are more likely to depend on visual as well as kinesthetic cues. Another group of falls was attributed to postural hypotension. These occurred when the person had quickly stood up with a corresponding drop in blood pressure. Sheldon also reported that almost one-fourth of his subjects experienced some problems with stability of posture. They had difficulty maintaining an erect position with their eyes closed. Many also had greater difficulty in recovering balance once equilibrium was lost.

J. Waller (1978) found that those persons who fell because of a precipitating medical problem suffered from more medical conditions than did those who fell because of other reasons. However, he did not identify any specific medical problems that may make the elderly especially vulnerable to falls other than the previous observation that the bones of many elderly are less dense. Furthermore, the muscle mass is less supportive so that the bones are more susceptible to fracture.

Environmental Factors. Sheldon describes a number of environmental factors that contributed to the falls he studied. Stairs were the major culprit, but slippery surfaces including ice and snow also figured prominently. Unexpected objects were also a factor and these were frequently moving objects such as grandchildren or pets. Darkness contributed to falls as did the edges of rugs and carpets, curbstones and steps, and irregularities in the pavement. J. Waller identified enviromental factors similar to those of Sheldon. However, he also found that prosthetic devices such as walkers, canes, and wheelchairs actually contributed to some of the falls. Only one of the falls he studied was in the shower.

Data from the Consumer Product Safety Commission (CPSC) National Electronic Injury Surveillance System (NEISS) consistently show that stairs are a major problem for all ages (Injuries Associated with Selected Consumer Products, 1981). Of injuries related to consumer products and treated in hospital emergency rooms, those associated with stairs head the list, with more than three-quarters of a million in 1981. Next to very young children (age four and under), the elderly have the highest population rates for injuries associated with stairs, steps, ramps, and landings. For fatalities, the elderly have by far the highest rate, accounting for 85 percent of fatal injuries from stairway falls.

Archea et al. (1979) developed guidelines for stair safety based on their careful observations of how stairs and steps are actually used by a variety of people. They conclude that, "many stairway accidents are caused by human perceptual and kinesthetic errors. These errors are frequently triggered by some correctable flaw in the design or construction of a stairway" (p. 101).

Countermeasures

The fact that aging is inevitable and that the probability of falling increases with age does not rule out the possibility of modifying the rate at which falls occur or the degree of injury that follows. Countermeasures may be divided into three major groups, namely, modifications of the individual, modifications of the environment, and availability of services.

Countermeasures that Modify the Individual. The evidence indicates that at least part of the vulnerability of the elderly to injury from falls is related to physical changes. Osteoporosis occurs in conjunction with aging and accelerates in postmenopausal women, particularly whites and Orientals. Although this association has been noted since the 1940s, it is only recently that the evidence has shown a clear relationship between estrogen replacement therapy and reduced osteoporosis and bone fracture. Long term use of such therapy has been linked to an increased probability of uterine cancer, but some physicians feel that under properly prescribed circumstances the demonstrated benefits outweigh the risks (Smith et al., 1981).

Hegsted (1968) has reported that the incidence of fracture of the spine is lower in areas with at least 3 ppm of fluoride in the drinking water, but questions remain concerning the safety of fluoride treatment (Smith et al., 1981).

There is strong evidence that dietary calcium treatment may be important in bone maintenance and prevention of osteoporosis at least for some persons. Such treatment should begin early as a preventive measure, since most women over the age of 35 are losing more calcium than they are taking in (Smith et al., 1981).

Calcium absorption is affected by Vitamin D, a vitamin in which the elderly are particularly likely to be deficient (Potts and

Deftos, 1974, in Hughes and Neer, 1981). Treatment with Vitamin D improves intestinal calcium absorption which should in turn lead to greater bone strength.

Hughes and Neer (1981) explain how lighting affects bone density and hence the occurrence of bone fracture in the elderly. They state that:

> Light has profound biological effects, and, since life evolved under the influences of sunlight, it is not surprising that the living organism has developed an array of physiological responses to the spectral energy distribution characteristic of solar radiation. (p. 76)

Problems are created by limited exposure to natural light, particularly for older people in winter climates. Seasonal variations have been observed in the proportion of femoral-neck fractures showing evidence of osteomalacia, and the differences are attributed to variations in hours of sunshine (Aaron et al., 1974). The usual sources of artificial light do not include some of the important elements in natural sunlight, particularly the ultraviolet radiation. Lighting that includes such radiation has been shown to improve calcium absorption which presumably would be reflected in stronger bones and a lower incidence of fracture. It should be noted that not all patients benefit from Vitamin D treatment. There are clearly other factors involved that remain to be discovered.

Hughes and Neer also report on Russian research that shows that lighting that includes the full spectrum of sunlight, especially in the ultraviolet region, has been found to facilitate immunologic responsiveness and promote good health. Presumably such lighting is associated with a reduced incidence of colds, viral infections, pneumoconiosis (black lung disease), and functional disorders of the nervous system. It also appears especially beneficial for persons recuperating from illness. Because of such findings, the Russians have set standards for minimal ultraviolet radiation in the workplace. Much of the research reviewed by Hughes and Neer was not conducted with elderly subjects, but it appears that lighting is an area that should be further investigated, since it offers a relatively low cost means to counteract some of the problems associated with aging.

The extent to which regular exercise can postpone or prevent loss of bone mineral needs to be further examined. Whedon (in Marx, 1980) and Smith (1981) report that deprivation of physical activity such as occurs in bedridden patients is associated with a dramatic loss of bone mineral. Likewise, exercise has been found to slow or prevent bone loss in astronauts living in a zero-gravity environment. In controlled studies, physical activity has been shown to be associated with an increase in bone mineral content of elderly subjects, suggesting that there would be a reduced likelihood of injury from falls (Smith, 1981). In addition, properly designed exercise programs have been found to increase range of motion in the elderly which may in turn reduce probability of loss of balance and ensuing falls (Munns, 1981).

Educational measures that inform the elderly of special hazards may also prove beneficial. Better information on diet and exercise, as well as on activities that should not be undertaken alone, may be useful.

Countermeasures that Modify the Environment. The most effective countermeasures are those that modify the environment in which the older person functions. Our homes, shopping centers, churches, and other public places have not been designed with the elderly in mind. With the exception of the addition of ramps to some of our public buildings, very little consideration has been given to this growing segment of the population. A number of steps can and should be taken to facilitate the mobility of the elderly and reduce their liability to injury from falls. Wall handgrips can be provided in bathrooms and other places where they may be of help. Other countermeasures include improved lighting; better designed stairways, steps, and landings; and modification of surfaces. These are described more fully below.

1. *Lighting.* Almost every kind of visual skill deteriorates with aging. While not all of the deficit can be compensated for, improved lighting can do much to help. Hughes and Neer review how visual performance varies with age and lighting conditions. Based on the available evidence, they conclude:

> The implication of the visual performance research is that the older population needs higher quantities of illumination to achieve higher contrasts to see as effectively as the younger population. While this is true, it should be noted that the visibility of the task can also be enhanced by improving the contrast of the task; increasing the duration of task examination; and/or improving the geometry of the lighting in the space to minimize veiling reflections and glare, and to maximize the distribution of brightness in the environment. (pp. 68–69)

For both younger and older workers, better illumination improves performance and increases worker satisfaction, but older
workers seem to benefit more. The quality of the light relates to
the distribution of brightness in space. Because older people cannot
adapt readily to changes in luminance, room surfaces should not
have excessive brightness contrast. An older person working on a
visual task is likely to look away to other parts of the room. If
these other areas are appreciably brighter or darker than the area
on which he or she is focusing to work, there will be a decrease in
the person's visual comfort and ability. Fozard and Popkin (1978)
believe that the older person's difficulty in coping with such tran-
sient changes in brightness contribute to accidental falls on stairs.
They report that most falls occur on the top landing or the first
step where the older person's visual control is particularly important. It is here that abrupt changes in luminance often occur. They
recommend that local lighting be used to illuminate the first few
steps to resolve this age-related problem.

Although stairways are a special problem that will be discussed more fully below, lighting on stairways is of crucial importance. Because glare is especially detrimental to the performance
of the elderly, Archea et al. (1979) recommend that stair treads
should not reflect bright patches of glare. While inadequate lighting is a problem, too much light may create glare. Stairways
should also be readily visible to both familiar and unfamiliar
users. In the case of stairs that are located in an area normally
used for sleeping, or stairs for which the upper landing or step is
obscured by a door that is normally closed, there should be a lumi-
nous cue that is clearly visible to the user approaching the stairs.
A night light can be used on the side wall of the stairway at least
one riser depth below the level of the upper landing in order to
communicate the sense of depth and alert the oncoming user. If
other illumination is used, it should light both the upper landing
and the treads themselves. Anywhere the elderly have to make
judgments about ground or floor surfaces, good illumination is
essential.

Night lights in a home can be especially helpful to older people
who get up at night. Such lighting is particularly important when
the older person is in unfamiliar surroundings.

Other lighting-related countermeasures recommended by
Hughes and Neer include modifications of windows and lighting
fixtures to reduce excessive brightness. While older workers particularly should not be required to work directly facing a window,

the use of reduced transmission glass, shades, or baffle systems for the windows should also help control brightness and glare. Lighting fixtures should include adequate shielding to reduce direct glare.

Artifical lighting varies in the extent to which it simulates natural lighting so far as accurate rendering of color is concerned. Conventional cool white fluorescent lighting renders color poorly and differs greatly from natural daylight. Research has shown that workers show better visual acuity and less physiological fatigue with daylight full-spectrum lighting as opposed to the conventional cool white. There is also some evidence that the elderly perform better with lighting that more accurately simulates natural lighting.

An abundance of research exists on how lighting can be used to facilitate functioning at all ages and particularly for the elderly. However, much of what has been discovered remains to be implemented (see Hughes and Neer, 1981; Fozard, 1981; Sekuler et al. 1980).

2. *Step, Stairs, and Landings.* Falls on stairways are the most frequent cause of fatal injuries from falls. Because stairs are such a major factor in fatal and injury-producing falls, the Consumer Product Safety Commission has sponsored an extensive investigation of stairway accidents (see Templer, Mullet, Archea, and Margulis, 1976; Carson et al., 1978; and Archea, et al., 1979). One of the primary study groups was elderly citizens. Based on review of the literature, in-depth investigation of stairway accidents, and videotape recordings of some 50 hours of people using stairs, the research has led to guidelines to stair safety. Recommendations cover the physical attributes and appearance of the surrounding environment, dimensional integrity and structural quality, and signs and symbols. A number of their recommendations are summarized below with additional comments by the author:

1. The height of the step should be between 4 and 7 inches, while the distance from front to back of the step (the tread dimension) should be between 11 and 14 inches.
2. The carpet, mat, tile, or other material covering any tread or landing should not slide when foot contact is made while either ascending or descending.
3. Tread covering should be tight and uniform from one tread to the next.
4. Stairs exposed to precipitation should have a nonslip finish or a well-drained surface.

5. The edge of each tread should be clearly differentiated. Elderly users particularly are likely to experience a blurring of the edges and difficulty distinguishing separate treads. A uniformly textured plain-colored surface should be provided on each tread throughout the run of a flight of stairs. Tread edges can be marked with a single built-in or painted stripe which contrasts noticeably with the rest of the tread. The stripe should extend no more than 1½ inches into the tread and should be flush with the remainder of the tread surface. Such striping should be especially helpful to persons who wear bifocals or who have had cataracts removed, since it is often difficult for these people to identify the edge of a step.

6. Handrails should be continuous, particularly at points where the stairs make sharp 90° or 180° turns.

7. Handrails should be comfortable to grasp. They should allow enough room so that the user's fingers or hand do not rub against a wall or mounting bracket when the railing is being grasped. Handrails should not be slippery to grasp, nor should they become too hot from sunlight or other heat sources to use comfortably.

8. Ideally handrails should be available on both sides of the stair so that both right-handed and left-handed users can use the railing with their favored hand. Handrails on both sides provide assistance to both ascending and descending users. Handrails not only provide guidance, but also provide assistance once a fall begins and can reduce the severity of the consequences. It may also be useful to indicate the ending of a handrail by a change in size or shape so that the user has an additional cue that the end of the steps has been reached. Such modification should reduce the number of falls that occur because the person has "missed the last step."

9. Stair, steps, and landings should be clear of obstacles. Doors should not open over stairs or landings and stairs should be clear of projections such as coathooks, picture hangers, or nails. There should be no glass areas in or near flights of stairs or landings. Of course stairs should not be used for storage.

10. Stairs should provide clear head room.

11. There should be no compelling points of visual interest that compete for a user's attention while approaching a

stair. The stair treads and handrails should be the most conspicuous objects in the user's visual field.

12. There should be no abrupt changes in light level between stairs and their surroundings. Older people particularly have difficulty adapting to rapid changes in light level. Even windows facing landings at the head of a first flight of stairs can create problems for ascending users because in the daytime the user is facing outdoor lighting while ascending the first flight and then may not be able to adapt readily to a rapid decrease in lighting during ascent of the second flight. Other comments concerning illumination of stairs are described in the previous section on lighting.

For more detailed discussion of these and other recommendations, the reader is referred to the reports mentioned above. The reports include suggestions for retro-fitting existing stairs and steps.

At least some of the recommendations for improving safety of stairs and steps may also be applied to curbs. For example, curb edges can be delineated particularly at corners where people are most likely to be crossing. Surfaces of streets and sidewalks in these areas should be well-drained to reduce slickness and the likelihood of ice formation in cold weather.

3. *Modifications of Surfaces.* Of course loose rugs are especially hazardous to the elderly. Uneven surfaces in pavements can lead to trips and falls. Because the elderly often do not lift their feet as high when they walk, they are more likely to come in contact with any protruding surfaces on floors or ground. J. Waller recommends that floors be entirely bare if possible, although he does not recommend that they be constructed of concrete or other extremely hard material. However, he questions the value of efforts to modify floors by making them "softer" through the use of carpets because he points out that in the case of the elderly bone breakage appears to be as likely to occur whether the person hits a hard or soft ground surface. Apparently, in the case of the elderly, whether a fracture occurs is more a function of the brittleness of the bone than the nature of the surface struck.

The fact that many falls occur as a result of slippery surfaces means that steps to reduce the slipperiness could reduce the probability of fall. Many of the victims in both Waller's and Sheldon's studies experienced their falls on public sidewalks and streets.

Clearly, there is a responsibility for proper maintenance of those public walkways used by the elderly.

Another intervention to combat slipperiness is modification of shoe soles. Different shoe sole materials interact differently with various types of floor surfaces. Certain synthetics have been found to be especially slip-resistant for all floor surfaces, but the shoe manufacturers have not yet utilized this information (Irvine, 1976a, 1976b). The implications for the elderly are obvious.

Availability of Services. Transportation services can reduce the exposure of the elderly to many of the hazardous circumstances that lead to falls. Likewise, services brought to the home can eliminate completely the necessity for exposure to hazards posed by curbs and icy surfaces. In an investigation of falls among the elderly in nursing homes, Hogue (1982b) found that a high proportion occurred during the first week and especially the first day of residence. She recommends that when new residents enter a long term care facility they should be given close attention from someone already secure in the surroundings. This service could be provided by another resident, a volunteer, or a family member, and not necessarily a member of the professional staff.

Once injury has occurred, the degree of impairment can be affected by the availability and quality of emergency medical services. J. Waller (1973) has found that young people are given preferential treatment in receiving emergency care. Furthermore, because elderly people so frequently are alone when an injury occurs, there is often a delay in receiving help. J. Waller reports that older victims often do not even seek help for an hour or more after the injury has occurred (1978). Finally, the quality of the medical care, including surgery and physical therapy, can reduce the extent of permanent disability resulting from the injury.

Motor Vehicle Injuries

Motor vehicle injuries are the leading cause of death due to unintentional injury from ages 65 through 74 and the second leading cause after age 74. The corresponding population death rates are 22 per 100,000 and 30 per 100,000 persons. If all persons age 65 and over are considered together, motor vehicle injuries rank second to falls in death rates due to unintentional injury. However, there is much more research information available on motor vehicle injuries.

It is well know that motor vehicle accidents and injury rates vary in association with age. While older people have lower population rates of involvement, once an incident occurs, it is more likely to have serious consequences. To understand the experience of older persons, the following materials will refer to the experience of other age groups as well.

Pedestrians

A possible difficulty for the current cohort of elderly pedestrians is that many of them, particularly women and minorities, are not fully aware of how drivers behave because many of them have little or no driving experience. As more experienced drivers become elderly pedestrians, they may have greater skill in this regard.

Should our society become more energy conscious as well as more appreciative of the benefits of physical exercise, we may witness an increase in pedestrian traffic. Future cohorts may walk more than present cohorts in their 60s and 70s. If so, pedestrian exposure, and hence risk, will be increased. At the same time, the increased exercise should improve fitness which in turn should decrease risk. Hence the outcome for older pedestrian injuries is uncertain.

In the case of the elderly, walking is sometimes the only major source of transportation. Failing physical and perceptual skills, combined with diminishing economic resources and increasing transportation costs, frequently eliminate other possible forms of transportation. Yet walking is also accompanied by hazards to the elderly person even beyond the inherent hazards present at any age.

Extent of the Problem. Pedestrian deaths account for close to one-fifth of all motor vehicle deaths in the United States. However, for older persons they account for an even larger proportion. In 1980, pedestrian accidents accounted for 27 percent of motor vehicle deaths occurring to persons aged 65–74 and 45 percent of motor vehicle deaths occurring to persons aged 75 and older. Put another way, persons over age 65 account for about 11 percent of the total population, yet they represent 21 percent of all pedestrian deaths.

It is clear that pedestrian travel is particularly hazardous to the health of our present older citizens.

Age and Sex Characteristics of the Victims. Pedestrian crashes may be characterized by three major groups of victims, namely, the young, the elderly, and the intoxicated. Even though children account for the highest proportion of pedestrian crashes, it is the elderly who are more likely to suffer serious or fatal consequences. When pedestrian fatalities are examined in terms of population death rates, persons aged 65 and older experience the highest rates. For the total United States population, the rate is 36 per million, but for persons aged 65 through 74 the rate is 56, and for persons aged 75 and older, it rises to 105.

At every age level, males are more likely to be victims of pedestrian accidents than females. For the population as a whole, the rates are 51 per million for males compared to 21 for females. For ages 65 through 74, the numbers are 83 compared to 35, and above age 74, they are 179 for males versus 63 for females, even after a lifetime of decimation of the male birth cohort by accidents of all types.

Major Types of Hazard. Pedestrians in traffic are unprotected, and the elderly pedestrian is especially vulnerable. However, certain factors are associated with changes in risk. Two such factors are alcohol and intersections.

1. *Alcohol.* Although alcohol is less likely to be present in elderly pedestrian victims than in younger adult victims, nevertheless, in the case of fatally injured pedestrians in the United States from 1977 through 1979, 18.8% of those aged 65 through 74 and 6.7% of those aged 75 and over had been drinking. Again, sex differences are evident. For male victims aged 65 through 74, 25% had been drinking compared to 7.4% of such females. Above age 74, the corresponding proportions are 8.8% for males and 3.3% for females (Wolfe and O'Day, 1981).

For all pedestrian victims (both fatal and non-fatal) in North Carolina in 1980, 41% of males aged 66 through 75 and 8.7% of males above age 75 had been drinking. None of the female victims above age 65 had been drinking.

A study conducted in New Orleans included alcohol data on both pedestrian victims and other pedestrians. Thirty-nine percent of the victims aged 60 through 69 and 22% of those aged 70 and older had blood alcohol concentrations of 0.10% or above (Blomberg et al., 1979). Research indicates that blood alcohol levels above 0.05% impair performance requiring divided attention, a skill necessary for coping with traffic. Such impairment, when combined with slower perceptual and motor speeds characteristic of the elderly, is sufficient to account for an increase in injuries in older age groups even at lower alcohol levels.

2. *Intersections.* While intersections pose special hazards for vehicles and pedestrians alike, they are considered the appropriate place for pedestrians to cross. Yet many intersections provide no special facilities such as pedestrian signals to assist pedestrians in crossing. Even when signals are available, signals are often not designed for use by people who do not respond quickly and maintain a fairly rapid pace in crossing. Because both pedestrians and vehicles may place an unwarranted trust in signals with a corresponding decrease in vigilance, intersections can become particularly difficult for the elderly to maneuver. The problem is confounded further when vehicles are allowed to turn on red traffic signals.

Intersections can be made even more difficult if buses stop just before reaching a pedestrian crosswalk. The stopped bus conceals the pedestrian who leaves the bus and crosses in front of it to cross the street. Because the elderly are more likely to have to rely on bus transportation and because many elderly suffer from sensory and motor deficits, this situation poses particular problems.

Countermeasures. An understanding of the circumstances surrounding pedestrian accidents should facilitate development of countermeasures. A study of rural and suburban pedestrian crashes by Knoblauch (1977) did not always identify the elderly victim separately, but examination of the accident type suggests those that are most likely to involve this group. Notable among these is one in which a vehicle is turning or attempting to turn and not attending to oncoming traffic and hence fails to see the pedestrian. Fifty percent of the pedestrians in such crashes were more than 50 years of age. In a second category, the vehicle strikes a pedestrian crossing the road at an intersection. Interestingly, the drivers were more likely to be turning right than left. A third accident type that was likely to involve older pedestrians (as well as very young children) involved a vehicle backing up into a pedestrian who did not realize it.

One potential countermeasure identified in an earlier study by Berger (1975) may have particular relevance for the elderly, namely, the relocation of bus stops so that the bus would cross through an intersection prior to stopping. In this way the pedestrian leaving the bus could walk behind it into the crosswalk and thus reduce the probability of walking into the path of traffic. Other countermeasures that may benefit the elderly, if drivers would comply, are the midblock crosswalk and the stop line relocation. The latter countermeasure would provide more room between the traffic stopped for a traffic signal and the pedestrians crossing in front.

Regardless of the pedestrian's skill and alertness, there are a number of countermeasures that can simplify the task of coping with traffic. These include improved and increased use of pedestrian crossing signals, separation of pedestrian and vehicular traffic, enforcement of existing laws and ordinances concerning pedestrians, improved vehicular design, better lighting of streets used by pedestrians, increased use of reflective materials, and quality and availability of emergency medical services.

1. *Pedestrian Crossing Aids.* Pedestrian signals often do not allow adequate time for the elderly person to cross. Current rules for cycling of the traffic lights, including pedestrian-activated buttons, assume that people walk at a rate of 4 feet/second. Such a standard is adequate for young healthy persons with normal vision and hearing. Older people move more slowly and need more time (J. Waller, 1980). Furthermore, the elderly frequently take longer to initiate action, thus increasing the total time required. Pedestrian islands may be used to provide refuge for the pedestrian who cannot cross in the time available. Studies in the United Kingdom suggest that older pedestrians are less likely to understand the operation and meaning of traffic signals (Wilson and Rennie, 1981). Some intersections combine an auditory signal with the pedestrian light to make use of more than one modality in alerting the pedestrian to the appropriate time to cross. Laws allowing right turn on red have led to an increase in pedestrian crashes, with the elderly showing especially high increases (Zador, Moshman, and Marcus, 1981). Pedestrian crashes are significantly lower when no traffic movement is allowed in any direction during the pedestrian signal (Zegeer et al., 1982).

2. *Separation of Pedestrian Traffic.* Clearly, to the extent possible, it is best to separate pedestrians regardless of their age from moving vehicles. Sidewalks are designed to do this. While overpasses and underpasses also separate traffic from pedestrians, they are expensive to construct and unless properly lighted and moni-

tored, they may pose their own hazards to pedestrian safety. Furthermore, they may require too much effort for the elderly to use. However, pedestrian malls that prohibit vehicles can be especially helpful to elderly shoppers so long as adequate transportation is available to enable the elderly to gain access to them.

A number of European countries are restricting traffic in residential areas and even closing streets in order to remove through traffic. In addition, streets are being redesigned so that traffic speed must be drastically reduced in order to navigate safely. These environmental modifications force changes in both the behavior of drivers and the probability of vehicle-pedestrian interactions.

3. *Enforcement.* Although all states have laws requiring that drivers give the pedestrian the right of way, a survey of states to determine actual practices found that with few exceptions there is little emphasis given to enforcement of pedestrian safety laws (Haight and Olsen, 1981). The authors point out that regardless of whether strict enforcement can be shown to be related to accident reduction, there is the question of equity in road use. Because pedestrians may learn to jump out of the way of vehicles and thus avoid becoming casualties does not argue against enforcement.

4. *Vehicle Design.* Because most pedestrian accidents occur at relatively low speeds ($\leq$ 20 miles per hour), modifications in vehicle design can make a difference in survival rates of the victims. Since impact with the bumper frequently causes broken leg bones, a softer structured bumper would reduce the rate of the initial rotation of the pedestrian and reduce the probability of broken bones. Once the pedestrian is hit, his body is likely to pass up over the hood and hit the windshield or other parts of the vehicle. There is considerable evidence that modifications in vehicle design can significantly reduce pedestrian morbidity and mortality (National Highway Traffic Safety Administration, 1979, 1980; Daniel, 1982).

5. *Lighting.* In urban and suburban areas street lighting can increase the visibility of pedestrians to drivers of oncoming vehicles. Although elderly pedestrian accidents usually occur before late evening, the improved lighting may be beneficial in the earlier hours. Polus and Katz (1978) examined the effect of a special crosswalk illumination and signing system that is presently used in Israel. The system identifies the location as a pedestrian crosswalk and illuminates it after dark. They found that the special crosswalks led to a significant reduction in pedestrian accidents compared to control crosswalks.

6. *Reflective Materials.* An immediately available countermea-

sure for nighttime pedestrian accidents is the increased use of white clothing (shoes, coats) or retroflective material. Strips of such material can be put on shoes, belts, jackets, vests, or other outer clothing that can readily be seen by oncoming traffic.

7. *Emergency and Follow-up Care.* As in the case of falls, the quality and quantity of emergency and follow-up services will affect the probability of survival and the degree of permanent disability.

Drivers

Driver licensing programs have been designed to qualify young people beginning their driving careers. Furthermore, the vehicle and highway components of the system have been designed primarily on the basis of measurements obtained from young or middle-aged people. In addition, the basic human performance data used in highway design were collected virtually entirely from male subjects. Yet when older drivers experience difficulty with this system, their problems are frequently dismissed as insoluble because of their age.

Extent of the Problem. Whether elderly drivers pose special problems depends upon how their performance is viewed. Society in general and the insurance industry in particular are primarily interested in the absolute number of crashes experienced regardless of miles driven. Thus a driver who drives 500 miles a year and has one crash is preferable to a driver who drives 100,000 miles a year and has two crashes. The actual crash rate of older drivers based on their presence in the licensed population is no higher or even lower than that of the driving population in general and lower than that for drivers below age 25. Thus the absolute number of crashes experienced by older drivers provides no basis for higher insurance rates. (However, because older drivers are likely to experience more serious injury in the same level crash, their medical expenses are likely to be higher.)

When crash rates are figured on the basis of mileage driven, the performance of the elderly driver is the worst of any driver group. However, North Carolina data show that mileage is a far more significant factor than age or sex in accounting for crash rates. High mileage drivers have lower crash rates per mile driven (Stewart, 1975). Older drivers who report high mileage have crash rates comparable to those of other age-sex groups with similar mileage. It appears that at least part of the higher crash rates based on mileage found for older drivers may be an artifact associated with their lower mileage driven.

Morbidity Versus Mortality. As in the case of pedestrians, elderly drivers are more likely to succumb to motor vehicle injuries than are younger drivers when the severity of the crash is taken into account. As a result, even though the crashes of older drivers occur at lower speeds the fatality rate per crash is higher. Baker and Spitz (1970) found that the proportion of drivers 60 years of age and older was five times as high among those who were fatally injured as among those who survived multivehicle crashes. Wiener (1972) has found that drivers aged 65 and older are at higher risk of injury and fatality in relation to their presence in the driving population. Older people are much more susceptible to death once a crash occurs.

Types of Violation Committed. The violations committed by older people of the current cohort are very different from those of younger ones. In relation to actual exposure, young males are overrepresented in every violation type, and young females are overrepresented in all types except reckless driving and alcohol-related offenses. In contrast, older drivers (age>64) are overrepresented in only failure to yield, failure to stop, and safe movement violations (Waller et al., 1977). Planek, et al., (1968) also report that older drivers have difficulty yielding right of way as well as turning and changing lanes. They indicate that older drivers make errors of omission such as failure to read traffic signs and observe red lights and stop signs. Older drivers are underrepresented in speeding and improper lane violations as well as following too closely violations. Thus the older driver can maintain his lane position and avoid reckless behavior, but he appears to have difficulty handling maneuvers that require a series of rapid judgments such as changing lanes.

Types of Crashes Experienced. In light of the violation types most frequently committed, it is not surprising that the crashes of older drivers are more likely to be multivehicle in contrast to the preponderance of single vehicle crashes experienced by young drivers. The older driver's crashes occur at lower speeds with less damage to the vehicle and are less likely to involve alcohol. However, as noted earlier, older drivers are more susceptible to injury than their younger counterparts (Planek, 1972; Wiener, 1972).

Self-Limitations. There is good evidence that on the whole older drivers restrict themselves when the driving task becomes too complex. Ysander and Herner (1976), studying elderly male drivers in Sweden, found that many of the licensed drivers no longer drove at all, even though they kept their licenses.

Those that do not stop driving entirely reduce the amount of driving. Studies of exposure show that after age 65, i.e., after retirement, drivers do not drive as much. There are also changes in the quality of exposure. Older drivers are less likely to drive in complex situations such as rush hours, on icy roads, or in unfamiliar surroundings (Planek, 1972; Ysander and Herner, 1973).

Perhaps the greatest change in type of driving that occurs with increasing age is the reduction in driving after dark. It appears that most of this reduction is the result of self-restriction that is undoubtedly related to the changes that are occurring in processing visual information. Rackoff and Mourant (1979) report that older drivers appear to need to take in more visual information than younger drivers. They also drive more slowly at night. The fact that older people need many times more illumination to see an object in darkness than what is required by younger people and require more time for dark adaptation, combined with changes in the ability of older people to recognize important features in a complex situation and their slowed overall performance, provide at least part of the explanation for the older individual's difficulty handling the driving task at night.

Cohort Effects. It would be a mistake to assume that descriptions of the current elderly population provide a complete basis on which to develop programs for future generations of elderly citizens. Those who are over age 65 today exhibit the effects not only of aging but also of shared cultural experiences. For example, there has been an increase in the availability and use of the automobile for transportation since these people were in childhood so that most of them did not spend so much of their early years as passengers in automobiles or as children moving in and about motor vehicles.

Furthermore, the social customs were such that many women did not learn to drive even when men did, and only a very few of today's elderly would have ever received any formal training in how to drive (Jones, 1978). As a result many of them continue driving habits more suited to low density traffic and absence of complex traffic controls and many of the women are not very experienced drivers. In contrast, when those who are young adults today become elderly they may not show some of the driving problems experienced by today's senior citizens.

Nevertheless there are some factors that are less likely to be different. These include some of the physiological factors that lead to diminishing sensory and motor function. Even these, however, may be subject to some modification as there is increasing awareness of the importance of proper diet and as physical fitness is pursued by larger and larger segments of the population.

Countermeasures. Because our highway transportation system was not designed for the elderly, it is not surprising that some elderly may experience difficulty with it. Apparently, the relatively good performance of the older driver may in part result from withdrawing from the system, that is, no longer attempting to cope with it. This type of solution is accompanied by other problems in that it leads to greater isolation of the elderly. It is past time that this growing segment of our population is given attention commensurate with their numbers and their needs.

Countermeasures may be divided into four major areas, namely, highway engineering, vehicle design, services and support systems, and driver measures.

1. *Highway Engineering.* The evidence shows that elderly drivers have more difficulty identifying relevant information from background variables, need much more illumination to perceive the information, take longer to process the information, and take much longer to respond to it. An adequate highway system must provide sufficient information in a form that can readily be located and identified. It must also provide sufficient illumination for the elderly driver to perceive it. Information must be introduced so as to allow the driver enough time to process it and respond appropriately. To accomplish these objectives would require that highways be adequately lighted where there is pedestrian traffic or other hazards and that roadway delineation be sufficient and clear. There have been great improvements in the technology of highway delineation which improve visual control greatly at night. Such delineation combined with improved signing may be the most promising highway countermeasures that can realistically be provided in a climate of scarce resources.

However, before large expenditures are made there is a need

for additional research to determine more precisely the signing and delineation needs of this age group. Sivak et al. (1981) studied the performance of young and old drivers responding to highway signing at night. Although the two groups had been equated on standard tests of visual acuity, the older drivers had to get much closer to the signs before they were able to read them. As a result they had less distance remaining in which they could act on the information transmitted by the sign.

A more recent study by Sivak and Olson (1982) examined the performance of older and younger drivers who had been equated not only on visual acuity under high luminance but also under low luminance, as well as for high and low contrast under each luminance condition. The few older subjects who could match the visual performance of younger subjects showed a comparable response to highway signs under nighttime conditions. Nevertheless, because most older drivers cannot meet such visual criteria, there remains a need to improve signing to enable more older drivers to function adequately.

2. *Vehicle Design.* As in the case of highway design, the elderly have not been included in the design of the vehicle. While younger drivers may have no problem with passenger car design that requires a 120 degree headturn to check overtaking traffic, the elderly may not be able to perform so well for a number of reasons such as arthritic conditions, circulatory problems, or limited peripheral vision. It may be feasible to design a system of mirrors that would go far in assisting the elderly in detecting what is going on around them.

Vehicle design, especially seat design and seat location in relation to controls, must take into consideration changes in body proportion that accompany aging. For example, most of the observed loss in height occurs in the trunk while the length of limbs remains relatively unchanged (Stoudt, 1981).

The controls on some passenger cars require extraordinary agility. Once again the elderly are likely to be handicapped by them. The development of onboard microcomputer systems for detecting approaching objects or issuing warnings when vehicle systems are not functioning properly has been discussed for some time, but the decreasing costs of such systems may make them a financially realistic possibility in the future.

When crashes do occur the elderly are in greater need of crash protection. Crash attenuators that enable the vehicle to absorb much of the impact energy can help protect the elderly occupant.

The elderly, like the rest of the population, show low rates of safety belt usage. Because this group is particularly vulnerable to injury, automatic restraint systems should be especially beneficial.

3. *Services and Support Systems.* As in the case of other injuries, the quality of the emergency medical system and follow-up services is crucial in mitigating the degree of injury and eventual disability. Adequate treatment following hospital discharge not only should meet the physical needs of the victim but should also insure that the person is not entirely cut off from normal social contacts as a result of any ensuing disability. Particularly in the case of the elderly, isolation and a feeling of helplessness can lead to rapid deterioration in overall health and well-being.

4. *Driver Measures.* Finally, there is the driver, the most difficult part of the highway transportation system to influence. However, programs can be implemented or made available on a voluntary basis that may affect this age group.

Driver licensing examinations currently do not measure the types of visual skill that appear to be most closely related to driving performance. Perhaps the most promising skill that should be included is dynamic visual acuity, that is, the ability to identify a moving object in the visual field. The study by Sivak and Olson (1982) found that older drivers are less likely to demonstrate adequate visual acuity under low luminance. Because this skill is important in nighttime driving, it might be appropriately included in driver license examinations, although the authors recommend further validation before new programs are implemented.

Every state has some form of medical review of drivers for whom there is some indication that there may be a medical problem that would affect driving performance. This program is not aimed specifically at older drivers, but because medical problems increase with increasing age it serves as one way of detecting potential problems and possibly bringing them under control.

Education and training have traditionally been aimed at younger drivers or those who have been identified as problem drivers. Yet many older drivers are receiving instruction on defensive driving and how to handle some of the special problems confronting the elderly. The National Retired Teachers Association/American Association for Retired Persons has promulgated one such program called the 55 Alive/Mature Driving (Seaton, 1979). While many elderly drivers do not have the capacity to match the skill of many younger drivers, their greater maturity and often superior judgment may make them more receptive and responsive to instruction. However, there is no objective evidence that the NRTA/ AARP program results in improved performance.

Finally, educational measures can be aimed at the general driving population who may contribute to the problems of the older driver. Younger drivers need to understand that older people cannot see as well or respond as quickly, especially after dark. Whether and to what extent such measures would be effective remains to be seen.

It must be recognized that there will be many instances in which the only appropriate decision will be to restrict the conditions under which any person with substandard capacities may drive or to remove licensure all together. Of course, older persons will be most affected by such a policy. Decisions must be made on an individual basis and only after careful review of all relevant information (Hogue, 1982b). Two further points need to be made in regard to the evaluation and restriction of older drivers.

First, decisions to restrict drivers always involve trade-offs. Traditionally driver licensing authorities are trained to review the situation solely in terms of highway safety. However, we would maintain that the evaluation should be more global in nature. In our society, particularly in rural areas, the denial of driver license is often tantamount to such severe restriction and sacrifice of independence that the consequences may be more devastating than the highway safety risk that would be incurred. If loss of a license requires an older person to move to unfamiliar surroundings (even though they may be more "convenient" and sanitary), it should be recognized that such a major change at an advanced age could trigger rapid deterioration in performance. Likewise, if loss of license requires that one become a ward of society or that one is no longer able to maintain reasonable independence, again the cost may be far greater than is warranted. While there are times when license removal is necessary, in other cases it may be more appropriate to risk the possibility of paying a price in highway safety in order to achieve a broader goal. Viewed in the larger sense it may be a worthwhile trade-off.

Our second point concerns the driving task as it relates to older people. Much has been said about the need to make the task such that it can be handled by older drivers who may be less able to turn their heads to engage in surveillance behavior or to process information provided by highway signing. The older driver's problem should be viewed as a barometer for the rest of us. Like the miner's canary, they give warning of where the driving task is overly complex and where the rest of us may be in greater danger. Appropriate modifications of the vehicle and driving environment will not only enable older drivers to perform more adequately but also enable the rest of us to drive with greater ease and perhaps reduce the possibility of crash involvement when we are functioning at less than optimum level. Should all go well, eventually we will be joining the ranks of older drivers. At that time we will be the beneficiaries of any improvements we can introduce into the system.

Burns

Burns are of much greater importance than their frequency would indicate. Because severe burns affect a number of different body systems, the treatment is complex and expensive. Furthermore, severe burns frequently leave both physical and psychological scars.

Extent of the Problem

Burns rank as a major cause of death due to accidental injury. In the 65–74 age group they rank third after motor vehicle accidents and falls, and in the 75 and over age group, they rank fourth. Hogue (1982a) reports that the elderly experience burns at a higher rate than is true for the general population, particularly from flames and hot surfaces or substances. Furthermore, older people are less likely to survive once a burn occurs (Slater and Gaisford, 1981). Hogue offers a number of possible explanations for the higher morbidity and mortality rates, including the fact that elderly people spend more time in their homes, where most burns occur. In addition, a higher proportion of older people have at least one chronic health problem and may be on medications that impair functioning and/or interfere with the healing process. The elderly are also characterized by a thinning of the skin that may result in more serious injury from the same amount of external heat. Whatever the reasons, when burns occur in the elderly, they are likely to be serious and to require extensive costly treatment.

Age and Sex Characteristics of the Victims

Burns are a major cause of accidental death at all ages, but very young children (less than age five) and people aged 65 and over have the highest population death rates. Those aged 75 and over have by far the highest rates of all.

Most studies report that males outnumber females by a ratio of about two to one (e.g., Hamit, 1978) in mortality figures from burns. However, Clark and Lerner (1978), describing a survey of burn patients treated by hospitals in central New York over a two-year period, report that above age 60 the percentage of burned females admitted to the hospital is greater than that for males, even though prior to that age, the two-to-one ratio held. They speculate that the finding may result from women continuing to work in the kitchen where so many burns occur while older males may discontinue many of their previous activities that expose them to the possibility of burns. In contrast, a Rhode Island study found a higher proportion of men among burn patients admitted to all hospitals over a five-year period (Avery, 1979). National figures on mortality reported by the National Safety Council (1982) still show an almost two-to-one male to female ratio for fatally burned victims aged 75 and over.

Vulnerability of the Elderly

The greater susceptibility of the elderly to burn injury is probably related, at least in part, to the many physical and biological changes that have been described previously. Once a hazardous situation has developed, the elderly are less well equipped to cope with it. J. Waller (1972) describes a situation in which a highly flammable item of clothing burst into flame. In one such instance the wearer was a young healthy alert person who quickly removed the clothing and doused the flame in water. In an almost identical situation, the wearer was older and crippled by arthritis and could not remove the garment. As a result he died.

Furthermore, the elderly are more likely to succumb once burn injuries occur. They may suffer from prior health problems that interfere with normal recuperation, and even under the best of circumstances the healing process does not progress as rapidly as in a younger person.

Studies describe the results of the greater vulnerability of the elderly to burn injury. With the exception of young children, for all types of burn, the mortality rate increases with increasing age. In a study of patients treated at a Charlotte, North Carolina hospital, patients over 65 comprised 7.2% of the burn patient population studied but accounted for 25.9% of the deaths. Nearly half the deaths occurred to persons aged 45 and over although they accounted for less than one-fourth of the total patient population. Likewise, a central New York study reported that the hospitalization rate for patients over 60 was not significantly different from that of the total population, but the death rate was substantially higher. In a study of burn victims, Levine and Radford (1977) found that the percentage of fire victims with fatal outcomes was much higher for the very young (less than 10 years of age) and the very old (60 and over), with those above age 70 experiencing almost a 40% fatality rate.

Major Hazards and Countermeasures

A major cause of burns to the elderly is hot liquids. Many of these burns occur as a result of spilling or dropping heated liquids in the kitchen while others occur in the bathroom where tap water drawn for the bath or turned on for a shower is sufficiently hot to cause damage to the skin (Avery, 1979). Baptiste and Feck (1980) describe such injuries and outline strategies for preventing them. They point out that liquid at 130°F causes injury to full thickness epidermis in 30 seconds, as reported by Moritz and Henriques in 1947. Yet a survey of residences in Seattle (Feldman, et al., 1978) found that 80% of them had water temperatures of more than 130°. Baptiste and Feck (1980) reported that of the tap water burns that were treated in hospitals in upstate New York, 95% had occurred in the home. Moreover, 54% of the homes were multiunit dwellings. It has been shown that most dishwasher detergents are effective at temperatures of 120° F or even lower, and, of course, many detergents for washing clothes are effective in cold water. There are no convincing reasons for heating home water to the higher temperatures. The control of the water temperature would do more than save energy. It would prevent unnecessary scalding (Hogue, 1982b).

Because so many burns occur in the kitchen by persons handling hot food and liquids, Avery (1979) suggests the use of specially designed aprons and/or food containers to protect against spillage. A further recommendation is to reduce the temperature of food and liquids served to the elderly.

Planek (1982) reports that cooking was named as the activity involved in over 56% of 4.5 million residential fire incidents reported to the National Household Fire Survey between April 1, 1973 and April 15, 1974. Stoves and ovens accounted for about 90% of the cooking fires. Electric burners were more often implicted than gas burners, although the reverse was true for oven fires. Fires caused by stoves being "accidently turned on or not turned off" were more frequently associated with electric stoves. In this regard, Chapanis and Lindenbaum (1959) and Chapanis and Mankin (1967) have studied the pattern of display of stove burners in relation to controls. There are major differences among such control-display linkages, with at least one tested pattern leading to no errors and consistently minimal response times. In contrast, some of the displays that are readily available on the market require a long period of learning and result in lengthy reaction times even after repeated use. The application of human factors methodology could reduce the probability of error and hence the likelihood of burn injury.

Another major source of hazard for the elderly, as well as other ages, is smoking or other uncontrolled ignition sources. Planek (1982) reports that for home fires smoking is the known source most often associated with injury and death. Although smoking has been shown to be heavily implicated in burns and burn deaths, much of the hazard can be mitigated through the use of nonflammable materials. These could be used not only in clothing for the elderly but also in rugs, bedding, mattresses, drapes, and furniture where the elderly will be living. It should be noted that it is not enough that the materials be nonflammable. They must also be such that they do not smolder and produce poisonous gases that may be even more lethal than flame.

Perhaps the most effective countermeasure for smoking-related burns and deaths would be the use of a self-extinguishing cigarette. Although the technology for producing such a product has long been available, there has been sufficient opposition to prevent its being marketed.

Another source of burn hazard is house fires. While they do not account for a large proportion of burn injuries, they are vastly overrepresented in burn fatalities. In the Charlotte study, house fires accounted for 8.1% of the burns but 29.6% of the deaths (Hamit, 1978). Another study conducted in southern California reported that house fires accounted for 5% of the adult burns but 44%

of such deaths (Kieran et al., 1977). Because some elderly are less able to remove themselves once a house fire occurs, and because they may be more vulnerable to both smoke and flame, it is important that measures be taken to reduce the probability of a fire breaking out.

Haddon (1972) has outlined a number of countermeasures specifically to reduce the probability of burn injury. Those that may have particular relevance to the elderly and have not already been mentioned are the following:

- Construct living facilities for the elderly using fire retardant or flame resistant materials. Use flame retardant paint, fire doors, and thermal insulation in the walls and roof. Do not use space or floor heaters, both of which have been found to contribute to burn injuries.
- Do not keep gasoline, old newspapers, or other flammable materials in the house. Alternatively, reduce the quantity of such items. Do not smoke in bed or in storage areas.
- Improve the stability of hot items and improve the handles on moveable hot items to increase the safety of their use. Reduce the brewing temperatures of coffee and tea. Contain the heat in material that does not transfer it to the user at a hazardous rate, as in the double walled (with air in between) design of some Japanese tea cups.
- Do not allow elderly people to cook or engage in other activities where burn hazards exist if the elderly are no longer competent to do so.
- Develop a quick response for bringing emergency medical care to the burned and ensure that emergency medical personnel are qualified to deal with burns. Provide grafting and cosmetic surgery as well as psychotherapy to burned victims where appropriate.

Accidental Hypothermia

Hypothermia, described briefly in Chapter 1, is abnormally low body temperature and is generally defined as existing when the deep body temperature falls below 95° F (35° C). It has been shown that the lower the deep body temperature, the greater the morbidity and mortality (Exton-Smith, 1981). Although it is not generally considered as an injury, accidental hypothermia, in contrast to that intentionally induced for medical or surgical purposes, is discussed in this chapter because it is a life threatening condition that may be induced by a physical environmental stress, namely, cold.

Extent of the Problem

There are no good figures on the extent of accidental hypothermia in the United States, but in Great Britain it has been estimated that accidental hypothermia may account for 0.68 percent of all hospital admissions (Exton-Smith, 1968). This figure does not take into account the number of persons who are treated at home or who may die in bed. Because patients are not routinely evaluated for this condition and because it may develop as a complication of some other condition, there are no concise data on morbidity and mortality. Nevertheless, population studies in Great Britain (see below) indicate that as much as ten percent of the population age 65 and over suffers from reduced temperature (below 35.5° C) and greater vulnerability to accidental hypothermia.

Major Sources of Hazard

While accidental hypothermia may result from a variety of causes, such as drugs, endocrine disorder, and neurological disorders, exposure to cold is the major cause, and the threat is greater during winter months. It has long been established that older persons are more vulnerable to this condition, but the rising costs of fuel in recent years have exacerbated the problem of keeping the elderly adequately warm.

Krag and Kountz (1950) studied hospitalized older patients (ages 57–91) and compared them with young healthy employee volunteers (ages 22–36). Subjects were subjected to prolonged exposure to a cold environment (5 to 15° C) and measures were made of oxygen consumption and oral, rectal, and surface temperatures. They found that even though older subjects were capable of increasing heat production, they were less able to maintain body temperature. This inability to cope with the cold environment was not related to how debilitated they were. Furthermore, the older subjects were less likely to report being chilly in the cold.

Studies of populations at risk have been conducted in Great Britain. Watts (1971) examined the relationship between reported thermal sensitivity in determining the thermal environment. He found that the homes of his elderly subjects were cool or even quite cold by standards established by the Institute of Heating and Ventilation Engineers, yet his subjects did not report feeling cold.

Other studies (Fox, MacGibbon, Davies, and Woodward, 1973; Fox, Woodward, Exton-Smith, Green, Donnison, and Wicks, 1973) have described in more detail the population of elderly persons living at home in Great Britain. These studies confirm that the elderly have lower deep body temperatures that those reported for young subjects. Generally, they found that the elderly are less likely to report feeling cold even when both internal body temperatures and external dwelling temperatures are low.

Deep body temperatures below 35.5° C were found in 10 percent of the population studied, and this group should be considered at elevated risk of hypothermia. Colder body temperatures were found to be associated with living alone, having inadequate heat, and receiving supplementary pensions, suggesting that these are among the poorer older people.

An illness or fall that renders the older person immobile for any length of time could be the precursor to hypothermia resulting in death.

Countermeasures

Persons responsible for the care of the elderly should be made aware of the vulnerability of this population to hypothermia. Because there is reason to believe that reduced resources are at least partly to blame for lower temperatures in the home of the elderly, special attention must be given to insuring that funds are available to provide adequate heating. The reduced ability to maintain body temperature means that the elderly need a warmer environment than do younger persons. The fact that older people are less likely to report feeling cold could lead to the impression that the temperature is sufficient even when it is not.

Other preventive measures include regular visiting of the elderly to insure that their needs are being met and greater attention to their clothing and nutritional needs.

It is also recommended that the lower limit on the standard clinical thermometer be extended down to 32 or 33° C so that incipient hypothermia may be more readily detected from mouth temperature readings.

Conclusion

Unintentional injury remains a significant health problem for the elderly. Aging is associated with an increased probability of problems with vision, hearing, memory, motor skills including balance, bone strength, and temperature regulation. These changes increase the likelihood that unintentional injury may occur. At the same time, the older person experiences decreases in recuperative power so that long term disability or even death may ensue from an injury from which a younger person would recover fully.

The three leading causes of injury to the elderly are falls, motor vehicle injuries, and burns. In addition, with the increasing overrepresentation of the elderly among the poor and underprivileged, there is growing recognition of the problem of accidental hypothermia. While there are specific countermeasures for each of these areas, there are some countermeasures that apply in all instances. First and foremost of these is a change in our society's view of old age which in turn will be reflected in the elderly's view of themselves. Our society is youth oriented and has deemed that certain behaviors are inappropriate for older persons. Furthermore, it is generally held that certain losses of function inevitably accompany old age. These attitudes create problems for the older person as well as for the larger society.

Fozard and Popkin (1978) hold that the most effective approach to a healthy productive old age requires lifelong preparation. Although ultimately there is no "cure" for aging, there are many circumstances that can greatly increase the probability that the later years will be healthier and happier. Lifelong habits concerning diet; exercise; use of tobacco, alcohol, and other drugs; handling of stress; and involvement in outside interests can, to a large extent, affect the health and satisfaction we experience in old age. The latter years should be viewed as part of the overall life sequence rather than as a relatively sudden withdrawal from the normal pattern of living.

In addition to changes in lifelong habits, there is a need for realistic environmental changes and modification in services and support systems to meet the needs of older persons who experience functional limitations. Chapanis (1974) points out that the human factors principles and methodologies that have illustrated their effectiveness in business, industry, and the military have yet to be applied to the special needs and capabilities of the elderly. Areas of potential application specified by Chapanis include the design of visual and auditory displays; design of controls, tools, and appliances; the layout of workplaces; the design of stairs, ramps, and passageways; and the specification and design of environments in terms of lighting, ventilation, airflow, temperature, and humidity. He also stresses the importance of considering human costs and benefits as well as financial ones in developing environments for the elderly. Thus social and psychological needs must be recognized as well as performance measures. Chapanis' recommendations would lead to more enriching as well as safer environments for the elderly.

Such an approach requires changes throughout the society, including health care, the work place, and leisure activities. It also requires that the performance abilities and social and psychological needs of older people be considered in the early stages of design of furniture, homes, neighborhoods, shopping centers, and transportation facilities. While it will take time to bring about such a social revolution, some changes are already occurring. Moreover, today's elderly and soon-to-be elderly can be helped to broaden their horizons regarding the possibilities for change in their own lives. The evidence indicates that changes in life style can produce a stronger, more viable cohort of older people who will be not only less likely to experience unintentional injury but also more resilient should such injury occur.

References

Aaron, J.E., Gallagher, J.C., and Nordin, B.E.C. Seasonal variation of histological osteomalacia in femoral-neck fractures. *The Lancet,* July 13, 1974, 2 (7872), 84–85.

Archea, J., Collins, B.L., and Stahl, F.I. *Guidelines for Stair Safety.* Washington, D.C.: National Bureau of Standards. May 1979.

Avery, C.E. Burn episodes, clothing, and the elderly: A survey of inpatient records in Rhode Island hospitals. *Journal of Safety Research,* 1979, *ll,* 98–108.

Baker, S.P. and Spitz, W.U. Age effects and autopsy evidence of disease in fatally injured drivers. *Journal of the American Medical Association,* 1970, *214,* 1079–1088.

Baptiste, M.S., and Feck, G. Preventing tap water burns. *American Journal of Public Health,* 1980, 70, 727–729.

Berger, Wallace G. *Urban Pedestrian Accident Countermeasures Experimental Evaluation. Volume 1. Behavioral Evaluation Studies.* Falls Church, Va.: BioTechnology, Inc. February 1975.

Birren, J.E., Butler, R.N., Greenhouse, S.W., Sokoloff, L., and Yarrow, M.R. *Human Aging I. A Biological and Behavioral Study.* (Publication No. (ADM) 77–122). Washington, D.C.: U.S. Government Printing Office, 1971.

Blomberg, R.D., Preusser, D.F., Hale, A., and Ulmer, R.G. *A Comparison of Alcohol Involvement in Pedestrians and Pedestrian Casualties. Executive Summary.* Darien, Ct.: Dunlap and Associates, Oct. 1979.

Botwinick, J. *Aging and Behavior: A Comprehensive Integration of Research Findings,* Second Edition. New York, N.Y.: Springer Publishing Co., 1978.

Campbell, A. J., Reinken, J., Allan, B. C., and Martinez, G.S. Falls in old age: A Study of frequency and related clinical factors. *Age and Aging,* November 1981, *10,* 264–270.

Carson, D.H., Archea, J.C., Margulis, S.T., and Carson, F.E. *Safety on Stairs.* Milwaukee, Wis.: Carson Consultants, Inc. Atlanta, Ga.: Georgia Institute of Technology. Washington, D.C.: National Bureau of Standards. November 1978.

Chapanis, A. Human engineering environments for the aged. *The Gerontologist,* June 1974, *14,* 228–235.

Chapanis, A., and Lindenbaum, L.E. A reaction time study of four control-display linkages. *Human Factors,* 1959, *1,* 1–7.

Chapanis, A., and Mankin, D.A. Tests of ten control-display linkages. *Human Factors,* 1967, *9,* 119–126.

Clark, W.R., Jr., and Lerner, D. Regional burn survey: Two years of hospitalized burned patients in Central New York. *Journal of Trauma,* 1978, *18,* 524–532.

Cole, D.G. *A Follow-Up Investigation of the Visual Fields and Accident Experience Among North Carolina Drivers.* Chapel Hill, N.C.: University of North Carolina Highway Safety Research Center, June 1979.

Corso, J.F. *Aging Sensory Systems and Perception.* New York, N.Y.: Praeger, 1981.

Daniel, S. *The Role of the Vehicle Front End in Pedestrian Impact Protection.* (SAE Technical Paper Series 820246), Warrendale, Pa: Society of Automotive Engineers, Inc., 1982.

Exton-Smith, A.N. Accidental hypothermia in the elderly. *The Practitioner,* 1968, *200,* 804–812.

Exton-Smith, A.N. The elderly in a cold environment. In Arie, T. (Ed.) *Health Care of the Elderly.* London, England: Croom Helm, Ltd., 1981, 42–56.

Feldman, K.W., Schaller, R.T., Feldman, J.A., and McMillon, M. Tap water scald burns in children. *Pediatrics,* 1978, *62,* 1–7.

Fox, R.H., MacGibbon, R., Davies, L., and Woodward, P.M. Problem of the old and the cold. *British Medical Journal,* 1973, *1,* 21–24.

Fox, R.H., Woodward, P.M., Exton-Smith, A.N., Green, M.F., Donnison, D.V., and Wicks, M.H. Body temperatures in the elderly: A national study of physiological, social, and environmental conditions. *British Medical Journal,* 1973, *1* 200–206.

Fozard, J.L. Person-Environment Relationships in Adulthood: Implications for human factors engineering. *Human Factors,* 1981, *23,* 7–27.

Fozard, J.L., and Popkin, S.J. Optimizing adult development: Ends and means of an applied psychology of aging. *American Psychologist,* 1978, *33,* 975–989.

Gibson, J.J. The contribution of experimental psychology to the formulation of the problem of safety—A brief for basic research. In *Behavioral Approaches to Accident Research.* New York, N.Y.: Association for the Aid of Crippled Children, 1961, 77–89.

Haddon, W. *Energy Damage and the Ten Countermeasures Strategies.* Washington, D.C.: Insurance Institute for Highway Safety. Oct. 1972.

Haddon, W. On the escape of tigers: An ecologic note. *Technology Review:* 1970, *72,* 45–47.

Haight, F.A., and Olsen, R.A. Pedestrian safety in the United States: Some recent trends. *Accident Analysis and Prevention,* 1981, *13,* 43–55.

Hamit, H.F. Fators associated with deaths of burned patients in a community hospital. *Journal of Trauma,* 1978, *18,* 405–418.

Hegsted, D.M. Fluoride and mineral metabolism. *Annals of Dentistry,* 1968, *27,* 134–143.

Hogue, C.C. Injury in late life: Part I. Epidemiology. *Journal of the American Geriatrics Society,* 1982a, *30,* 183–190.

Hogue, C.C. Injury in late life: II. Prevention. *Journal of the American Geriatrics Society,* 1982b, *30,* 276–280.

Hughes, P.C., and Neer, R.M. Lighting for the elderly: A psychological approach to lighting. *Human Factors:* 1981, *23,* 65–85.

Injuries Associated with Selected Consumer Products Treated in Hospital Emergency Departments by Quarter and 12 Months Ending 12/31/81. *NETSS Data Highlights:* 1981, *5,* 2–3.

Irvine, C.H. Evaluation of some factors affecting measurements of slip resistance of shoe sole materials on floor surfaces. *Journal of Testing and Evaluation,* 1976a, *4,* 133–138.

Irvine, C.H. A simple method for evaluation of shoe sole slipperiness. *ASTM Standardization News,* 1976b, *4,* 29–30.

Iskrant, A.P., and Joliet, P.V. *Accidents and Homicide.* Cambridge, Ma.: Harvard University Press, 1968.

Jones, M.H. *Driver Performance Measurers Across Age.* Los Angeles, Ca.: University of Southern California Traffic Safety Center. Oct. 1978.

Kieran, M.J, Bartlett, R.H., Danet, R., and Allyn, P. Burn epidemiology: A basis for burn prevention. *Journal of Trauma,* 1977, *17,* 943–947.

Knoblauch, R.L. *Causative Factors and Countermeasures for Rural and Suburban Pedestrian Accidents: Accident Data Collection and Analysis.* Falls Church, Va.: BioTechnology, Inc., Mar. 1977.

Krag, C.L., and Kountz, W.B. Stability of body function in the aged. I. Effect of exposure of the body to cold. *Journal of Gerontology,* 1950, *5,* 227–235.

Levine, M.S., and Radford, E.P. Fire victims: Medical outcomes and demographic characteristics. *American Journal of Public Health,* 1977. *67,* 1077–1080.

McFarland, R.A. The sensory and perceptual processes in aging. In Schaie, K.W., (Ed.), *Theory and Methods of Research on Aging.* Morgantown, W.V.; West Virginia University, 1968, 9–52.

Marx, J.L. Osteoporosis: New help for thinning bones. *Science,* 1980, *207,* 628–630.

Miller, E. Memory and aging. In Gruneberg, M.M. and Morris, P.E., (Eds.) *Applied Problems in Memory.* New York, N.Y.: Academic Press, 1979.

Moritz, A.R., and Henriques, F.C., Jr. The relative importance of time and surface temperature in the causation of cutaneous burns. *American Journal of Pathology,* 1947, *23,* 695–720.

Munns, K. Effects of exercise on the range of joint motion in elderly subjects. In Smith, E.L., and Serfass, R.C. (Eds.), *Exercise and Aging: The Scientific Basis.* Hillside, N.J.: Enslow Publisher, 1981, 167–178.

National Highway Traffic Safety Administration. *Proceedings of the Eighth International Technical Conference on Experimental Safety Vehicles,* Washington, D.C.: National Highway Traffic Safety Administration, Oct. 1980.

National Highway Traffic Safety Administration. *Proceedings of the Seventh International Technical Conference on Experimental Safety Vehicles.* Washington D.C.: National Highway Traffic Safety Administration, Dec. 1979.

National Safety Council. *Accident Facts, 1982 Edition.* Chicago, Il.: National Safety Council, 1982.

Planek, Thomas W. The aging driver in today's traffic: A critical review. In Waller, P.F. (Ed.), *Aging and Highway Safety: The Elderly in a Mobile Society.* Chapel Hill, N.C.: University of North Carolina Highway Safety Research Center, 1972, 3–38.

Planek, T.W. Home accidents: A continuing social problem. *Accident Analysis and Prevention,* 1982, *14,* 107–120

Planek, T.W., Condon, M.E., and Fowler, R.C. *An Investigation of the Problems and Opinions of Aged Drivers.* Chicago, Il.: National Safety Council. Dec. 1968.

Polus, A., and Katz, A. An analysis of nighttime pedestrian accidents at specially illuminated crosswalks. *Accident Analysis and Prevention,* 1978, *10,* 223–228.

Potts, J.R., and Deftos, L.J. Parathyroid hormone, calcitonin, vitamin D, bone and bone mineral metabolism. *Duncan's Diseases of Metabolism* (7th Ed.). Philadelphia, Penn.: W.B. Saunders Co., 1974, 1225–1430.

Prudham, D. and Evans, J. Grimley. Factors associated with falls in the elderly: A community study. *Age and Aging,* 1981, *10,* 141–146.

Pulling, N.H., Wolf, E., Sturgis, S.P., Vaillancourt, D.R., and Dolliver, J.J. Headlight glare resistance and driver age. *Human Factors,* 1980, *22,* 103–112.

Rackoff, N.J., and Mourant, R.R. Driving performance of the elderly. *Accident Analysis and Prevention,* 1979, *11,* 247–253.

Salthouse, T.A. Adult age and the speed-accuracy trade-off. *Ergonomics,* 1979, *22,* 811–820.

Schonfield, D. and Stones, M.J. Remembering and aging. In Kiholstrom, J.F. and Evans, F.J. (Eds.), *Functional Disorders of Memory.* Hillsdale, N.J.: Lawrence Erlbaum Associates, 1979, 103–139.

Seaton, M. 55 Alive/Mature Driving. *Proceedings of Twenty-Third Conference of the American Association for Automotive Medicine,* Morton Grove, Il.: American Association for Automotive Medicine, 1979, 235–241.

Sekuler, R., Hutman, L.P., and Owsley, C.J. Human aging and spacial vision. *Science,* 1980, *209,* 1255–1256.

Sheldon, J.H. On the natural history of falls in old age. *British Medical Journal,* 1960, *2,* 1685–1690.

Sivak, M., Olson, P.L., and Pastalan, L.A. Effect of driver's age on nighttime legibility of highway signs. *Human Factors,* 1981, *23,* 59–64.

Sivak, M., and Olson, P.L. Nighttime legibility of traffic signs: Conditions eliminating the effects of driver age and disability glare. *Accident Analysis and Prevention,* 1982, *14,* 87–93.

Slater, H., and Gaisford, J.C. Burns in older patients. *Journal of the American Geriatrics Society,* 1981, *29,* 74–76.

Smith, E.L. Bone Changes in the exercising older adult. In Smith, E.L. and Serfass, R.C. (Eds.), *Exercise and Aging: The Scientific Basis.* Hillside, N.J.: Enslow Publishers, 1981, 179–186.

Smith, E.L., Sempos, C.T., and Purvis, R.W. Bone mass and strength decline with age. In Smith, E.L. and Serfass, R.C. (Eds.), *Exercise and Aging: The Scientific Basis.* Hillside, N.J.: Enslow Publishers, 1981, 59–87.

Stewart, J.R. *An Analysis of Annual Mileage Self Reported by Renewal Applicants.* Chapel Hill, N.C.: University of North Carolina Highway Safety Research Center, Aug. 1975.

Stoudt, H.W. The anthropomety of the elderly. *Human Factors,* 1981, *23,* 29–37.

Templer, J.A., Mullet, G.M. Archea, J., and Margulis, S.T. *An Analysis of the Behavior of Stair Users.* Atlanta, Ga.: Georgia Institute of Technology. Washington, D.C.: National Bureau of Standards, Nov. 1978.

Waller, J.A. Emergency care for fatalities from injury and illness in nonhighway setting. *Journal of Trauma,* 1973, *13,* 4–60.

Waller, J.A. Falls among the elderly—Human and environmental factors. *Accident Analysis and Prevention,* 1978, *10,* 21–33.

Waller, J.A. *Medical and Related Issues in Driving by Elderly Persons.* Burlington, Vt.: Vermount University College of Medicine, 1980.

Waller, J.A. Nonhighway injury fatalities. II. Interaction of product and human factors. *Journal of Chronic Disease,* 1972, *25,* 47–52.

Waller, P.F., House, E.G., and Stewart, J.R. *An Analysis of Accidents by Age.* Chapel Hill, N.C.: University of North Carolina Highway Safety Research Center, Jan. 1977.

Watts, A.J. Hypothermia in the aged: A study of the role of cold-sensitivity. *Environmental Research,* 1971, *5,* 119–126.

Welford, A.T. Motor Performance. In Birren, J.E. and Schaie, K.W. (Eds.), *Handbook of the Psychology of Aging.* New York, N.Y.: Van Nostrand Reinhold Co., 1977, 450–496.

Wiener, E.L. Elderly pedestrians and drivers: The problem that refuses to go away. In Waller, P.F. (Ed.), *Aging and Highway Safety: The Elderly in a Mobile Society.* Chapel Hill, N.C.: Highway Safety Research Center, 1972, 53–95.·

Wilson, J.R., and Rennie, A.M. Elderly pedestrians and road safety. In Foot, H.C., Chapman, A.J., and Wade, F.M. (Eds.), *Road Safety Research and Practice.* New York, N.Y.: Praeger, 1981, 143–149.

Wolbarsht, M.L. Tests for glare sensitivity and peripheral vision in driver applicants. *Journal of Safety Research,* 1977, *9,* 128–139.

Wolf, E. Glare and age. *Archives of Ophthalmology:* 1960, *64,* 502–514.

Wolfe, A.C., and O'Day, J. *Factbook on U.S. Pedestrian Accidents.* Ann Arbor, Mi.: Highway Safety Research Institute, Feb. 1981.

Ysander, L., and Herner, B. Elderly male automobile drivers in Gothenburg and their traffic behavior in the year 1971. *Proceedings of First International Conference on Driver Behavior,* Oct. 1973, SM3.

Zador, P., Moshman, J., and Marcus, L. Adoption of right turn on red: Effects on crashes at signalized intersections. *Accident Analysis and Prevention,* 1982, *14,* 219–234.

Zegeer, C.V., Opiela, K.S., and Cynecki, M.J. Effect of pedestrian signals and signal timing on pedestrian accidents. In *Transportation Research Record,* No. 847, 1982, 62–72.

4

Housing and the Elderly

MICHAEL A. STEGMAN*

Introduction

In the United States as well as Great Britain there are those who reject both the notion that old people should be a protected class within national housing policy and the view of aging which they believe gives credence to large, age-segregated housing construction programs for the elderly (Butler et al., 1979). The so-called disengagement theory developed by Cumming and Henry posits that:

> ... aging is an inevitable mutual withdrawal or disengagement, resulting in decreased interaction between the aging person and others in the social systems he belongs to (Cumming and Henry, 1961, p. 14).

Some view the implications of this theory in terms of political economy, as a reflection of society's unwillingness to accord the elderly the measure of respect and dignity they deserve after their economically productive years. The concept of disengagement, according to Blau,

> ... deserves to be publicly attacked, because it can so easily be used as a rationale by the non-old, who constitute the 'normals' in society, to avoid confronting and dealing with the issue of old people's marginality and rolelessness in American society (Blau, 1973, pp. 152–153).

*Written with the editorial assistance of Anne Hafrey.

Whether, as Fennell argues (1977), old people are forced to be passive or not, and whether national housing policy embodies the anti-social tenets of the disengagement theory or not, it is true that the general basic pattern of Federal housing programs in the United States has been to promote projects designed exclusively for the elderly.

A public health perspective in national housing policy deliberations concerning the elderly would not result in the abandonment of traditional building programs. Rather, it would encourage us to reduce our emphasis on building new housing for the elderly in favor of enriching the services available to them both in their own homes and neighborhoods, and in housing built especially for them. In short, a public health perspective on housing should favor a continuum of housing services which, in Lawton's terms, would "match the level of support to the level of competence [and therefore] need of the individual" (N. Lawton et al., 1980).

This chapter is intended as a primer for public health professionals concerned with the housing needs of the elderly. It should also help move us closer to the policy approach reflected in the principle of the housing continuum. It describes the present needs of the elderly in the United States, how these are likely to change during the next 10 to 20 years, and the importance of developing policy responses to meet changing needs. There are three sections in the chapter. The first discusses the relationship between the socioeconomic and demographic characteristics of the aged and then presents a detailed analysis of the elderly's housing conditions, homeownership rates, and housing expense burdens. The section concludes with a look at the neighborhood considerations, such as displacement and crime, that affect the housing and housing satisfaction of the elderly.

The second section deals with such issues as the expected growth and continued aging of the elderly, and the redefinition of housing policy and programs that these trends will require. In focusing on the increasing suburbanization of the aged, the section points up the importance of housing services to older people in communities that are just beginning to face the permanent decline of their school-age populations and their inadequate services for the elderly.

A discussion of public health-related policy considerations for the aged concludes the chapter. There is a need for new forms of housing for older people and a need to institutionalize the link between housing and such services as home maintenance or personal care that would enable the elderly to live independently, or at least to live outside of an institution.

Housing Conditions of the Elderly

As is true with other age groups, the housing conditions of the elderly vary according to income and household composition, the latter referring to whether the elderly live alone, with a spouse, or with other relatives or non-relatives. These same variables are related to whether the elderly own or rent their houses or live in government-assisted housing or an institution. As is the case for younger people, the housing conditions of the elderly also vary significantly according to the resident's race, as well as region and urban or rural location.

Household Composition

Because the elderly are more likely than younger people to live alone, they comprise a much larger proportion of all households than of the total population. In 1979, the 23 million people in the nation aged 65 or more accounted for just 11% of the total population but 20% of all households (Muller et al., 1980, p. I. 9). Forty-five percent of all older households contained both husband and wife, while an almost equal percentage consisted of only one person. Seventy-seven percent of these single-person households were women, and 23% were men (U.S. DHUD, 1979, p. 3).

As the high rates of single households imply, the tendency of older people to live with their children or other younger relatives has declined in recent years. In 1940, 15% of all elderly men and 30% of elderly women lived with their kin, compared to 4 and 13%, respectively, in 1975 (Mindel, 1979). Soldo and Mindel, among others, interpret the rise in independent living among the elderly to be a "matter of choice rather than default." (Soldo, 1978, p. 8). "[A]ttitude studies," according to Mindel, "have indicated that most individuals, both younger and older, prefer not to maintain multigenerational living arrangements" (Mindel, 1979, pp. 461–462). This does not mean, however, that kinship ties between the old and young have necessarily deteriorated. On the contrary, the growing economic independence of older people, coupled with longer life expectancy and more relatively disability-free years, have made it possible for more elderly to live by themselves and still maintain strong family ties. According to Soldo:

> Sussman, Litwak and Adams all present evidence to suggest that the elderly are quite successful in actualizing their preferences for kinship ties while maintaining their household independence. . . . Intergenerational bonds of affection and responsibility, coupled with frequent exchanges of visits and services are the rule rather than the exception for the vast majority of older persons (Soldo, 1979, p. 8).

While the incidence of multigenerational households has declined over the years, this arrangement is still more common among the elderly than is institutionalization. Indeed, an older person's moving into the home of a relative can be an "alternative to movement into an institution," or perhaps, an intermediate step, ". . . being neither as satisfactory . . . as independent living nor as threatening and guilt-inducing as institutionalization" (Mindel, 1979, p. 462).

The Incomes of Older People

The composition of older households influences income. In 1975, the median income of all older households ($8,720) was 58% of that for all households ($14,960), while single old people had a median income just 42% of that of older families ($3,640) (U.S. DHUD, 1979 pp. 3, 6). Not surprisingly, couples are much less likely to be poor than single people living alone because both may still be earning. While only 9% of all older families had incomes below the federal poverty level in 1975, 25% of all single old men and 31% of all single old women were poor. Due primarily to changes in the social security system, such as the indexing of social security benefits and the fact that women may now receive benefits on the basis of their own earnings, the economic circumstances of older people have improved over the past 10 years, relative to the total population (U.S. DHUD, 1980a, p. 9). In 1970, ". . . the elderly poor constituted 24.5 percent of all elderly persons and 18.5 percent of all poor people. In 1977, the elderly poor numbered 14.1 percent of all elderly and 12.9 percent of all poor persons" (U.S. DHUD, 1980a, p. 9). According to the Bureau of the Census, the poverty rate for the elderly was 15.3% in 1981, compared to 14% for all Americans.

The economic fortunes of the nation's minority elderly, however, have deteriorated. In 1970, 83% of the elderly poor were white and about 17% were black or Hispanic. By 1977, the proportion of the elderly poor who were white fell to 76%, while the percentage of black or Hispanic elderly poor climbed to 24%. In both 1970 and 1977, the likelihood of poverty for an elderly individual was over twice as great for Hispanics and blacks as for whites (Struyk and Soldo, 1980, p. 25). The differences are even more dramatic among women. Forty percent of all older black women have incomes below the poverty level, compared to 16% of all older white women (Struyk and Soldo, 1980, p. 26).

From a regional standpoint, "the rates of poverty among the older population are twice as great in the South as in the North and West—and metropolitan areas show lower proportions of elderly in poverty than do nonmetropolitan areas, regardless of region" (Struyk and Soldo, 1980, p. 27). Among owners and renters alike, median incomes are lowest for rural residents, somewhat higher in central cities, and highest in the metropolitan suburbs. In 1975, the median income of elderly central city homeowning families was $6,708. Suburban owners enjoyed incomes 40% greater than that ($7,514). Residents of small cities had incomes 94% of the central-city median ($6,276), and rural homeowners received incomes that were only 80% that of central city families ($4,363). For renters the range was narrower but still substantial. For central-city families the median income was $4,209, 8% less than the suburban renter median income ($4,561), while the rural median income of $3,245 was 77% that of central city renters (Gutowski and Feild, 1979, p. 21).

Clearly, older renters are much more likely than owners to be poor. Nearly 55% of all elderly suburban renters and 60% of all central city renters had incomes below $5,000 in 1975. It is not only elderly renters who are poor, however. Twenty-nine percent of all elderly suburban owners and more than 35% of central city owners had incomes of $5,000 or less in 1975. Indeed, more than one out of every five elderly suburban renters had incomes of less than $3,000 (Gutowski and Feild, 1979, p. 21).

Despite high levels of poverty among the elderly, it is important to recognize that not all older households are poor. Nearly 18% of aged suburban homeowners and 9% of suburban renters had incomes of at least $15,000 in 1975. Somewhat less than half of these owners and almost two-thirds of the renters had incomes of $25,000 or more. The percentages of elderly central city owners and renters with incomes of at least $15,000 are nearly matched in the suburbs (16 and 7% respectively). Only 3% of central city owners and 6% of central city renters have incomes above $25,000 (Gutowski and Feild, 1979, p. 21).

Substantial differences in incomes resulting from location (regional, intra-, and intermetropolitan) and housing tenure notwithstanding, Struyk and Soldo (1980, p. 27) conclude that "the major predictor of income adequacy appears to be family status. Depending on region and place of residence, one-quarter to one-half of persons age 65 or over who are not living in a family have incomes below the poverty level." In other words, "The factors which determine income in retirement are the same ones that determine income before retirement"—family background, education, occupation, duration and consistency of employment, and marital status (Henretta and Campbell, 1976 p. 990).

These variables strongly determine income and are evident in a superficial examination of differences in household composition among older people in the central cities and suburban communities of our metropolitan areas. As just noted, incomes of the elderly are higher in the suburbs than in the cities, and are higher for families than for single individuals. Not surprisingly, then, older people in the suburbs are more likely to be living in families than are those in central cities. One-half of all suburban individuals 65 years or older are married, compared to 40% in the central cities (Gutowski and Feild, 1976, p. 45). These differences are even more pronounced within the 65–74 year age cohort. Fifty-seven percent of all suburban household heads in this age group are married, compared to 43% of those in central cities (Gutowski and Feild, 1976, p. 46).

The Quality of Housing

It is almost axiomatic that older people live in older housing. This is principally due to declining mobility as retirement approaches, a phenomenon often referred to as "aging in place" (Struyk and Soldo, 1980, p. 160). Cowgill notes the centrifugal growth of cities, which finds young families on the "growing edge while older persons stay behind in shrinking households and aging housing structures" (Cowgill, 1978, p. 447). As of 1973, one-third of all older families had been living in their dwellings for at least 20 years (Struyk and Soldo, 1980, p. 160), while nearly half of all elderly-occupied housing was built before the Second World War (Struyk and Soldo, 1980, p. 42). In nonmetropolitan areas, the "aging in place" phenomenon is even more pronounced. In 1973, two out of every three older farm families had been living in their dwellings for at least 20 years (Struyk and Soldo, 1980, p. 161).

Despite the disproportionately high concentration of elderly in older housing, the physical conditions in which they live are probably no worse, and in some cases are better, than those of younger people, at least according to traditional definitions of housing adequacy.

"Traditional definitions" refer to such census-based indicators of physical condition as the absence of complete plumbing and kitchen facilities in a dwelling, or families having to share complete bathrooms and kitchens with other families.

While older households are more likely than younger ones to live in housing lacking complete plumbing, the differences are not large (4.6% of the elderly versus 2.6% of all households). Similarly, while they are also more likely to lack complete kitchens, the difference is only one percentage point (2.9 versus 1.8 percent) (U.S. DHUD, 1979, p. 8).

As is the case with the rest of the population, the incidence of housing problems differs greatly between older renters and owners, and again between urban and rural residents. Almost 8 percent of all older renters live in housing without complete plumbing, while 6 percent have incomplete kitchens. The comparable deficiency rates among homeowners are just 3.3 and 1.6%, respectively. The reported incidence of housing deficiencies for older households is much greater in the South than elsewhere, and is substantially higher in nonmetropolitan than metropolitan areas (Struyk and Soldo, 1980, p. 46). Fifteen percent of older renters in nonmetropolitan areas live in housing with incomplete plumbing, compared to just 4% in metropolitan areas (Struyk and Soldo, 1980, p. 48).

In addition to these indicators of housing deficiencies, the Department of Housing and Urban Development (HUD) has defined inadequate housing more broadly to include not only those units with incomplete facilities, but also those with one or more of the following defects: no public sewer, septic tank, cesspool, or chemical toilet for sewage disposal; no heating, or heating provided by unvented room heaters burning gas, oil, or kerosene, or by a fireplace, stove, or space heater; a leaking roof, open cracks or holes in interior walls or ceilings, holes in the interior floor, broken plaster or peeling paint (over one square foot) on interior walls or ceilings;

exposed wiring and fuses, or circuit breakers which blew three or more times in the past 90 days; or no wall plugs in one or more rooms. The unit may also have more than one of the following defects in the public halls: no light fixtures, loose or missing steps, loose or missing stair railings (Gutowski and Feild, 1979, p. 65).

Because the definition of inadequate house put forth by HUD is more inclusive than the above two measures, one would expect to find significantly more inadequate housing being occupied, by all groups and by the elderly alone, when the HUD criteria are applied. This is indeed the case. According to a recent Urban Institute analysis, occupancy rates of substandard housing are higher for nonelderly than for elderly central city residents (13.8 versus 8.7%), while housing conditions do not vary significantly in the suburbs and in rural areas for those under and over 65. For both groups, between 6 and 7 percent of suburban residents occupy inadequate housing, and 16% of the elderly and 14% of nonelderly households in rural areas live in inadequate housing (Gutowski and Feild, 1979, p. 66).

Regardless of an individual's age, the housing conditions of renters are far worse than those of owners. A city versus suburban location makes little difference in the housing condition of older people, unlike the case for younger households. Fourteen percent of all older central city, and 12% of suburban, renters live in housing with at least one of the structural or maintenance deficiencies described above. Among older homeowners, the incidence of inadequate housing is about one-third as high (4.1% for central city and 4.6% for suburban households) (Gutowski and Feild, 1979, p. 68). The authors of the Urban Institute study conclude that, coupled with the lower incomes, "the greater intensity of problems with housing adequacy experienced by elderly renters is further support for the hypothesis that . . . elderly renters, regardless of location, represent a major target group for housing, income and social service assistance" (Gutowski and Feild, 1979, p. 67).

In light of this conclusion it should be noted that while the incidence of physical housing problems among the elderly, especially renters in central cities, is high, it is lower than for the nonelderly. Because the data on housing defects are derived from household responses to census questions, however, and not through independent housing inspections, the resulting rates of housing inadequacy may not be highly reliable. Households vary in their housing expectations, in their tolerance for various kinds of inconveniences, maintenance problems, and difficulties with the plumbing, electrical, and mechanical systems in their buildings. Given their relative immobility, generally limited incomes, and lack of viable housing alternatives, older households might understate the number of maintenance deficiencies in their housing to a greater degree than the younger population does. This would be particularly true for homeowners (who have no landlords to blame for maintenance problems). Little systematic work has been done on the relation between objective and subjective evaluations of housing conditions, but Lawton cites a recent HUD study that documents a high rate of underreporting of housing problems by the elderly. Trained inspectors followed up a HUD household survey of maintenance problems with an inspection of the sampled dwellings and found that "elderly household heads reported only about half the [defects] found during inspection" (Lawton, 1980, p. 56). In short, it is likely that more older families occupy physically inadequate housing than the limited data imply.

More important, perhaps, than the fact that older people might be underreporting the frequency of various defects in their physical environment is the insensitivity of many conventional measures of housing quality to such correlates of advanced age as rheumatism, impaired vision, and various other physical disabilities. Not all older people suffer from these infirmities, but for those who do, otherwise minor maintenance deficiencies become major housing burdens. Lawton notes, for example, that "in one study done at the Philadelphia Geriatric Center, 8 percent of the applicants for planned housing mentioned the necessity of climbing stairs as a reason for wishing to leave their current residences" (Lawton, 1980, p. 61). Other studies also imply that the adequacy of housing should be judged relative to the needs and capabilities of the occupants. This is particularly the case for physically handicapped people and the elderly. Again, according to Lawton,

> Some physical features of the residence become deficiencies only when the user is himself limited in competence. . . . Put another way mild problems that are solved almost without thinking by a person with the full vigor and resources of middle adulthood may constitute insuperable barriers to an elderly occupant with fewer personal, social and economic resources (Lawton, 1980, p. 57).

It is important to distinguish between the concept of relative housing quality, or the lack of person-environment consequence, as Carp would describe it (Carp, 1976), and the much maligned theories of the late nineteenth-century social reformers and their counterparts in the 1930s. They posited causal links between poor housing conditions and "many of the social and physical problems confronting the poor" (Weicher, 1980, p. 5). According to Weicher, these housing advocates believed that "tearing down the slums and replacing them with good new housing [would] reduce crime, delinquency and antisocial behavior generally and improve the mental and physical health of the poor" (Weicher, 1980, p. 5). In rejecting this notion, he cites Kasl's exhaustive evaluation of 178 studies in the fields of public health, medicine, and social psychology which purport to link housing and health:

> The link between parameters of housing and indices of psychological health has not been well supported by the reviewed evidence, at least not in any direct sense . . . the relationship between housing and chronic conditions and disability is not at present supported by any firm evidence . . . the association between housing and mental health (excluding housing satisfaction) is ' supported only by the weakest, most ambiguous studies. . . . The best-designed studies do not demonstrate any mental health benefits, and it now appears that some of our most cherished hopes—such as raising educational and occupational aspirations by moving people out of slums—will never be realized (Kasl, 1976, p. 6).

Poor housing conditions may not cause many of the elderly's problems, but few would dispute that aging makes individuals more sensitive to their physical surroundings and less able to adapt to otherwise unimportant environmental changes. The elderly's reduced levels of physical competence also make them less able than younger people to modify their dwellings to remove whatever physical barriers might arise as a result of their infirmities. Thus, while poor housing might not cause poor physical and mental health, certain housing conditions can contribute to the health problems of older people and limit their independence. A couple of examples should clarify this point. Poorly insulated housing causes most people some discomfort. If older people are indeed more likely than others to be susceptible to hypothermia, a lack of insulation could make an otherwise adequate dwelling unfit for them. Similarly, since older people are less likely than younger people to recover from a serious fall and are more likely to suffer serious health consequences from a fall, raised thresholds, loose stairs, or even poor lighting constitute more serious housing problems for them than for others.

The exaggerated claims of the housing reformers are not the only reason efforts to redefine housing adequacy typically meet with policy resistance. More often than not, redefinition has involved higher rather than lower minimum standards. Thus, for example, while the proportion of all American families who are ill-housed fell from nearly half to less than 3% between 1940 and 1979, using incomplete plumbing as the measure of substandard quality, 7.5% of the population live in housing which needs rehabilitation if one uses a variant of the HUD definition of housing conditions as the standard (The President's Commission on Housing, 1981, pp. 12–17).

As long as proponents of subsidized housing use the higher counts of families with housing problems to lobby for ever larger production programs, any redefinition of housing quality that would swell the national estimates of substandard housing is bound to meet heavy resistance from a skeptical, cost-conscious Congress.

From a public health perspective, therefore, it is important to break the policy link between the count of inadequately housed elderly and the optimal size of subsidized housing production programs. More and better information on the housing conditions of the elderly would probably show that many of their housing problems can be remedied inexpensively through such housing-related services as housekeeping, home management, personal care, repair and maintenance services, and adult day care rather than by traditional rental housing construction programs. Reliance on nonhousing programs to solve the elderly's housing problems would lessen the need for expensive new construction and, perhaps, lower the need for intermediate care facilities as well.

Homeownership Rates Among the Elderly

Mention was made earlier of the fact that owner-occupied housing tends to be in better condition than rental units, but the extent of homeownership among the elderly was not discussed. The vast majority of old people, even those whose incomes are below the federal poverty level, own their houses (Welfeld and Struyk, 1978, p. 19). Seventy-one percent of old people overall and 83% of elderly couples own their homes. Homeownership rates are lower for single elderly and lowest of all for single men, although even half of them own a home. Because renters tend to occupy worse housing than owners, the high rate of tenancy among single elderly—espe-cially men—explains the greater incidence of substandard housing for single people than for couples.

Homeownership rates not only vary by household composition, but by regional and metropolitan location as well. As with the nonelderly, elderly people are more likely to own their own homes in smaller cities and communities than in metropolitan areas. In 1973, for example, 62% of all older residents of large metropolitan areas owned their homes. Ownership rates increased to 74% in urban nonmetropolitan areas, climbed to 83% for rural nonfarm communities, and peaked at 90% among older farm residents (Lawton, 1980, p. 54).

A far higher proportion of elderly suburban than core city residents own their homes, which is consistent with higher overall homeownership rates in the suburbs. In 1976, the suburban elderly homeownership rate was 73%, compared to 55% for all older cen-tral city households (Gutowski and Feild, 1979, p. 31). In both cities and suburbs, the rental stock occupied by older people is dominated by single-person households—63% of all older renters in the cities and 62% in the suburbs. While a majority of older metro-politan homeowning households contain at least two people, a size-able percentage are made up of one person—36% in the cities and 33% in the suburbs (Gutowski and Feild, 1979, p. 48). These high rates among single individuals probably reflect in part the increas-ing tendency "for elderly women, mostly widows, to live alone" (Mindel, 1979, p. 459).

Housing Expenses

Due principally to long-term occupancy in their present houses, nearly 83% of all older people own their own homes free and clear, compared to just 25% of the nonelderly (Struyk and Soldo, 1980, p. 58). Of the 15% of all older owners with incomes below the poverty level (compared to 27% of all older renters) (Struyk and Soldo, 1980, p. 26), 87% also own their houses free and clear (Struyk and Soldo, 1980, p. 58). Despite these high rates of debt-free ownership, however, the asset position of most older homeowners is not very strong. One-quarter of these owners without mortgages live in houses valued at less than $15,000 in 1976, while another quarter had between $15,000 and $25,000 equity in their houses (Struyk and Soldo, 1980, p. 5).

Largely because so many older people own their house out-right, the average housing expense burden of older households is not very different from that of the nonelderly population. In 1976, the average older household spent 23% of its income for housing, compared to 20% by the nonelderly (Struyk and Soldo, 1980, p. 55). Still, however, 2.3 million older households spent more than 35% of their incomes on housing in 1976 (Struyk and Soldo, 1980, p. 4). The housing expense burden was far greater of course among renters. About 24% of all elderly suburban renters, 12% of rural renters, and 29% of elderly central city renters spent more than half of their income on housing (Gutowski and Feild, 1979, p. 31).

In summary, while older people account for approximately 11% of the total population and 20% of all households, they own around 25% of all owner-occupied housing in the country (Haley and Wiseman, 1980, p. 2). "In rural farm areas, however, where the elderly represent 12 percent of the population, they own almost one-third of the housing stock" (Struyk and Soldo, 1980, p. 159). In part because housing conditions are worse in rural areas than in cities, and homeownership rates among the elderly are much higher there than elsewhere, older people are reported to own around 40% of the nation's substandard housing units (Mayer and Olson, 1980, p. 10). It must be emphasized, however, that the housing problems "seem linked much more to elderly homeowners' incomes than their age" (Mayer and Olson, 1980, p. 10). Indeed, among renters and owners, "race, ethnicity, sex . . . are the factors that, far more than age, affect the chances of a poor household living in physically deficient housing" (U.S. DHUD, 1979, p. 15). Like the total population, all elderly households have one chance in 10 of living in substandard housing, but that probability rises to one in five for older blacks and Hispanics. ". . . [A] poor Hispanic man, if he is at least 65 years old and living alone . . . has better than a 50-50 chance of being ill-housed" (U.S. DHUD, 1979, p. 15).

Neighborhoods

As difficult as it is to assess the physical conditions of the elderly's housing reliably, measuring the attributes of their neighborhoods is far more challenging. Any serious discussion of the situation of older people must address neighborhood considerations. "By virtue of their location, housing units serve more than the simple need for shelter . . . proximity to stores, recreational facilities, churches and neighbors is predicated on residential location" (Soldo, 1981, p. 15), for the elderly and young alike. Access and proximity to a wide range of services and facilities may be even more important to older people than to younger ones. Long trips are more difficult for older people with failing vision or difficulty in walking. Hansen, for example, estimates that older persons spend 80 to 90 percent of their time in their immediate home environment (Hansen, 1971). Newcomer (1976) has shown that elderly public housing tenants use services more intensively when these are located nearby, and that optimal use of such resources often requires very close proximity. Berghorn et al. (1978) demonstrate that "the condition of the neighborhood . . . has been shown to be positively related to the morale . . . of older persons" (Struyk and Soldo, 1980, p. 165). The work of Kahana et al., like Rosow (1967) indicates that when persons "evaluate their living situations, complaints are usually focused on the social environment and features of the neighborhood rather than the dwelling unit per se" (Kahana et al., 1977, p. 126). Given the importance of location and the convenience of the neighborhood in an assessment of the quality of life enjoyed by older people and the proposition that "an older person living in a structurally sound unit in an unsafe neighborhood has a housing problem just as much as an older person whose home lacks adequate plumbing or heat" (Struyk and Soldo, 1980, p. 147), it is important to know where the elderly are most likely to live.

Because of their long occupancy in old houses, the centrifugal growth pattern of cities and the flight of young people from the countryside, the elderly tend to be disproportionately concentrated in older central cities and rural communities with populations below 2,500. Cowgill (1978) defines these areas as gray ghettos. In the cities, these gray ghettos typically exhibit high rates of building abandonment, inadequate housing, high rates of unemployment, poverty, and crime, poorly maintained streets and sidewalks, and limited municipal services (Struyk and Soldo, 1980, p. 5).

Despite these obvious environmental limitations, Struyk and Soldo report that, like their younger counterparts, most older people are satisfied with their neighborhoods (Struyk and Soldo, 1980, p. 5). When central city elderly express dissatisfaction with their neighborhoods, the most frequently cited problems are excessive street noise (33%), airplane noise (21%), neighborhood crime (19%), and industrial activities. Among suburban elderly, neighborhood crime (15%) drops out of the top four problems, and is replaced by inadequate street lighting (19%) (Gutowski and Feild, 1979, p. 73).

Respondents to the Annual Housing Survey were also asked about the adequacy of six types of neighborhood services: transportation, schools, shopping, police and fire protection, and medical clinics. Not surprisingly, suburban "households are far more likely to report inadequate services than central city households" (Gutowski and Feild, 1979, p. 79). Thus, according to Gutowski and Feild, "while neighborhood conditions may be better in the suburbs, neighborhood services appear to be better, or at least more widely available in the cities" (Gutowski and Feild, 1979, p. 79). Even in the suburbs the frequency of negative responses is quite low. One-third of older suburban residents think that public transportation is inadequate, compared to just 10% in central cities; around 13% of city and suburban dwellers rate their neighborhood shopping services as inadequate, and 12% of all suburbanites and 7% of all city residents think that their neighborhoods lack sufficient medical clinics (Gutowski and Feild, 1979, p. 82). Only with respect to the inadequacy of police protection do older suburbanites rate their neighborhood services much more favorably than do old people living in cities. One out of 10 elderly city residents are dissatisfied with their neighborhood police services, compared to just one out of 17 older suburban residents (Gutowski and Feild, 1979, p. 84).

In assessing the significance of these low levels of acknowledged dissatisfaction with both neighborhood conditions and available services, Struyk and Soldo, like Lawton and Carp, warn against "the easy acceptance of subjective evaluations that are likely to be contaminated by the perceived lack of realistic alternatives, by reduced aspirations, and by self-protective denial" (Struyk and Soldo, 1980, p. 15). Whether a lack of realistic alternatives explains why older people seem more content than they ought to be with their neighborhoods, however, is still unclear.

Neighborhood Crime. While Gutowski and Feild's Annual Housing Survey-based analysis of neighborhood inadequacies showed excessive street and airplane noise to be of greater concern to older people than crime, other researchers have singled out the problem of neighborhood crime as a pressing and pervasive problem facing the elderly. As far back as 1974, for example, Goldsmith and Tomas wrote that "criminal behavior has a chilling effect upon the freedom of older Americans. Fear of victimization," they said, "causes self-imposed 'house arrest' among older people" (Goldsmith and Tomas, 1974).

Even when the probability of nonreporting by the elderly is taken into account, Clemente and Kleiman (1976, p. 208) found that "victimization rates for crimes against the person are lower for the elderly than for any other age group over 12." While concluding that fear of crime is even more of a problem for older people than crime itself, Clemente and Kleiman (1976) indicate that the level of fear varies with the characteristics of the elderly and their neighborhoods. Blacks of all ages have a greater fear of victimization than do whites, and this is especially true for the elderly. Poor people, including the elderly poor, exhibit higher levels of fear than do those with higher incomes, although income is more of a factor among the nonelderly than the elderly. Similarly, education makes some difference in fear of victimization among the nonelderly but not among the elderly. Finally, fear of crime varies directly with the size of the community. More than three-quarters of all older people in cities with at least 250,000 people are afraid of crime, compared to 68 percent of the aged in cities with between 50,000 and 250,000 people. Fear of victimization declines to 43 percent in communities of between 2,500 and 50,000 people and touches only 24 percent of the old in towns with populations below 2,500 (Clemente and Kleiman, 1976, p. 209).

Lawton cautions that the proposition that "the fear of crime keeps the urban elderly 'prisoners in their own homes' has as yet had no empirical support" (Lawton, 1980, p. 46), but there is a consensus in the literature that fear of crime seriously limits the mobility of older people in their own neighborhoods. In Newcomer's (1976) terms, ". . . barriers, such as . . . local crime, may perturb the use/proximity relation . . .; that is, low use may be made of some very near facilities" (Lawton, 1980, p. 40). Neighborhood crime or fear of criminal activity rules out the use of facilities in certain areas and thus has the potential to cut off the flow of important support services to frightened older people. According to Cutler, "supportive programs which might otherwise have served and benefited the elderly have been rendered ineffective by what Faulkner (1975) refers to as an 'omnipresent sense of danger'" (Cutler, 1979–1980, p. 374).

Lawton and others have found that the availability of social supports seems to reduce the fear of crime among the elderly (Sundeen and Mathieu, 1976). This is consistent with Gubrium's (1974) notion that supportive personal relations in age-homogeneous communities lessen anxiety about victimization. This proposition was later confirmed in Sundeen and Mathieu's (1976) study of crime in three different settings, one of which was a walled, age-segregated retirement community. The study, which also included a lower income, central city neighborhood dominated by apartment buildings and a middle class urban neighborhood containing a mix of single family homes and apartments, found that the central city elderly took more low-cost precautions against crime than did others. This included buying guns, installing more locks and staying home more frequently. The higher income retirement community residents had more confidence in their private security force than did the central city elderly in their municipal police forces. Feelings of security were quite high inside the walled community. Once outside, though, approximately the same percentages of these older people as those in the other environments feared being the victims of crime. Finally, despite the fact that social networks tend to reduce the level of anxiety, a high enough fear of crime in a neighborhood or community can cause the social-support system to erode (Conklin, 1975).

Forced Displacement. Struyk does not discuss the "gentrification" of inner city and suburban neighborhoods which is a result of private reinvestment, and the conversion of rental buildings to condominiums and cooperatives, which has resulted in the forced displacement of those who are unable or unwilling to pay the higher prices necessary to remain in their buildings or neighborhoods (see for example, U.S. DHUD, 1980b). There are few hard data on the phenomenon of displacement, but the Annual Housing Survey shows that in 1976, 8 and 9%, respectively, of all city and suburban individuals who moved within the previous year were displaced by private actions (Gutowski and Feild, 1979, p. 55). Private investment was the reason that 4% of nonelderly central city households gave for moving, but it was not among the top eight reasons for younger suburbanites (Gutowski and Feild, 1979, p. 56). This is consistent with HUD's recent finding that around half of all condominium conversions in the country have occurred in suburbs and that older people are more likely than others to move when their buildings are converted (U.S. DHUD, 1980b).

Around one-fifth of all households in buildings that have been converted are elderly, and not all of them are either poor or forced out (U.S. DHUD, 1981a). HUD reports that as of January 1, 1980,

23% of all elderly households residing in buildings converted between 1977 and 1979 bought their units, 29% continued to rent their old apartment, and 49% moved (U. S. DHUD, 1981a). Many of those who bought did so out of a reluctance to move, and the housing costs for their converted dwellings increased an average 11%, compared to 40% among nonelderly tenant buyers (U.S. Department of Housing and Urban Development, 1981a). This large difference is due to the bigger down payments made by older buyers, 20% of whom paid over 50% of the total purchase price in cash at closing (U.S. DHUD, 1981a).

In one of its most socially disruptive forms, the revitalization of downtown neighborhoods involves the redevelopment or conversion of single-room occupancy hotels (SROs). (See, for example, Eckert, 1979.) According to Hartman et al. (1981 p. 54), these hotels house people "who don't have the money or the family support to live anywhere else, especially the single, pension-dependent elderly." In New York City, for example, the number of SRO hotel rooms, most of which rented for under $50 a week, declined from around 50,000 in 1975 to 28,000 in 1978. Inflation and the pressures of economic development are expected to all but eliminate the SRO hotel in New York by 1984 (Hartman et al., 1981 p. 55). Similarly, the pressures from tourism and industrial development in San Franciso have contributed to the substantial decline of the SRO hotel in that city, where nearly 6,000 SRO hotel rooms were converted to tourist accommodations between 1975 and 1979 (Hartman et al., 1981 p. 55).

The decline of the SRO hotel seriously disrupts the social networks of occupants and management that enable tenants to maintain their independence. According to Lally, hotel employees are largely sympathetic to the tenants and often provide them with care and special favors, such as meal delivery or, at times, rent reductions (Lally et al., 1979). Eckert reinforces this view in his case study of the redevelopment of a SRO hotel district in San Diego, where tenants of all ages relied on themselves despite high levels of functional impairment (Eckert, 1979). In yet another study, Cohen and Sokolvsky (1980) report that the general perception of SRO tenants as social isolates is incorrect. Many of these self-proclaimed loners have extended social networks that go beyond the hotel, and these can be permanently damaged by the loss of their housing.

The close proximity of inexpensive eating places, and discount clothing and drug stores enables most SRO hotel tenants to remain independent despite their low incomes and physical and psychological disabilities. Thus, according to Eckert, SRO hotels function as semi-institutional facilities which "provide numerous services to their residents at a price and in some cases with a finesse that is not available in many formal extended-care facilities" (Eckert, 1979, p. 501). The loss of these inexpensive hotels throughout the country may thus mean the loss of affordable housing to marginally independent people, and the loss of their ability to survive outside of an institution as well.

Housing-Related Trends: The Next Twenty Years

Before considering the policy implications of this analysis, one should recognize several important trends in national housing policy discussions regarding the elderly. These trends relate to the growth, changing age composition, and location of older people in this country during the next 20 years. First, with the continued decline in mortality rates, the number and proportion of elderly in the total population will continue to increase. There were around 9 million people aged 65 or more in 1940 and 24 million in 1978. This number is expected to reach 45 million by the year 2020 (U.S. General Accounting Office, 1981, p. 1). The elderly are a small fraction of the population, but one that is growing, from 11% in 1978 to an expected 13% or more in 1990—i.e., an increase of nearly 20% (Muller et al., 1980, p. I-9). The aged have recently become an effective political force at all levels of government. Their political leverage at the national level has been reflected in such highly visible convocations as the decennial White House Conferences on Aging which began in 1960 and which heavily influenced the enactment of such major social legislation as the Older Americans Act, Medicare, and Medicaid.

Political Influence

In the housing realm, as well, the political influence of the "elderly lobby" can scarcely go unnoticed. Despite strong administration opposition to continuing deep-subsidy housing construction programs, the Section 202 elderly housing direct-loan program survived the budget cuts in Fiscal Year 1982 after HUD argued that "it would be politically impossible to win Congressional approval of a recession of the $830.8 million 1982 program which is expected to finance construction of 17,200 units of housing for the elderly" (Bureau of National Affairs, 1982, p. 614). Section 202 was also the only deep-subsidy new construction housing program to be included in the Administration's FY 83 budget.

The elderly's political strength at the state level is best reflected in homestead exemptions and so-called "circuit-breaker" programs which reduce property taxes for older homeowners. The aged also flex their political muscle over local housing issues. In New York City, for example, the rent control program disproportionately benefits the elderly. The median age of tenants in rent-controlled housing is 64, and lower-income elderly tenants are exempt from rent increases that the City permits landlords to pass on to nonelderly tenants (Stegman, 1982, p. 214). In the case of cooperative or condominium conversions, elderly tenants who desire to remain in their units are guaranteed lifetime tenure.

At least as important as their increasing numbers is the dramatic extent to which the age composition of the elderly population is changing. In 1979, about 40% of all older people were over 75 years old (U.S. General Accounting Office, 1981, p. 1). Heumann reports that the proportion of the elderly in this age group will increase by over 60%, while the Commissioner on Aging has predicted a growth in this cohort to between 40 and 45% of all elderly by 2020 (Heumann, 1980, p. 320; U.S. General Accounting Office, 1981, p. 1). The importance of these numbers lies in the fact that "significant levels of impairment are most evident in persons aged 75 and over" (Heumann, 1981, p. 320).

The National Center for Health Statistics, for example, estimates that the rate of functional disability among the noninstitutionalized elderly is 39% for those between the ages of 65 and 74, 50% for those 75 to 84, and 63% for those 85 and older (U.S. General Accounting Office, 1981, p. 1). The relative growth of the older cohorts, therefore, has wide ranging implications for housing policy. Individual mobility is more limited for the very old. Golant has shown, for example, that a much lower percentage of people over the age of 70 have driver's licenses than do those in the 65–69 year age group (Golant, 1976). Congress has explicitly recognized the importance of maintaining the mobility of the elderly by mandatory improved access to, and more responsive forms of, public transportation (Schmitt, 1979).

If older people are to maintain independent living arrangements, more attention will have to be paid to housing-related services. Government-assisted rental housing for the aged was built and subsidized without the space, facilities, or services needed by tenants whose levels of competence have declined during their years of residence, and now requires a major effort to retrofit it with the necessary support systems. New housing for the elderly must be designed and financed to include a range of health and social services.

Suburbanization

Another factor in the development of future housing policies is the increasing suburbanization of the elderly. In 1976, 32% of the 3.8 million elderly households in the U.S. lived in the central cities, and 24% lived in the suburbs (Gutowski and Feild, 1979, p. 5). A substantially larger share (29%) of those in the 55 to 64 year age group also lived in the suburbs (Gutowski and Feild, 1979, p. 5). In addition, some empirical studies on the migration of older households have documented an increasing suburbanization of the elderly, which some analysts believe will accelerate in the future. Between 1965 and 1979, 80% of all metropolitan moves by the elderly were either wholly within the central cities or the suburbs (Gutowski and Feild, 1979, p. 9). Six percent were from suburb to city, and the remaining 14% were from city to suburb. The net effect of these moves was the net migration of around 275,000 older people to the suburbs (Gutowski and Feild, 1979, p. 9). These moves are prompted by what Gutowski and Feild call push and pull factors. Push factors include the perception that neighborhoods are becoming increasingly unsafe, traffic congestion is worsening, and getting around is becoming more difficult (Gutowski and Feild, 1979, pp. 10–11). Among the pull factors are the growing number of apartments in the suburbs and the availability of smaller houses that were built in the early building-boom years of the 1950s. Gutowski and Feild believe that these push and pull factors will continue to result in the net emigration of older people, particularly white elderly, from the central cities.

While the policy implications of this trend toward suburbanization are not all clear, one thing seems certain: despite presently high rates of ownership among the elderly, more older people will be homeowners in the future because the elderly today are less likely to have owned homes when they were between 55 and 64 than are today's 55–64 year age group (U.S. DHUD, 1980a, p. 6).

This latter cohort is more heavily suburbanized than the former. The homeownership rate among households in the 55–64 year age group is one-third higher in the suburbs than in the central cities (83% compared to 63%) (Gutowski and Feild, 1979, p. 8). Since mobility rates are quite low for this age group, overall homeownership rates among the elderly will rise over the next ten years.

Future Homeownership Rates

Continuing high rates of homeownership among the elderly are all but assured, at least for the next twenty years, based on the existing rates of today's middle-aged and near-elderly households. The one qualification to the above statement concerns the increasing difficulty which lower- and moderate-income elderly have in paying rising property taxes and energy costs. Should these and other related burdens cause enough older people to sell their houses or otherwise relinquish ownership rights to them, homeownership rates among the elderly could drop in the next ten to twenty years. Over the long term, spiraling housing costs, high interest rates, and the shrinking ability of housing to compete for capital in ever more deregulated financial markets may make it more difficult for younger families to buy a home. While there is no long-term significance in the possibility that the average age of the first-time home buyer might increase by the year 2000, a decline in homeownership rates among the nonelderly could have important implications for the future elderly and their housing. Without their own homes and the stored wealth that equity represents, the savings and investment patterns of older families will change a great deal. Mobility patterns may also vary significantly from what they would have been otherwise.

Despite the broadening of housing choices available to suburban households in the form of low-rise garden apartments, townhouses, and apartment towers, it is likely that as many as eight out of 10 older households will be homeowners by the year 2000 (U.S. DHUD, 1980a, p. 7) and nearly 90 percent of them may be living in single-family housing. The significance of this fact is hard to overstate in terms of the demands it will generate for home-based housing services ranging from homemaking and housekeeping to home maintenance. Also, because much of the newer suburban housing stock was built around 30 years ago when energy was cheap, it is probably energy-inefficient and, unless retrofitted, is now quite expensive to heat and cool. There have been no systematic studies of the financial problems this might pose to people living on fixed incomes. There are, however, indications that the combination of excessive living space, high and rising property taxes, and excessive fuel and utility costs has already forced many suburban householders to change their living arrangements by subdividing their single-family houses into duplexes or multifamily dwellings. According to the Census Bureau, American homeowners created about 2.5 million such accessory housing units between 1979 and 1980 (Owen, 1982, p. E-46). This number is large enough to represent a substantial source of potential housing for small households in this country.

A Tristate Regional Planning Commission study of the New York City area (Metropolitan Housing Institute, 1980) indicates that 70 percent of the 186 communities in the Commission's planning jurisdiction that responded to its survey reported accessory housing conversions, virtually all of which violate local fire and safety codes. The town of Islip, in Nassau County, reported between 5,000 and 8,000 conversions; Babylon, also in Nassau County, noted 4,000 conversions, a number that is "growing daily."

A creative response to the accessory housing movement is but a small part of the larger challenge to inner suburban governments which must now meet an entirely different set of housing and municipal service needs than, say, 20 years ago, when they "were scrambling to build the infrastructure to provide educational and recreational services for their growing school-age population" (Gutowski and Feild, 1979, p. 15).

Finally, it is important to understand that one cannot simply extrapolate the elderly's current problems and circumstances 5 or 10 years into the future and then fit a set of policy responses to these scenarios. The previous analysis notwithstanding, the next generation of older Americans will differ significantly from today's. They will be more independent economically because of nearly universal coverage of the social security system and the supplementary support provided by private retirement plans and Individual Retirement Accounts (IRAs). The older population of 1990 will also be more mobile than today's, a higher percentage of them having driven all of their adult lives. They may therefore depend less than preceding generations of elderly on the immediate neighborhood environment for all support services. The educational level of the next generation of elderly will be higher than is the case today, as will their level of political awareness, organization, and activism. All of these cohort effects will exert important influences on the evolution of the housing policy agenda for the next 20 years.

Policy Considerations

The first legislative initiative in the area of housing policy for the elderly came in 1956 with an amendment to the National Housing Act to permit elderly individuals to occupy public housing that, up to then, had been reserved for families. In 1959, Section 202 of the National Housing Act provided direct below-market interest rate federal loans to nonprofit sponsors of housing for lower- and moderate-income elderly people. The Section 202 and the low-rent public housing projects which were later authorized for the aged were both designed with the elderly's physical limitations in mind. Among the design features of these projects were electric wall outlets raised above floor level, lower kitchen cabinets, and built-in grab-bars in the bathroom. This housing was not, however, designed or financed to accommodate on-site congregate dining, or routine health or recreational services. (See Lawton, 1980, Chapter 4.)

Whether responsive to the actual pattern of housing needs among the elderly or not, federal housing programs have certainly succeeded in housing large numbers of them. The scale of government-built or -sponsored housing in this country is small compared to that in Britain and the socialist countries of Northern and Eastern Europe; but the elderly's share of the American subsidized inventory is quite large. Including Section 202, which is the principal construction program for the older population and now consists of over 100,000 units (U. S. DHUD, 1981b), more than 30 percent of the units developed under all other federally-assisted rental housing programs are currently occupied by elderly families and individuals. Altogether, more than 700,000 older households in the United States live in federally-assisted housing (Welfeld and Struyk, 1978). According to Welfeld and Struyk, "using the eligibility criteria of current HUD-administered programs [indicates that] the elderly are certainly receiving their fair share of the subsidized housing resources in this country" (Welfeld and Struyk, 1978).

It is not so much that national housing policy makers set out over the years to favor the elderly, although the Section 202 program is more resistant to deep budget cutbacks than other subsidized housing programs. Rather, developers of assisted housing favor elderly households over equally needy nonelderly families with children. Because of their built-in design features, HUD permits higher construction costs and rent structures in projects for the aged. These translate into higher developer fees, larger cash flows, and bigger tax shelters for investors. Managers also prefer older tenants over families with children. Finally, housing for the elderly attracts less local political opposition on such matters as siting and necessary zoning changes than does housing for low-income families.

Moreover, the elderly can take advantage of housing assistance like the Section 8 existing housing program, which subsidizes rents in private dwellings. Programs like Section 8, housing allowances and vouchers, which were recently endorsed by the President's Commission on Housing (1981), all provide limited cash assistance to income-eligible households occupying rental housing that meets the minimum quality standards defined in the programs. Because older households are more likely than, say, single-parent minority families to live in housing that already meets these minimum standards, or which the landlord could bring up to standard at relatively little expense, they are likelier to qualify for housing allowances at higher rates than other low-income population groups. Income-related housing assistance is also likely to be allocated on the basis of high housing expenses, and older renters are more likely than lower-income working families to be paying disproportionately high proportions of their incomes for rent.

The challenge in the mid-1980s and beyond will not be how to attract housing policy makers' attention to the aged, but how to sharpen the policy focus and encourage the design of programs and service delivery systems that will be responsive to the elderly's changing needs, health, and location. While there is little disagreement that elderly low-income renters suffer more serious housing problems than other older people, it is also true that this group receives more than its fair share of the resources directed at solving the elderly's housing problems. As already indicated, most older people own their homes, and large numbers of them have serious housing and housing-related problems. Moreover, HUD has found that inadequately housed homeowners are unlikely to take advantage of government-assisted rental housing:

> Elderly renters are almost 12 times as likely as elderly owners to move from unsubsidized to subsidized housing. About 20 percent of all elderly low rent public housing move-ins are previous owners, yet there are about three times as many elderly owners as renters in the total elderly populations (U.S. DHUD, 1980, p. 3).

This glaring inequity in federal assistance programs has not gone unnoticed. Welfeld and Struyk, for example, have argued that, by categorically excluding homeowners, current housing programs exclude the majority of households headed by the elderly, the majority of households living in units that are physically deficient, and those who devote a disproportionate share of their income to housing. This situation means sharp inequities between elderly renters and elderly homeowners and results in substantial deterioration of the existing housing stock (Welfeld and Struyk, 1978, p. 63).

A comprehensive national housing policy for the elderly should have two objectives: to enable those who want and are able to remain in their own homes to do so for as long as possible, and to provide the necessary assistance to others so they can find suitable housing. For this policy to be effective, it must provide program options for elderly homeowners and renters whose needs are not being met by conventional rental construction.

To remedy some of the limitations of existing policy, Welfeld and Struyk have proposed a wide range of innovative housing assistance programs that would help accomplish both policy objectives. They recommend that the federal government sponsor condominium developments which would offer elderly homeowners small, easily maintained units bought with the equity from their present houses. Rather than subsidizing their purchase, HUD would contribute to operating costs to the extent that these exceeded some set percentage of household income. The houses which the elderly would then vacate would become available for larger families or could be subdivided into subsidized or unsubsidized multifamily rental units (Welfeld and Struyk, 1978, pp. 68–69). Welfeld and Struyk also call for the development of "granny flats," which are separate, self-contained dwellings like modular units to allow aged parents to live on their children's land. Granny flats consist of "a bedroom, bathroom, living room, and kitchen facilities . . ." (Welfeld and Struyk, 1978, p. 84). In Australia, where this kind of housing is available, occupants rent granny flats from the local housing authority, which delivers the houses to the site and removes them when they are no longer needed (Welfeld and Struyk, 1978, p. 84). The barriers to a successful test of the concepts of the granny flat and accessory housing in the United States arise at the local rather than the federal level. As presently constituted, most municipal zoning ordinances would not permit the addition of second dwellings on residential lots zoned for single-family housing, while fire and housing codes make it difficult to subdivide units. In light of the "graying of suburbia" (as Gutowski and Feild refer to the aging suburban population), it would seem to be only a matter of time before the elderly challenge the rigid and outmoded municipal land-use controls that bar reasonable solutions to their housing problems.

Recognizing the high cost of conventional rental housing built for the elderly and the fact that two-thirds of all income-eligible aged are single, Welfeld and Struyk propose that the federal government build more two-bedroom dwellings that could be shared by two unrelated adults. Although the development cost of these larger units is about 15 percent greater than for one-bedroom apartments, the unrelated households in them would be able to pay twice as much rent as formerly so that average rents per person would decline. Not only would such a program permit a much larger number of older people to be housed from a given appropriation, but shared apartments would enable older tenants to provide each other with physical and emotional support (Welfeld and Struyk, 1978, pp. 66–67).

For single males, most of whom live alone and many of whom have been forced out of their inexpensive SRO hotel rooms, Welfeld and Struyk recommend that the federal government build high-rise rooming houses similar to SRO hotels. These centrally located projects would be built without kitchens because most SRO hotel occupants cannot or tend not to want to cook for themselves. The buildings would, however, include a "snack bar with vending machines and microwave ovens" (Welfeld and Struyk, 1978, p. 85). According to Welfeld and Struyk, a 13-story prototype project in Toronto,

> offers single rooms with a stove, refrigerator and toilet. There is one communal bathroom for every five rooms. Double rooms have a bathroom with a shower. Each room has individually controlled heating and an intercom. Coin-operated laundries are available in the basement, and a small, privately owned supermarket is located just off the lobby (Welfeld and Struyk, 1978, p. 85).

While more and better-designed housing must continue to be a vital component of national policy, only a very small fraction of elderly households will ever live in subsidized housing, no matter how much of it is built. As Lawton and others have indicated, only around 5 percent of all old people live in institutions at any one time, and about 4 percent in age-segregated housing. The remaining 91 percent live in "individually chosen homes scattered among homes occupied by people of all ages" (Lawton, 1978, p. 39). Thus, if the housing needs of most older people are to be met in the next decades, it will have to be through the delivery of support services directly to homes and neighborhoods.

Not only is the need for support services great, but it is time to develop a service-oriented housing policy for the elderly. For one thing, "[s]ervices to older people not living in planned housing might involve costs that cannot be borne by a staggering economy" (Lawton, 1980, p. 101). Equally as important, as the elderly population continues to age in place, increasingly large numbers of older tenants in public housing, Section 202 and other federally-assisted housing projects will become less able to care for themselves. While there are little data on the extent of the dependency problem, Heumann reports that "over 12 percent of current elderly public housing tenants suffer from multiple impairments (and) can no longer be accommodated in conventional public housing, and most of them have no family support and will have to transfer to nursing homes in the absence of sheltered housing" (Heumann, 1980, p. 321). The need for support services in assisted housing will therefore be felt sharply very soon, forcing federal housing policy for the elderly to lose some of its bricks and mortar character in the next five years.

Intermediate and long-term care facilities will always be needed to serve the needs of the dependent elderly population, but there is growing evidence that "persons in nursing homes do not need skilled care and could have avoided institutionalization if homemaker and personal care services had been available to them" (U.S. General Accounting Office, 1981, p. 21). The Congregate Housing Services Program (CHSP), created by Title IV of the Housing and Community Development Act of 1978, is a potentially significant policy response to the problem of premature institutionalization. The CHS program gives funds to "public housing and Section 202 housing for the elderly and nonelderly handicapped persons to ensure availability and accessibility of nonmedical supportive services needed by residents who are at risk of institutionalization" (DMH Associates, 1980, p. i). The CHS demonstration program currently underway includes "full meal services and those additional supportive services such as housekeeping aid, personal assistance or other services deemed essential for eligible individuals to maintain semiassisted independent living standards" (U.S. DHUD, 1981b, p. 27). Although Congress assigned responsibility for the CHS program to HUD, which has funded 28 congregate housing projects, the Department has already appealed to Congress to transfer the program to the Department of Health and Human Services (HHS) because "the needs of the elderly and nonelderly handicapped will be better met by HHS," (Bureau of National Affairs, 1981, p. 1095) presumably because HUD is equipped to deliver housing and non-social services. Thus far, at least, HHS has shown as little official enthusiasm for the program as HUD, presumably because its principal mission is to deliver social services and not housing.

If lack of fit between agency and service clouds the future of the Congregate Housing Services program, similar political difficulties and bureaucratic indifference could undermine the further development and testing of much-needed preventive home maintenance and repair services for lower- and moderate-income elderly homeowners. Preventive home maintenance programs for the aged that deliver no new housing, that would support the building industry, and that provide more of a housing than a social service, have few natural allies in HUD, HHS, or Congress. While the research division at HUD is carrying out a demonstration program of maintenance services to elderly homeowners to test local administrative and delivery mechanisms (see for example Curtin et al., 1981), there is no division at HUD to which a successful pilot program could be transferred should the Secretary ever accord such a program priority over more traditional housing efforts in the Department's budget.

The importance of the lack of constituency for such services for the aged cannot be overstated in regard to national policy. First, inexpensive home repair is one of the few affordable program responses to undermaintenance, which seems to be "the most widely used method(s) of dissaving for elderly homeowners" (Guttentag, 1975). In addition to preventing minor maintenance deficiencies from becoming major housing defects, preventive maintenance service programs can readily be expanded to remodel the houses of mildly disabled people. If we could prolong the elderly homeowner's independence and reduce the demand for planned housing and nursing homes by removing raised thresholds or installing grab-bars in the bathroom, or even installing a stair-based elevator, extending the concept of home maintenance would be cost effective.

Conclusion

It is important that we move toward a housing policy for the elderly that is based on the idea of continued residence in the same dwelling. Because of entrenched political interests and federal bureaucratic regulations, however, the momentum for such a shift in policy will not come from the federal government. The impetus for change will probably be strongest at the community level, where health and housing practitioners are struggling to create service oriented housing programs for the aged by combining their resources in ways not envisioned by national policy makers. This public health housing partnership must be strengthened at the local level so that it may become a force for policy change.

References

Berghorn, F. J., Shafer, D. E., and Wiseman, R. F. *The Urban Elderly: A Study of Life Satisfaction.* New York, N.Y.: University Books, 1978.

Blau, Z. S. *Old Age in a Changing Society.* New York, N.Y.: New Viewpoints, 1973.

Bureau of National Affairs. *Housing and Development Reporter.* Washington, D.C.: Bureau of National Affairs, May 25, 1981.

Bureau of National Affairs. *Housing and Development Reporter.* Washington, D.C.: Bureau of National Affairs, Jan. 4, 1982.

Butler, A., Oldman, C., and Neight, R. *Sheltered Housing for the Elderly: A Critical Review.* Leeds, England: University of Leeds, 1979.

Carp, F. M. Housing and living environments of older people. In R. H. Binstock and E. Shanas (Eds.), *Handbook of Aging and the Social Sciences.* New York, N.Y.: Van Nostrand Reinhold Co., 1976, pp. 244–271.

Clemente, F. and Kleiman, M. B. Fear of crime among the aged. *The Gerontologist,* 1976, *16,* 207–210.

Cohen, C. I. and Sokolvsky, J. Social engagement versus isolation: the case of the aged in SRO hotels. *The Gerontologist,* 1980, *20,* 36–44.

Conklin, J. E. *The Impact of Crime.* New York, N.Y.: MacMillan Publishing Co., 1975.

Cowgill, D. O. Residential segregation by age in American metropolitan areas. *Journal of Gerontology,* 1978, *33,* 446–453.

Cumming, E. and Henry, W. E. *Growing Old: The Process of Disengagement.* New York, N.Y.: Basic Books Publishing Co., 1961.

Curtin, R., Newman, S., and Chin, A. *Home Repair Services for the Elderly: An Evaluation of Baltimore's Home Maintenance Program (Phase One), Draft Report.* Ann Arbor, Mi.: Institute for Social Research Survey Research Center, University of Michigan, June 1981.

Cutler, S. J. Safety on the streets: cohort changes in fear. *International Journal of Aging and Human Development*, 1979–1980, *10*, 373–384.

DMH Associates. *A Preliminary Report on the Planning and Implementation Process of the Congregate Housing Services Program.* Submitted to the Department of Housing and Urban Development, Washington, D.C.: December 16, 1980.

Eckert, J. K. Urban renewal and redevelopment: high risk for the marginally subsistent elderly. *The Gerontologist*, 1979, *19*, 496–502.

Faulkner, A. O. The Black aged as good neighbors: an experiment in volunteer services. *The Gerontologist*, 1975, *15*, 554–559.

Fennell, G. *Social interaction in grouped dwellings for the elderly.* Paper for the British Sociological Association Social Policy Study Group meeting, in Birmingham, England, May 21, 1977.

Golant, S. M. Intraurban transportation needs and problems of the elderly. In M. P. Lawton, R. J. Newcomer, and T. O. Byerts (Eds.), *Community Planning for an Aging Society.* Stroudsberg, Penn.: Dowden, Hutchinson, and Ross, 1976.

Goldsmith, H. and Tomas, N. E. Crimes against the elderly: a continuing national crisis. *Aging*, 1974, *236*, 10–13.

Gubrium, J. Victimization and three hypotheses. *Crime and Delinquency*, 1974, *20*, 245–250.

Gutowski, N. and Feild, T. *The Graying of Suburbia.* Washington, D.C.: The Urban Institute, 1979.

Guttentag, J. M. Creating new financial instruments for the aged. *Bulletin for the Center for the Study of Financial Institutions*, (New York University), 1975.

Haley, B. and Wiseman, R. *Repair Responses of Elders (Draft).* Washington, D.C.: Department of Housing and Urban Development, 1980.

Hansen, G. D. Meeting housing challenges: involvement—the elderly. In *Housing Issues*, Proceedings of the Fifth Annual Meeting, American Association of Housing Educators, Lincoln, Ne.: University of Nebraska Press, 1971.

Hartman, C., Keating, D. and Legates, R. *Displacement: How to Fight It.* Berkeley, Ca.: National Housing Law Project, 1981.

Henretta, J. C. and Campbell, R. T. Status attainment and status maintenance: a study of stratification in old age. *American Sociological Review*, 1976, *41*, 981–992.

Heumann, F. L. Sheltered housing for the elderly: the role of the British warden. *The Gerontologist*, 1980, *20*, 318–330.

Kahana, E., Liang, J., Felton, B., Fairchild, T., and Harel, Z. Perspectives of aged on victimization, "ageism," and their problems in urban society. *The Gerontologist*, 1977, *17*, 121–129.

Kasl, S. V. Effects of housing on mental and physical health. In *National Housing Policy Review, Housing in the Seventies: Working Papers*, 1976, *1*, 286–304.

Lally, M., Black, E., Thornock, M., and Hawkins, J.D. Older women in single room occupant (SRO) hotels: a Seattle profile. *The Gerontologist*, 1979, *19*, 67–73.

Lawton, M. P. The housing problems of community resident elderly. In *Occasional Papers in Housing and Community Affairs, Volume 1*, Washington, D.C.: Department of Housing and Urban Development, 1978, pp. 39–74.

Lawton, M. P. *Environment and Aging*. Monterey, Ca.: Brooks/Cole Publishing Company, 1980.

Lawton, N., Greenbaum, N., and Liebowitz, B. The lifespan of housing environments for the aging. *The Gerontologist*, 1980, *20*, 56–64.

Mayer, N. and Olson, L. *The Effectiveness of Home Repair and Improvement Programs in Meeting Elderly Homeowner Needs. (Executive Summary)*. Washington, D.C.: The Urban Institute, 1980.

Metropolitan Housing Institute. *A Study of Means for Promoting and Legalizing Conversions of Single Family Structures—As a Way of Increasing the Nation's Housing Supply*. A research proposal submitted to the U.S. Department of Housing and Urban Development by Metropolitan Housing Institute, Nov. 26, 1980.

Mindel, C. Multigenerational family households: recent trends and implications for the future. *The Gerontologist*, 1979, *19*, 456–463.

Muller, T., Soble, C. and Dujack, S. *The Urban Household in the 1980s: A Demographic and Economic Perspective*. Washington, D.C.: The Urban Institute, 1980.

Newcomer, R. J. An evaluation of neighborhood service convenience for elderly housing project residents. In P. Suedfeld and J. S. Russell (Eds.), *The Behavioral Basis of Design (Volume 1)*. Stroudsberg, Pa.: Dowden, Hutchinson, and Ross Publishing Co., 1976.

Owen, L. Accessories: old idea has come around. *Washington Post*, April 17, 1982, p. E-46.

President's Commission on Housing. *Interim Report*. Washington, D.C.: The White House, October 30, 1981.

Rosow, I. *Social Integration of the Aged*. Glencoe, Il.: Free Press, 1967.

Schmitt, R. Transportation and the urban elderly: local problems, ameliorative strategies, and national policies. In S. N. Golant (Ed.), *Location and Environment of Elderly Population*. New York: N.Y.: John Wiley and Sons, Publishers, 1979, pp. 127–134.

Soldo, B. J. Housing and characteristics of independent elderly: a demographic overview. In *Occasional Papers in Housing and Community Affairs*, Vol. 1. Washington, D.C.: Department of Housing and Urban Development, 1978, pp. 7–38.

Soldo, B. J. Impact of neighborhood change and age-related adaptations. In P. S. Taylor (Ed.), *Long-Range Research Agenda for Elderly Housing and Related Services*. Washington, D.C.: The Gerontological Society, March 1981, pp. 15–25.

Stegman, M. A. *The Dynamics of Rental Housing in New York City.* New York, N.Y.: New York City Department of Housing Preservation and Development, 1982.

Struyk, R. H. and Soldo, B. J. *Improving the Elderly's Housing.* Cambridge, Ma.: Ballinger Publishing Co., 1980.

Sundeen, R. A. and Mathieu, J. T. The fear of crime and its consequences among elderly in three urban communities. *The Gerontologist,* 1976, *16,* 211–219.

U.S. Department of Housing and Urban Development. *How Well Are We Housed? No. 4.* Washington, D.C. Department of Housing and Urban Development, 1979.

U.S. Department of Housing and Urban Development. *Elderly Unsubsidized Housing: A Needs Perspective.* Washington, D.C.: Department of Housing and Urban Development, 1980a.

U.S. Department of Housing and Urban Development. *The Conversion of Rental Housing to Condominiums and Cooperatives: A National Study of Scope, Causes and Impacts.* Washington, D.C.: Department of Housing and Urban Development, 1980b.

U.S. Department of Housing and Urban Development. *The Conversion of Rental Housing to Condominiums and Cooperatives: The Impacts on Elderly and Lower Income Households.* Washington, D.C.: Department of Housing and Urban Development, 1981a.

U.S. Department of Housing and Urban Development. *FY82 Budget, Summary.* Washington, D.C.: U.S. Department of Housing and Urban Development, January 1981b.

U.S. General Accounting Office. *Improved Knowledge Base Would be Helpful in Reaching Policy Decisions on Providing Long-Term, In-Home Services for the Elderly.* Washington, D.C.: U.S. General Accounting Office, 1981.

Weicher, J. C. *Housing: Federal Policies and Programs.* Washington, D.C.: American Enterprise Institute, 1980.

Welfeld, I. and Struyk, R. J. Housing options for the elderly. In *Occasional Papers in Housing and Community Affairs, Volume 3,* Washington, D.C.: Department of Housing and Urban Development, 1978, pp. 1–104.

PART III

PSYCHOSOCIAL ASPECTS OF AGING AND PUBLIC HEALTH

Life style is part of the dynamic which raises or lowers the level of wellness. It is an expression of the way individuals and groups interact with their physical and social environments. From a biological perspective, life style largely determines the viability of the basic anatomy and physiology which we inherit; from the public health perspective, life style is a plastic variable which we can shape in accordance with emerging epidemiological knowledge.

Life style behavior is the resultant of numerous forces: biological, psychological, and social. In this section we are concerned with the effect of psychosocial factors on individual and community well-being. Until recently, little scientific emphasis has been placed on the role that personal behavior or life style plays in one's state of health.

In Chapter 5, the author discusses the current state of knowledge of the effects of life style on the health and well-being of the aging individual.

The social sciences have stressed the need to increase knowledge and to change attitudes in order to modify behavior. Traditional health education has effectively utilized this model: for example, mass media campaigns in the last two decades on the negative effects of cholesterol have resulted in drastic reductions in the national consumption of animal fats. In Chapter 6, the authors stress that to make fundamental changes in favor of the well-being of the older population, the elderly themselves must be primarily involved in changing their attitudes and beliefs, and in increasing their knowledge, in order to make profound changes necessary to alter individual health as well as the system of health care.

A major change in the attitude to the elderly, both as individuals and as a group, is apparently still needed if people are to maximize their potential for a full life.

Behavior and Life Style as Determinants of Health and Well-Being in the Elderly

VICTOR J. SCHOENBACH

Introduction

The public health approach to maintaining and improving health and effective functioning emphasizes the *identification* of the determinants of health and *intervention,* often in the form of some modification of the environment, to affect these determinants. It frequently happens, however, that the determinants consist not of alien substances to which the individual is exposed involuntarily, but rather substances or behaviors that the individual deliberately seeks out and embraces. Furthermore, even where the exposure is not sought, modification of behavior may be the most effective or the only available strategy to reduce exposure.

For these reasons, behavior and life style are important epidemiologic variables affecting the collective health and well-being of the public, and especially, of the elderly. The elderly are of prominent concern because they are generally more physically vulnerable, due to the age-associated decline in physiological reserves, defenses, and repair processes (Finch and Hayflick, 1977). For many elderly, accumulated exposures to physical, chemical, and microbial insults will have hastened this decline and perhaps led to unmanifest or even manifest chronic diseases, so that behavior may be crucially important for maintaining adequate functioning.

The importance assigned to behavior as a determinant of health depends upon what is known and what other interventions are available. When behavior has constituted the only line of defense against a feared illness, the role of behavior has occupied center stage. Thus, the emphasis on hygienic and aseptic practices followed the acceptance of the germ theory, and then declined with the advent of effective antiseptics and antibiotics. The resulting casualness in sanitary practices led to a rise in nosocomial and other transmitted infections, leading in turn to a renewed concern for, among other things, simple handwashing (Albert and Condie, 1981).

The recent growth in the appreciation of the role of behavior in health has its roots in a number of societal developments:

1. Epidemiological, clinical, and laboratory evidence linking major illnesses and causes of death with smoking, alcohol abuse, sedentary living, and other life style behaviors;
2. Dissatisfaction with the provision of health care, giving rise to the self-care movement;
3. Escalating health care costs, prompting organizations that provide the financing to pursue means of prevention;
4. Limitations of health care technology in preventing or curing life style-related illnesses;
5. Demands on patient involvement in and compliance with many preventive and therapeutic regimens.

Behavior in its relation to health may be examined within the following conceptual categories:

1. Behavior related to health services—seeking and acceptance of preventive services (immunization, screening) and adherence to treatment regimens;
2. Health directed behaviors—personal hygiene, diet, exercise, and other actions (e.g., use of automobile seat belts and other safety equipment) pursued with a health motivation;
3. Life style behaviors with significant health effects—habits and activites pursued (or avoided) for purposes other than their health impact but which nevertheless strongly affect health (smoking, alcohol abuse);

4. Coping and adaptive behavior—modes of adjusting to life events, to changes in oneself, and to the environment, including the development and preservation of adaptive resources.

Of course, certain behaviors will fit into more than one of these categories, and depending upon the particular circumstances, a behavior may logically be classified differently for different individuals. Nevertheless, the above is a useful organizing scheme.

Given their greater vulnerability to serious disease and their greater burden of chronic illness, the elderly are a priority group for all of these areas, but particularly for the first category since the health of the elderly is more bound up with medical care than is that of younger persons. In contrast, many of the habits, activities, and behavioral patterns in categories two, three, and four are established during the first three decades of life (Wheeler, 1974; Uhlenberg, 1979). Therefore, the fostering of healthy habits, activities, behavior patterns, and environments for children and young adults today is the most strategic opportunity to make major contributions to the health of tomorrow's elderly population. The legacy of environmental and behavioral insults contributes greatly to the health problems of the elderly.

Some may take the above analysis as a justification for discounting the role of life style in the elderly, or even for holding the elderly responsible for the effects of their deleterious past behaviors (i.e., "blaming the victim"). But neither of these positions is fruitful. Definite knowledge of the effects of various behaviors is relatively recent (and in many cases still being explored). Moreover, the balance of life's demands and resources has often constrained the adoption of optimal behaviors. Today's elderly have lived through economic depression and at least one world war. But regardless of the level of responsibility for past behaviors, there are two compelling reasons for a concern with the life style of the elderly: behavioral changes have the potential to safeguard the health and functioning of the elderly, and the behavior of the elderly often provides the role models for younger generations.

In this chapter, research in each of the conceptual categories of behavior will be reviewed. Their importance and potential for promoting health of the elderly and their public health implications will be discussed.

Behavior Related to Health Services

Breslow and Somers (1977) have proposed a Lifetime Health Monitoring Program to identify specific professional services appropriate at different points in the life cycle. This proposal was soon followed by the Canadian Task Force Report on the Periodic Health Examination (1979), a comprehensive analysis of the evidence at that time for the carrying out of particular screening tests and examinations for each age-sex group, and by the American Cancer Society's "Guidelines on the Cancer-Related Checkup," giving age-sex-specific recommendations for type and scheduling of cancer screening tests (American Cancer Society, 1980). A recent review article (Allen, 1982) recommends the following test procedures for persons age 51 to 80: measurement of height, weight, blood pressure, hearing, and vision, tonometry, stool guaiac, sigmoidoscopy, tetanus-diptheria booster, influenza vaccine, pneumococcal vaccine, tobacco usage history, alcohol use history, accident counseling, and, for women, breast examination and mammography. These procedures are recommended annually or less frequently, depending upon the patient's age and previous medical history. The review by Kane et al. (1983) gives additional background regarding the evidence bearing on the efficacy of these preventive procedures, but does not present a specific schedule. The results of the Lipids Research Clinics Coronary Primary Prevention Trial (1984) will probably lead to the addition of serum cholesterol to the above list.

In addition to regular medical check-ups, prompt reporting of symptoms is essential to preventing functional decline and prolonged disability from health problems in the elderly, who possess lower homeostatic reserve (Weksler, 1981) and often have chronic medical conditions. Yet studies of illness behavior suggest that the elderly, especially the frail elderly, fail to report legitimate symptoms heralding serious yet treatable diseases (Besdine, 1981). Proposed explanations for nonreporting include: (1) the pervasive belief that illness naturally accompanies old age; (2) depression and loss of desire to regain vigor; (3) intellectual and cognitive loss; and (4) fear of the resultant medical interventions.

To the health professional, the last of these reasons may provoke a feeling of dismay. But indeed many diagnostic maneuvers involve a considerable degree of discomfort and some assault on personal dignity, despite the great advances in medical technology in recent decades. Furthermore, major chronic diseases, such as diabetes or circulatory disorders, require continuing medication, dietary, and exercise regimens, adherence to which can present a considerable challenge.

Medication Regimens

From a public health perspective the elderly are a priority target group, since many of them have medication regimens to which they must adhere. Medication taken for chronic disease may have both therapeutic and preventive functions. For example, antihypertensive drugs reduce hypertension but also prevent sequelae such as stroke, kidney disease, and heart attacks. The effectiveness of medications depends largely upon the level of adherence to an appropriately prescribed regimen. Such adherence is often problematic, particularly for complex regimens involving multiple drugs taken on different schedules—regimens common among elderly patients. For example, in a study of 46 physicians and 357 patients (234 with diabetes and 123 with congestive heart failure), Hulka et al. (1976) found that both types of patients were, on the average, omitting 18 percent of drugs prescribed, taking 19 percent more drugs than their physicians realized, and making scheduling errors on 17 percent of drugs, for an overall average total error for all doctor-patient pairs of 58 percent.

Whereas many studies of patient compliance have assumed that patient motivation is the key obstacle, data on physician-patient discrepancies suggest that much of the total problem of medication misuse may be attributable to the lack of accurate information and understanding by the patient of drug purpose, dose, and frequency (Hulka et al., 1975). Characteristics of patients most likely to be making errors are: living alone, having a lower educational level, receiving treatment in clinic settings, interacting with multiple providers, and receiving complex treatment regimens. In addition to reducing or eliminating effectiveness as therapeutic and preventive agents, errors in medication use may increase the likelihood of adverse drug reactions including toxic ones.

Possible approaches to reducing medication errors and noncompliance among elderly patients would include: (1) efforts to simplify treatment regimens where possible; (2) improvements in physician-patient communication; (3) packaging, dispensing, and educational measures to maximize understanding of the purpose, dosage, and frequency for medications; (4) behavioral and educational measures to enhance motivation and recollection for complying with the regimen; (5) involvement of family members, friends, or community volunteers to remind, encourage, and assist. Such measures as routine review of patient understanding of current prescriptions, simplified and easy-to-read labels on medicine containers, illustrated and easy-to-read personalized instruction sheets, use of drugs more distinctive in color, shape, and type of container, use of medication dispensers, increased opportunities for patients to ask questions about their medication regimen that may arise after the visit to the doctor, and increased attention to communicating to the patient the importance of taking the medications as directed may improve patient understanding and compliance. The creativity that was applied to developing the birth control pill dispensers over a decade ago could now be enlisted in the greater challenge of assisting an elderly patient, possibly poor-sighted and forgetful, to take perhaps four to five separate medications each on different schedules (plus others as needed). The challenge is greater but should be susceptible to innovative approaches and technologies, perhaps involving microelectronic devices or timed release preparations.

The other side of the relationship of drugs to health is the effects of the drugs on the elderly, including their effects on "behavior-related health." Drug toxicity and drug interactions may cause or contribute to many behavioral difficulties in elderly persons, including some of considerable severity and impact on functional ability. The July 1978 consensus development conference at the National Institute on Aging (NIA) agreed that drug toxicity was one of the most common reversible causes of mental deterioration (NIA Task Force, 1980). Among the reported behavioral side effects of commonly prescribed drugs in the elderly are hypotension, disorders of muscle tone and movement, agitation, confusion, disorientation, delirium, forgetfulness, unsteady gait, anorexia, nausea, blurred vision, muscular weakness, lethargy, deafness, tinnitus, irritability, and impaired psychomotor performance (Filner and Williams, 1979).

Despite the limited research that has been done on the handling of standard drugs by the elderly, evidence suggests that the uptake, distribution, and retention of many drugs are quite different in the elderly as compared with the younger adults who are generally the subjects in drug trials (Filner and Williams, 1979). The elderly may therefore be especially prone to adverse drug reactions, though the true magnitude of the problem is difficult to assess due to methodologic limitations in the available studies (Klein et al., 1981).

Drug interactions, a phenomenon about which there is at present limited firm data, may be of particular concern for the elderly since they often suffer from multiple chronic diseases with associated complicated drug regimens. The sedative effects of various drugs and of alcohol may be enhanced by other drugs, producing drowsiness, apathy, withdrawal, and speech and motor retardation (Filner and Williams, 1979). Even where side effects must be tolerated in order to obtain an important therapeutic effect, it must be remembered that many of the side effects listed can impair the functional ability of the elderly, particularly in respect to the matters discussed later in this chapter, such as adaptation, maintenance of social ties, and so forth. A review of the broader topic of the impact of health and illness on behavior in the elderly, particularly on personality, intellectual function, reaction time, and learning and memory, may be found in Siegler and Costa (in press).

Non-Pharmacologic Regimens

Adherence to dietary and other behavioral regimens, such as a low sodium and/or low fat diet, can be even more challenging than complying with a drug regimen. In extreme cases (e.g., less than 1 gram of sodium per day from all sources), very few processed or prepared foods (including commercially baked bread and cereals) can be consumed; liquid and even powdered milk (except when specially processed to remove sodium) must be used only sparingly; many vegetables (e.g., carrots and celery) must be restricted; home baking cannot use baking powder; and restaurant meals become an exercise in negotiation with the chef. Obviously, adherence to such a diet requires a major adjustment in eating habits and food preparation practices. The challenge is increased by the frequent unavailability of sufficiently detailed information on sodium content of foods, especially foods eaten out. Even hospital-prepared meals may have a limited selection of low sodium foods.

Severe dietary restrictions can readily introduce discord into family and social interaction, with constraints on when and where food can be eaten (because restaurant meals may not be suitable) and the need to prepare special foods that will frequently not appeal to the patient, let alone to his or her family. Nor will it aid family harmony to have one member make liberal use of the salt shaker while another dines on salt-free bread. The degree of adaptation involved and its continuing duration can impair morale and perhaps lead to depression. It has been said that growing old is a process of "gentle renunciations." But the renunciations may not be perceived as gentle.

Health-Motivated Behaviors

Health-motivated behaviors are those actions, practices, and habits whose original stimulus was the health benefit they are believed to afford. There is obviously overlap among the categories of behaviors presented in this chapter, since many behaviors in the previous section are undertaken for presumed health benefit, and actions to be discussed in subsequent sections may also be. Similarly, some of the behaviors discussed under the present heading may be adopted for reasons unrelated to health.

For convenience, health-motivated behaviors may be divided into three subclasses: hygienic, fitness, and safety.

Hygienic Behaviors

Bathing and grooming have obvious importance for health, though the national variations in frequency of bathing and standards of cleanliness that are compatible with apparently equivalent health indicate that there are important cultural components in these matters. Furthermore, bathing and grooming have implications for social interaction as well as personal morale, which can therefore be compromised if functional disability interferes with an individual's ability to care for him or herself.

Less culturally enshrined but also important for health are oral hygiene and foot care. Both of these practices are related to important sources of discomfort and disability in the elderly. Among the elderly, periodontal disease is the principal reason for loss of teeth, which has implications for nutrition, social interaction, communication, pain, and health care costs. The disease has a high incidence and prevalence in this country, increasing with age so that by age 65, 90 percent of the population is affected (Dental Research Institute, 1979). Oral hygiene (brushing, flossing, and professionally administered deplaquing) are effective in controlling the bacterial plaque that is a principal component of the disease process. The elderly are more at risk in that plaque accumulates faster in older subjects when they abstain from oral hygiene procedures, and older subjects develop gingivitis faster and more severely. But when active oral hygiene is reinstituted, the state of the gingiva returns to its earlier level (Dental Research Institute, 1979).

In addition to the obstacles that keep younger persons from utilizing proper oral hygiene practices (lack of motivation, lack of knowledge, competing demands on time, cost, embarrassment) many elderly lack sufficient strength and dexterity to manipulate dental floss or to practice effective brushing techniques. Electric toothbrushes, "water piks," and other devices may be of some assistance. Testing of antiseptic agents and antibiotic therapies has been carried out, but such alternative approaches are not currently available for regular use (Dental Research Institute, 1979).

Fitness

Under the heading of fitness, diet, exercise, and rest are considered. With respect to diet, several dimensions are of interest: (1) nutritional adequacy in terms of protein and calories, vitamins and minerals, and other essential nutrients; (2) balance of overall caloric intake with activity level, so that an appropriate weight level is maintained; and (3) avoidance of excessive intake of saturated fat, salt, and other dietary constituents that may contribute to or aggravate chronic diseases.

Nutritional aspects of health in the elderly have been discussed in a previous chapter, so only salient points will be briefly mentioned. Protein-calorie malnutrition and/or nutrient deficiencies appear to be primarily phenomena of poverty, living alone (with accompanying nonuse of social services), depression or loss of morale (so that appetite and interest in meal preparation are suppressed), and/or chronic disease (which may interfere with appetite, ability to prepare food, or ability to absorb nutrients). Poor dietary practices may also reflect lack of knowledge, indicating a strategic intervention opportunity.

Obesity is an important and recognized risk factor for a variety of diseases and complications of disease, being related to the onset and maintenance of elevated blood pressure, elevated serum cholesterol, elevated serum uric acid (and higher prevalence of gout), and elevated blood glucose (and higher prevalence of diabetes) (Sorlie et al., 1980). Recently there has been growing awareness that increased risk is also associated with underweight and that the traditional life insurance industry standards for "ideal" body weight may be set too low (Sorlie et al., 1980; Vaisrub, 1980). Indeed, in 1983 the Metropolitan Life Insurance Company revised its widely used weight tables, but the advisability of the higher values is being disputed.

Belloc (1973), in a study of five-and-one-half year mortality in the Human Population Laboratory cohort in Alameda County, California, reported data showing a U-shaped curve relating mortality rates to relative weight, with the minimum risk for persons 65 and over falling between 5 and 20% above their Metropolitan ideal weight. In the nine-and-one-half year follow-up (Breslow and Enstrom, 1980), the lowest age-adjusted mortality rates occurred between 5 and 30% *above* ideal weight (for males) and between 10% *below* and 30% above ideal weight (for females).

Weight control remains an important component of therapeutic blood pressure control measures, as well as a preventive measure (Stamler et al., 1980). Inasmuch as elevated blood pressure is one of the most potent risk factors for cardiovascular disease in the elderly (Kannel and Gordon, 1980), the avoidance of obesity must remain of concern, though apparently not to the point of the pursuit of slenderness.

In view of the importance of hypertension as a cardiovascular disease risk factor in the elderly, salt intake may be of concern. A definite causal role for salt intake in hypertension remains to be demonstrated, but there is much supportive evidence in animal and human studies. It may be that only a subset of the population is susceptible to sodium-induced elevation of blood pressure, but in the absence of a method to identify such a subgroup, the only preventive strategy currently available is to recommend limitations in salt intake for all. For the elderly this may be particularly problematic, since with the decline in sensory acuity there may be a tendency to increase the use of salt in order to enhance flavor. Thus the goal of controlling salt intake may run counter to that of promoting adequate nutrition. Drastic sodium restriction constitutes a great challenge, as discussed above, and the joint restriction of salt and sugar, or salt, sugar, and fat, is more difficult still.

Since the relationship of total serum cholesterol and serum triglyceride with cardiovascular disease risk appears to wane with increasing age (Kannel and Gordon, 1980), there may be less concern with restricting intake of saturated fat and cholesterol among the elderly. High density lipoprotein (HDL) cholesterol levels, however, remain inversely associated with coronary heart disease (CHD) incidence in both men and women at least to age 80. Adjustment for other lipids and other risk factors did not remove the observed relationship.

One factor that appears to affect both HDL-cholesterol and physical health is regular exercise. There is a sizable and growing body of evidence, from both laboratory and population studies, that supports the notion that regular exercise is protective against cardiovascular disease, promotive of general health and well-being, valuable in rehabilitation after illness, and associated with longer life and ability to function (Shephard, 1978). In the absence of intervention studies, this body of evidence cannot be taken as definitive, and there remain important questions concerning the requisite levels of physical activity, the age at which such activity must be begun, and what kinds of exercise will be most suitable for elderly persons, particularly those with existing illness.

Health professionals and various organizations have been advocating and encouraging greater levels of physical activity among the public, including the elderly public. Some concern has been voiced with regard to the possibility of injury from exercise that is too vigorous for an individual's physical condition (Shephard, 1978, p. 119), as well as with regard to intrusions on personal choice. In a recent report for the Administration on Aging, Lee, Franks, and Fullarton (1983) review the existing literature on the need for, effects of, and benefits from exercise in elderly persons. Their report includes basic principles of fitness for the elderly, policy recommendations, and an annotated bibliography of references on innovative fitness and exercise programs for older people.

In addition to cardiovascular and muscular endurance, which are the focus of aerobic exercise programs, fitness involves strength, flexibility, balance, coordination, and agility (Lee et al., 1983). Some declines in these fitness components are age-related; in other cases, regular exercise can probably prevent or forestall the decline. Physical activity may prevent involutional loss of bone and muscle and osteoporotic fractures (Aloia, 1981).

Various studies have reported small, short-term reductions in systolic and/or diastolic blood pressure, both in normotensive and hypertensive persons, in association with such relaxation practices as Jacobsonian deep muscle relaxation, yoga, Transcendental Meditation, the "relaxation response" practice devised by Benson, and other techniques (Peters et al., 1977; Shapiro et al., 1977). The benefits reported from some of these practices constitute evidence for the view that some regular relaxation practice may promote health and well-being in the elderly (Orme-Johnson and Farrow, 1977; Wallace et al., 1982). Methodologically rigorous studies of the effects on the elderly would be highly desirable, particularly since some of these practices convey additional benefits, such as introduction to a philosophical system, access to educational activities, and membership in a social group (Campbell, 1974; Truch, 1977).

Safety

Unintentional injuries are a leading cause of death among the elderly, though in general injury rates are lower in the elderly than in younger persons (Hogue, 1980). Chapter 3 has dealt with this topic, so only a few key issues will be considered here.

Seven out of 100 injury deaths in people 65 and older are related to fire or other hot substance contact (Hogue, 1980). Cigarettes left burning by an individual who has fallen asleep, often under the influence of alcohol, are a major cause of residential fires. Alcohol intoxication is also an important factor in falls (the source of more than half the deaths due to unintentional injury in people 65 and older) and vehicular crashes (nearly one-quarter of all injury fatalities in persons 65 and older, including approximately 2,000 pedestrian deaths) (Hogue, 1980). The involvement of alcohol in crashes by elderly drivers appears to be much less than in crashes by younger drivers, however.

Seat belt use has been shown to reduce risk of fatality and serious injury, but voluntary use of seatbelts remains low (Nichols, 1982). Increasing the use of seatbelts by the elderly could be expected to improve their survival in vehicular collisions and would set a desirable model for younger persons.

Life Style Behaviors with Significant Health Effects

Since we have already discussed fitness, diet, and relaxation, this section will be restricted to two celebrated life style behaviors, the use of tobacco and alcohol.

Tobacco

There is an overwhelming body of epidemiological, clinical, and laboratory evidence, demonstrating that use of tobacco, especially cigarettes, is an important contributor to the risk of cancer (respiratory, bladder, oral), cardiovascular disease (coronary heart disease, stroke, hypertension, sudden death), and respiratory diseases other than cancer (emphysema, bronchitis). For some of these conditions, for example coronary heart disease, the increased risk due to smoking appears to decline after age 65 (Kannel and Gordon, 1980). Due to other smoking-related conditions, particularly cancer, bronchitis and emphysema, and to the effects on general physiological function, mortality in smokers remains higher than that in nonsmokers at least to age 75 or 80 (Advisory Committee to the Surgeon General, 1964; Belloc, 1973).

The conflict between the extremely strong scientific case against smoking, particularly cigarette smoking, and the economic, political, and personal forces that support the practice is a continuing saga in the history of worldwide public health efforts in the twentieth century (New York State Journal of Medicine, 1983). Whereas tobacco's prominent economic role[1] has obstructed governmental actions to control it, the physiological addiction and psychological rewards of cigarettes obstruct individual efforts to give up the habit. In some cases, giving up smoking may be easier for an elderly person if situational factors, such as job stress, were important in his or her smoking behavior; in that case, smoking may be naturally reduced as retirement brings a reduction in such job stress. In other cases, however, the habit becomes increasingly firmly rooted by the passage of years, so that even a dramatic and personal threat, such as a heart attack, may not lead to sustained abstinence.

Since there are strong gratifications associated with smoking, albeit often due to established addiction, it can be argued that a trade-off between health and such gratifications is in the province of individual choice. Additionally, whereas the recommendations for smoking cessation among the elderly appear eminently justified, most studies of the benefits of cessation have involved middle-aged men (Kane et al., 1983). For the elderly, information, encour-

---

[1]According to the Tobacco Institute, tobacco products provided, directly or indirectly, two million jobs, $30 billion in wages and earnings, $22 billion in taxes, and 2.4 percent of America's gross national product. ("America's Golden Leaf." Washington, D.C.: The Tobacco Institute, n.d.)

agement to quit, and assistance in smoking cessation are very much appropriate, but the use of fear and/or penalties are probably not. However, a tolerant stance toward smoking by the elderly must be balanced by the need to respect the rights of elderly non-smokers for freedom from ambient air tobacco smoke.

Alcohol

There is convincing evidence that heavy alcohol consumption increases the risk of serious diseases of the liver, pancreas, brain, and gastrointestinal, cardiovascular, and endocrine systems, and of injury and death from motor vehicle collision, falls, burns, and violent behavior (Eckardt et al., 1981). A major difference between smoking and alcohol in their relationship to health risks, however, is that most smokers have elevated risks of adverse health effects, whereas most persons who consume alcohol do not appear to have increased health risks. With alcohol, risks appear to be associated with "excessive" consumption (variously defined) rather than with "light" or "moderate" drinking when such drinking takes place over reasonable time periods and not in circumstances conducive to injury (i.e., when or prior to operating machinery, driving, walking near traffic, etc.). Indeed, there is a growing though controversial body of evidence suggesting that light or moderate consumption of alcoholic beverages may be beneficial with respect to CHD risk (LaPorte et al., 1980), social interaction, and insomnia (Epstein and Solomon, 1981). Marmot et al. (1981) reported a U-shaped curve in the relationship between ten-year mortality and alcohol consumption, with excess mortality for nondrinkers and for persons imbibing an average of four drinks or more per day. Chien et al. (1973) showed in a double-blind, crossover experiment that small quantities of alcohol in a cabaret-type setting promoted socialization among elderly nursing home patients.

Most of alcohol's numerous metabolic and physiological effects, however, have not been specifically examined in the elderly (Vestal, 1981). Older subjects do develop a higher blood concentration of alcohol for a given dose than do younger persons, probably due to the decline in total body water with increasing age (Vestal, 1981). Older subjects also experience greater impairment in simple reaction time and in some memory functions, even when the comparison is restricted to a subset matched for comparable alcohol levels. Alcohol-induced decrements in cognitive and psychomotor performance may persist longer in older subjects (Parker and Nobel, 1980). Also, the elderly may be more susceptible to medical problems resulting from heavy consumption and from alcohol-drug interactions, about which there is little information concerning the elderly (Vestal, 1981). The extent of drug use by the elderly and the wide variety of prescribed and over-the-counter drugs with which alcohol can interact (Eckardt et al., 1981) make the latter issue of considerable concern.

Coping and Adaptive Behavior

Life is a process of adaptation. Long life reflects a history of successful adaptation. In some respects the adaptive challenges become more formidable in the later years, as bereavement and serious physical illness become statistically more prevalent. But general statements concerning life stress and the elderly are hazardous due to their heterogeneity, the great range of their adaptive resources, and the diversity of actual life experiences they encounter.

Among the changes to which all adults must adapt as they age are declines in physical strength, endurance, speed, and in many instances, mental performance. The onset of this decline is approximately coincident with the attainment of adulthood, so that professional athletes may be "over the hill" by their mid-thirties. Despite large differences in initial endowments and great variation in the rate of decline, most persons will eventually feel its effects in everyday activities, such as lifting, carrying, bending, stooping, and working. Perceptual acuity, particularly vision and hearing, also decline with age, as do agility and dexterity, especially in the presence of arthritis.

Adaptation to these changes takes place throughout adulthood. As they increase in degree, however, the burden becomes significantly greater, so that among elderly persons physical constraints may importantly affect the older person's interaction with his/her physical and social environment. Even so, it is primarily the degree of accommodation available in the environment that determines whether lack of strength or rapidity of performance is a significant problem for the well elderly individual. Urbanization and weakening of respect for the aged have made some environments quite unsupportive, so that being relatively slow in activities such as walking, driving, alighting from a bus or automobile, paying for a purchase, or understanding an explanation can stimulate feelings and even expressions of hostility despite the fact that in terms of the activity itself the speed of performance is largely irrelevant.

Persons with perceptual and/or motor limitations are also more affected by the physical and technological environment, which can create, aggravate, or alleviate difficulties in functioning. For example, the reduction in levels of illumination in response to the increase in the cost of electricity during the 1970s has probably meant that many elderly do not see as well in public places. Poor telephone connections interfere with long distance communication. Liquid crystal displays (LCD) and touch-sensitive buttons located close together can make calculators and other devices difficult to operate for persons with poor vision or unsteady hands.

To the extent that the elderly as a group are put at a disadvantage by an unaccommodating social and technological environment, they may naturally feel that their status in society has eroded. Inasmuch as social respect in our society is linked to productivity (Maddox, 1974), such erosion does indeed occur. At least as important, however, is that marginal declines in functional ability have simply created difficulties in environments that were neutral with respect to age. Successful performance at any age involves an interaction between the individual's ability and the situation; the more limited the individual's resources, the more important the situation (Maddox, 1974). It is therefore appropriate to consider the range of adaptive resources and where they may need reinforcement.

Adaptive resources include personal (knowledge, skills, abilities, health), economic (income, wealth, and possessions), social (family, friends, neighbors, or organizational participation), vocational (employment, hobbies, and volunteer work), and mental/spiritual (religious, intellectual, philosophical, and artistic) abilities. Clearly each of these reflects experiences and behavior throughout life, not merely after age 50, 65, or 75. Furthermore, each reflects an interplay of individual and environmental factors, and is therefore susceptible to improvement through intervention.

Knowledge and Skills

For people who have been coping sucessfully all along, there are two respects in which additional knowledge, skills, and abilities will be required. The first involves resources to deal with tasks and demands that arise from biological and institutional aspects of becoming elderly, and which therefore typically call for new skills. Examples of such tasks include adapting to the physical changes discussed above, coping with government programs specific to the elderly (especially Medicare and Social Security), coping with retirement, and often adjustment to disabilities and medical care regimens. Of course, throughout adulthood, and especially in the middle years, education and planning for the years ahead, with allowance for possible changes in health and life circumstances, should address financial and estate matters, housing, vocational and avocational pursuits, and family relations.

Ironically, public programs designed to assist the elderly may themselves present coping problems. The Medicare and Social Security bureaucracies can tax the coping abilities of even sophisticated and able professionals. With Medicare, for example, patients rather than providers must often carry out the details of applying for benefits. Benefit claims may need to be resubmitted multiple times, due to errors by one party or another, lost forms, or other reasons. Regulations and procedures are often complicated and confusing. Moreover, elderly patients may have supplemental coverage from employer health insurance plans, necessitating a second application, often with different deductible amounts, coverage restrictions, and procedures. The frequent observation by well-educated professionals who must negotiate these systems on their own behalf or for an elderly relative is to wonder how a person with less education could succeed. The situation is not improved by the frequent situation of long delays in processing applications, understaffed, inadequate facilities, and unwillingness to resolve matters by telephone, so that clients must often attend in person, sacrificing a morning or longer to resolve an error that may have originated with the Social Security Administration. Indeed, many of the relationships between old people and their children and relatives revolve around helping the elderly to handle the normative demands of bureaucratized human services systems (Sussman, 1976).

A second subgroup of resources are those needed to cope with tasks formerly carried out by spouse, offspring, or other persons no longer available. The dissolution of the marital partnership is particularly significant in this area. Even relatively simple tasks, such as moving a piece of furniture, often require two persons. But more significantly the division of responsibility in marriage means that a surviving spouse may be unequipped to carry out various tasks and responsibilities, such as cooking, cleaning, mending, minor home repairs and maintenance, dealing with repair persons, and management of business and financial affairs, simply through lack of knowledge or familiarity. It may be that education and training in these areas can be carried out in an anticipatory mode, perhaps as part of preretirement programs, if the fear of bereavement does not unduly interfere. Such training can also be presented in the positive light of rounding out one's abilities now that the work role no longer determines them. Since most surviving spouses are women and bereavement may precede retirement, consideration of other avenues is also necessary.

Instruction and assistance to persons living alone may be a fruitful area for volunteer work, particularly since it need not continue on a daily or weekly basis, as does the actual provision of services. The use of volunteers to help elderly persons to prepare their income tax returns is an example of a successful, though specialized, type of assistance. The need for supplementation of personal resources will increase in the future, as today's smaller families translate into fewer adult offspring to assist their elderly parents (Treas, 1977).

Economic Resources

Financial resources are, along with health status, a fundamental determinant of life satisfaction among the elderly as well as among young persons. Though financial resources are often discussed in the context of income support programs, many of the elderly would have greater resources at retirement had they been able to make better decisions concerning investment and saving before retirement. On a macrolevel, economic growth tends to produce a relative disadvantage in the economic status of nonworkers, including retirees, while inflation has led to an absolute decline in the real income of the elderly (Kreps, 1976). Information, education, and counseling through employers could perhaps improve the retirement savings program of the future elderly. Also, training or development of part-time employment capabilities could provide opportunity to supplement retirement income.

Social Support

Cassel (1976) referred to the presence of members of one's own species as an important factor in the development of disease and disorder. Drawing largely from the findings of animal studies, Cassel elaborated a hypothesis according to which social environments in which individuals were unable to obtain meaningful feedback that their actions were leading to desired consequences increased the individual's susceptibility to a wide range of environmental insults. This idea has been formulated in terms of "social support" as a possible modifying factor of the impact of life stresses on health (Cobb, 1976). Since everyone is exposed to life stresses, however, social support may also be regarded as a main effect in its own right (Cobb, 1979).

Though no single definition of social support has emerged, and no comprehensive method of measuring it has been developed, the various conceptualizations have substantial overlap (Broadhead et al., 1983). In a recent formulation, Cobb (1979) defines social support as a purely informational phenomenon consisting of three components:

1. Emotional support leading the recipient to believe that he or she is cared for and loved;
2. Esteem support leading the recipient to believe that he or she is esteemed and valued;
3. Network support leading the recipient to believe that he or she has a defined position in a network of communication and mutual obligation.

He distinguishes social support from three other forms of support:

1. Instrumental support or counseling, which involves guiding persons toward better coping and/or adaptation and toward maximization of their participation and autonomy;
2. Active support or nurturing, which is what parents do for infants and nurses do for patients;
3. Material support, the provision of goods and services.

Admittedly, these other forms of support may also imply social support, since in addition to the direct support they provide they may be taken as showing that the giving person cares for the recipient. Other writers (e.g., Minkler, 1981) do not attempt to differentiate among different forms of support.

Most of the attention in the literature has been devoted to social support in the above sense. Social support has attracted so much attention for at least two reasons. For one, it seems far more likely that social support mechanisms can be strengthened than that social stress can be decreased (Cassel, 1976; Kaplan et al.,

1977). Furthermore, certain factors often accompanying the aging process highlight the probable need for social support: loss of significant attachments, greater dependency needs leading to more importance for the perception of dependability of supportive relationships, cognitive impairment increasing the opportunity for misinterpreting feedback from the social environment and possibly resulting in heightened suspiciousness or caution, geographical isolation and limitation of mobility (Blazer and Kaplan, 1983). Blazer and Kaplan suggest that social support leads to the development of the following perceptions, which result from the satisfaction of social strivings by the environment:

1. A dependable social environment ("I am and will be taken care of.")
2. Social participation and interaction ("I am active and effective in changing my social environment; I can gain guidance from the environment.")
3. Belongingness (knowing one's role, being comfortable and "at home", having a sense of membership in a network of concern)
4. Intimacy ("I am close to someone.")

Although much informal information has been published about the importance of social support at this time of life, there is relatively little hard evidence. Nevertheless, the circumstantial evidence is convincing (Cobb, 1979): studies suggest that depression is less frequent in the presence of social support; adaptation following bereavement is improved by the availability or provision of social support; recovery from various diseases (cardiac failure, tuberculosis, psychosomatic illness, and various psychiatric illnesses) is accelerated or facilitated by high levels of social support. The association of compliance with medical treatment regimens and social support is one of the best documented relationships in all of medical sociology (Cobb, 1979). Support systems (Brody et al., 1978; Dunlop 1976) or the availability of a confidant (Lowenthal and Haven, 1968) can be a major factor in enabling an elderly person to live in the community.

A specific source of interpersonal support of which the elderly are often deprived is sexual intimacy. Information in this area is severely limited (Ludeman, 1981), due to the taboo against sex in old age (Pfeiffer, 1969) and the many obstacles to sex research generally. There is nevertheless ample circumstantial evidence for the assertion that the elderly frequently lack sexual intimacy: the imbalance in the ratio of elderly males to females, the constraints on privacy for older persons living with relatives or in homes for the aged, the prevalence of misconceptions about sexual functioning in the elderly, and the generally unsupportive social attitude toward sexual behavior of the elderly (Pfeiffer, 1969; Masters and Johnson, 1981). Even a minimum of education about the physiology of sexual functioning and aging could make a substantial contribution to removing misconceptions and lifting the taboo concerning this important area of living (Masters and Johnson, 1981).

Further discussion of the topic of social support and health in the elderly, including recommendations for research, can be found in Satariano and Syme (1981) and in Kasl and Berkman (1981). One important research topic is how the physical and institutional environment can facilitate the development, maintenance, and participation of social relationships. Lawton (1977) cites several studies in which the number of friends, level of social interaction, and morale among elderly persons were all related to the age-density of the apartment complex or surrounding neighborhood, though these relationships were not found among all studies of groups. He also reports that contact with friends has been found to be greater for elderly persons living in smaller communities towns, possibly due to the longer residence of people living in smaller communities in their dwelling units. Such findings may reveal opportunities for "social prevention," whereby alteration of the architectural environment can enhance social support within a population. Opportunities of this sort are of particular significance for the public health approach to health promotion.

Vocational and Avocational Activity

A common characteristic of persons who age successfully seems to be that they remain "in training" in their physical activities, psychological and intellectual activities, and social relationships (Pfeiffer, 1974). Work satisfaction is one of the strongest predictors of longevity (Palmore, 1980). Since the measure of "work" satisfaction includes housework, hobbies, and volunteer activities, the relationship with longevity might really reflect satisfaction with a meaningful role, rather than specifically with employment. Level of activity, including social activity, has also been consistently reported as one of the most important correlates of subjective well-being or life satisfaction (Larson, 1978), and has been shown to be related to life satisfaction even when reported health status is taken into consideration (Markides and Martin, 1979). Interpretation of these findings is complicated by the difficulty in excluding the possibility that activity itself reflects constitutional differences that may themselves account for the more favorable functioning of those who remain active.

Investigation of the effect of employment and retirement on health encounters additional obstacles. First, the decision to continue working or to retire is strongly affected by health itself as well as by economic resources (Morgan, 1979), both major influences on life satisfaction and longevity. Second, work, particularly high-status employment, conveys power and social status that may increase satisfaction more than the activity itself. Third, those who continue to work despite the opportunity to retire may be more energetic persons who would be expected to report more life satisfaction whether they work or not.

The relationship of work to satisfaction in the elderly has been investigated primarily in connection with retirement. The impact and desirability of the latter are the subject of a continuing debate (see Kasl and Berkman, 1981). The main (nonfinancial) problem in retirement is the loss of identification with the work role and the separation from the network of relationships which the work role involved (Back, 1969). It is difficult to maintain a positive identity when one's usual props, such as social and occupational role, have been taken away (Busse and Pfeiffer, 1969). Though regarded historically as a privilege and fought for as a just reward for long years of toil, the right to retirement has subtly shifted to an obligation to retire at the time retirement pay becomes effective (Back, 1969). Increasingly, retirement has come to be regarded as the proper role for the aged.

On the other hand, except for professionals and the few who enjoy work, those who can afford to retire do so, and will do so early if possible (Morgan, 1979). There is little evidence of a desire to keep on working or of a desire to return to work following retirement; furthermore, retired people do not report doing more volunteer work after they retire than before (Morgan, 1979).

Both the attitude toward and the effect of retirement depend upon financial circumstances and occupational status. Pre-retired individuals in high-prestige occupations are least enthusiastic about retirement, but several years later such individuals find retirement more attractive than they had thought they would. In contrast, those in low-prestige jobs are most enthusiastic about their approaching retirement, but after a few years do not find it as attractive as they thought they would (Back, 1969). Greater availability and acceptance of part-time employment could enable people to make a more gradual transition between full-time work and complete retirement. However, gradual retirement does not appear to ease the transition nor to be associated with being happier (Morgan, 1979).

For individuals who do retire, the ability to use leisure time effectively becomes very important. Volunteer work, hobbies, or avocational interests, if regarded as meaningful and satisfying by the individual, may have much of the supportive value of work without the demands and rigors of the workplace. The key phrase is "meaningful and satisfying." The better record of professionals in adapting to retirement may arise partly from their greater facility at developing avocational interests, particularly ones related to their previous professional work and linked to the previous network of social relationships or an alternate one.

Mental/Spiritual Resources

A common aspect of social relationships and work is that they tend to keep the individual's awareness from being entirely focused on his or her personal concerns. The same can be said for avocational interests if seriously engaged in. This broadening or diverting of the awareness may have considerable importance for increasing the individual's morale and resilience.

Studies of mortality and disease rates of Mormons, Seventh-Day Adventists, and other religious groups suggest that persons who belong to a social group and share common religious, ethnic, or cultural interests with other members experience lower morbidity and mortality and greater longevity than those who do not (Cohen and Brody, 1981). Differences in life style behaviors, such as dietary, alcohol, and smoking habits, tend to accompany different religious affiliations, however, and undoubtedly contribute to the wide religious differences in rates for specific types of illness. Nevertheless, the impact of religious affiliation and participation appears to be generally favorable, even if some of the impact is mediated through known health-related behaviors.

Despite assertions of the growth in the importance of religion in the lives of the elderly, buttressed by surveys showing that somewhat more of those over 65 said that religion is "very important" in their lives, nearly all studies of religious activity and leadership roles in the church agree that there is no general increase in religious activities among the aged (Palmore, 1969). Instead, the general tendency is for religious habits of the midyears to persist into the later years as long as physical health permits. The decline in participation that is often observed is generally attributed to poor health, though there is some suspicion that this reason is also used as an excuse. There is also some conflict in the evidence for the relationship of religious activities to personal adjustment and increased satisfaction in the aged. Here, though, the prevailing picture is that church attendance and other religious activities are associated with good personal adjustment and that they continue to be important for those for whom religion was important earlier in life (Palmore, 1969).

Leighton (1971) has included having a system of values as an "essential striving sentiment" for the avoidance of psychiatric disorder. Though scientific research has not paid much attention to the phenomenon, strong and developed philosophical convictions, artistic pursuits, and spiritual beliefs appear to convey considerable support in the face of adversity. The dynamics of this support may reside in several aspects. Most obviously, if an individual truly believes that God or some other supernatural force is acting to protect his/her personal well-being, that faith must convey great emotional support. Second, the belief system may provide a framework within which certain events have meaning, making them less feared and perhaps more readily accepted. Third, if an individual feels connected to and part of a larger system—especially one that is universal and eternal—then he or she may appraise events in a more positive manner. For example, to the extent that an individual feels part of a larger enterprise, he or she need not regard a personal reversal as a threat to everything that has meaning for him or her. Death itself can threaten only individuals, not large organizations, movements, or belief systems. A belief in life after death, a trust in religious support, a close but nonambivalent relationship with grandchildren all contribute to adaptation to the end of life (Jeffers and Verwoerdt, 1977).

Conclusion and Implications for Public Health Policy

The public health approach emphasizes prevention rather than care, and modification of the environment rather than provision of services. In applying this approach to the relationship of behavior to the health and effective functioning of the elderly, we must take account of the essential continuity or predetermination of the behavior of the elderly. Health in the elderly largely reflects past exposures including past behaviors and skills (Wheeler, 1974). Therefore a comprehensive approach to the elderly requires intervention at earlier stages of the life cycle (Uhlenberg, 1979).

There is also an essential role for interventions aimed at the elderly themselves. Whatever the health, skills, and behaviors a person possesses, time may eventually bring a degradation of performance and supports. So the health and well-being of the elderly will also depend upon general and specific measures to maintain functioning. A significant component of such measures includes the alleviation of the adverse impact on the elderly of a competitive society.

The needs of the elderly, as of all persons, include both material resources and a supportive social environment. Financial resources are fundamental, but not sufficient. Left to itself, American society produces and provides what a market system demands; important needs may go unsatisfied if they are of insufficient scale in a given economic and institutional environment. On the whole, the older consumer has had access to the same goods and services as have other age groups, with very little differentiation offered (Kreps, 1976). Therefore, to the extent that their needs differ from those of the majority of consumers, the elderly may have difficulty obtaining goods and services that may be important to them, such as homemaker services, food preparation and delivery, small portion sizes in restaurants and grocery stores, taxi services, home repair, and for elderly persons on salt-restricted diets, low sodium foods. Cooperative purchasing organizations can provide some assistance. Political influence can also make a difference, as can increasing the awareness of commercial enterprises about the extent of the existing market among the elderly. The most satisfactory solution will be the market response that can be anticipated to growing aggregate expenditure by the elderly (Kreps, 1976).

Collective goods, such as public transportation, sidewalks,

street lighting, cultural and recreational facilities, and police protection, are also not readily obtained in the market place. Galbraith, in *The Affluent Society,* criticized the American political-economic system's inadequate provision of such goods, and the elderly experience this shortcoming most directly. Obtaining collective goods requires organization, including political organization. But given strained budgets, political provision for the elderly often must come at the expense of other constituencies. Indeed, many earlier recitations of the needs of the elderly have a hollow ring in these times of budgetary cutbacks. Though the political influence of the elderly is already considerable, and can be expected to grow as their numbers increase, the U.S. economic and political situation of the past decade suggests that spending even on behalf of powerful constituencies will be constrained by the availability of real economic resources. In this regard, it will be to the advantage of the elderly if they continue to play a gainful economic role so as to strengthen their claim on community resources as well as to increase the total amount of such resources.

Enhancement of social supports is a key area for consideration, especially where this can be carried out through strategic interventions rather than provision of elaborate case management services. Increasing survival to old age, smaller families, growing employment of women, and increasing financial independence are eroding the capacity of the family to meet the support needs of the elderly, particularly of the frail elderly (Treas, 1977). Direct subsidies to families who care for elderly persons may be warranted in addition to the various services designed to offer a measure of relief.

Societal support in a more general sense is important as well. "User-friendly" bureaucracies (an analogy with "user-friendly" computers) and a greater awareness of the needs of the elderly on the part of designers and architects can help reinforce the feeling of being welcome and cared for. Greater consciousness of the needs and feelings of the elderly could be generated through increased social bonds, along with greater exchange of information and dispelling of myths about aging and the elderly. In improving the relationship, all participants will have to both give as well as take.

Fostering opportunities for interaction between youth and the elderly may yield benefits to both generations. It has been suggested that adolescents and the elderly have a natural affinity with each other, perhaps because they are both generational rivals of middle-aged adults, or because they both experience difficulty in finding satisfactory social roles (Wheeler, 1974). Activities such as tutoring, day care, and cultural endeavors can facilitate intergenerational communication, especially for persons without nearby grandchildren of their own.

Education of the elderly has important potential in several regards. By anticipating needs and situations, and imparting skills to meet them, education can enhance the adaptive ability of the elderly (Bates and Willis, 1979). Education for the elderly can also provide opportunities for growth in practical knowledge (e.g., personal computers), occupational skills, and academic learning. For the universities, elderly students represent a growth market that may offset the decline in the traditional college-age population (Kreps, 1976). The spread of cable television and other electronic technologies holds out all sorts of possibilities for media-based education with audience participation, increasing learning, and social interaction even for mobility-impaired elderly.

Citing the trend over this century to remove older people from constructive roles, thereby encouraging the waste of the resources they have to offer, Uhlenberg (1979) proposes that the greatest challenge to society may be the provision of meaningful social roles in which the elderly accept new responsibilities for constructive activity. Leisure activity, he writes, cannot be made the major developmental task of the last stage of life. People need to be needed.

Nevertheless, despite the apparent importance of work satisfaction, the majority of elderly persons who can afford to retire do so. What is the explanation for this seeming paradox? As noted earlier, the association between activity and well-being may reflect constitutional differences between the active and the nonactive rather than an effect of activity. It may also be that people take the easier course even though greater effort would produce more health and ultimate satisfaction, analogous to the omission of vigorous physical activity. It is also conceivable that what retirees seek to escape is often not the work itself but the way it is structured, including inflexibility of hours, pace, lack of autonomy, and other features against which employees chafe.

Much has been written about restructuring work to make it more meaningful and satisfying for workers of all ages. Part-time jobs and job-sharing arrangements also have considerable appeal for persons not needing a full-time salary. But making work more attractive to the elderly will not come easily. Not withstanding the accumulated knowledge and skills of elderly employees, employers are reluctant to hire them and encourage others to take early retirement. Although the minimum compulsory retirement age has been raised from 65 to 70, various economic and institutional disincentives as well as established practices and opinions remain. A younger worker may be more productive, better educated, more acquiescent, and much less expensive than someone who has accumulated seniority privileges, vacation days, salary increases, and whose statistically greater medical risk raises the premiums for employer-provided medical insurance. At the departmental level, supervisors may take pleasure in bringing in young employees and helping them to grow, may prefer the "attractiveness" and energy of youth, and may feel uncomfortable supervising a parent figure. Unlike Japan, America has never established a system of loyalty between employer and employee, so these circumstantial advantages tend to be unopposed. A strong economy is probably a key factor in increasing employment opportunities for the elderly as well as for other groups.

There are, of course, many limitations in the research base that underlies the foregoing recommendations, particularly with regard to behavioral and psychosocial variables. Some of this research base has been critically reviewed in a recently completed study by the Aging Health Policy Center (under a contract to the Administration on Aging). This study includes reports on fitness, nutrition, injury control, drug and alcohol misuse, policy issues (Pardini et al., 1984), a sourcebook (Fallcreek and Mettler, 1984), and an annotated bibliography. These and other materials are being made available to state and local health departments and agencies on aging as part of a Federal Government national health promotion initiative for the elderly that began in 1984.

While the need for further and more rigorous research is great, it is important that expectations be realistic. Research can detect consequences of specific behaviors, help to shape program components, and often indicate what specific components contribute to realizing what specific outcomes. But recommendations concerning such constellations of behavior as social relations, family structure, and vocational activity will necessarily involve considerable dependence on judgment, philosophy, and values. The disparity between what social epidemiology has been able to demonstrate and what writers on policy for the aged would like to draw from it is considerable. There is no single formula for success in growing old (Neugarten, 1974).

References

Advisory Committee to the Surgeon General. *Smoking and Health.* Report of the Advisory Committee to the Surgeon General of the Public Health Service. Washington, D.C.: U.S. Department of Health, Education, and Welfare, 1964.

Allen, D.W. Health maintenance procedures in family practice: A critical appraisal. *Family Medicine Review,* 1982, *1,* 46–66.

Aloia, J.F. Exercise and skeletal health. *Journal of the American Geriatrics Society,* 1981, *29,* 104–107.

Albert, R.K. and Condie, F. Hand-washing patterns in medical intensive-care units. *New England Journal of Medicine,* 1981, *304,* 1465–1466.

American Cancer Society. Guidelines on the cancer-related checkup: Recommendations and rationale. *CA—A Cancer Journal for Clinicians,* 1980, *30,* 194–240.

Back, K.W. The ambiguity of retirement. In E.W. Busse and E. Pfeiffer (Eds.), *Behavior and Adaptation in Late Life,* Boston, Ma.: Little, Brown, and Co., 1969, pp. 93–114.

Baker, S.P. and Dietz, P.E. Injury prevention. In D.A. Hamburg (Ed.), *Healthy People. The Surgeon General's Report on Health Promotion and Disease Prevention. Background Papers.* Washington, D.C.: U.S. Department of Health, Education, and Welfare, (PHS) Pub. No. 79-55071A, 1979, pp. 54–80.

Bates, P.B. and Willis, S.L. Lifespan developmental psychology, cognitive functioning, and social policy. In M.W. Riley (Ed.), *Aging from Birth to Death.* Washington, D.C.: American Association for the Advancement of Science, and Boulder, Co.: Westview Press, 1979, pp. 15–46.

Belloc, N.B. Relationship of health practices and mortality. *Preventive Medicine,* 1973, *2,* 67–81.

Besdine, R.W. Health and illness behavior in the elderly. In: D.L. Parron, F. Solomon, and J. Rodin (Eds.), *Health, Behavior, and Aging.* Washington, D.C.: National Academy Press, 1981, 15–24.

Blazer, D.G. and Kaplan, B.H. The assessment of social support in an elderly community population. *American Journal of Social Psychiatry,* 1983, *3,* 29–36.

Breslow, L. and Somers, A. The lifetime health monitoring program. *New England Journal of Medicine,* 1977, *296,* 601–608.

Breslow, L. and Enstrom, J.E. Persistence of health habits and their relationship to mortality. *Preventive Medicine,* 1980, *9,* 469–483.

Broadhead, W.E., Kaplan, B.H., James, S.A., Wagner, E.H., Schoenbach, V.J., Grimson, R., Heyden, S., Tibblin, G., and Gehlbach, S.H. The epidemiologic evidence for a relationship between social support and health. *American Journal of Epidemiology,* 1983, *117,* 521–537.

Brody, S. F., Poulshock, W.S., and Masciocchi, C.F. The family caring unit: a major consideration in the long-term support system. *The Gerontologist,* 1978, *18,* 556–561.

Busse, E.W. and Pfeiffer, E. (Eds.). *Behavior and Adaptation in Late Life.* Boston, Ma.: Little, Brown, and Co., 1969.

Campbell, A. *Seven States of Consciousness.* New York, N.Y.: Harper and Row, 1974.

Canadian Task Force Report on the Periodic Health Examination. Periodic (vs. annual) health examination. *Canadian Medical Association Journal,* 1979, *121,* 1–45.

Cassel, J. The contribution of the social environment to host resistance. *American Journal of Epidemiology,* 1976, *104,* 104–123.

Chien, C.P., Stotsky, B.A., and Cole, J.O. Psychiatric treatment for nursing home patients: drug, alcohol and milieu. *American Journal of Psychiatry,* 1973, *130,* 543–548.

Cobb, S. Social support as a moderator of life stress. *Psychosomatic Medicine,* 1976, *38,* 300–314.

Cobb, S. Social support and health through the life course. In M. W. Riley (Ed.), *Aging from Birth to Death.* Washington, D.C: American Association for the Advancement of Science, and Boulder, Co: Westview Press, 1979, pp. 93–106.

Cohen, J.B. and Brody, J.A. The epidemiologic importance of psychosocial factors in longevity. *American Journal of Epidemiology,* 1981, *114,* 451–461.

Dental Research Institute. The present and future prospects for the prevention of the principal oral diseases. In D.A. Hamburg (Ed.), *Healthy People. The Surgeon General's Report on Health Promotion and Disease Prevention. Background Papers.* Washington, D.C.: U.S. Department of Health, Education, and Welfare, (PHS) Pub. No. 79-55071A, 1979, pp. 81–133.

Dunlop, B.D. Need for the utilization of long-term care among elderly Americans. *Journal of Chronic Diseases,* 1976, *29,* 75–87.

Eckardt, M.J., Harford, T.C., Kaelber, C.T., Parker, E.S., Rosenthal, L.S., Ryback, R.S., Salmoiraghi, G.C., Vanderveen, E., Warren, K.R. Health hazards associated with alcohol consumption. *Journal of the American Medical Association,* 1981, *246,* 648–666.

Epstein, L. and Solomon, F. Alcohol use as a health problem in aging. Workshop summary. In: D.L. Parron, F. Solomon, and J. Rodin (Eds.), *Health, Behavior, and Aging.* Washington, D.C.: National Academy Press, 1981, 99–108.

Fallcreek, S. and Mettler, M. *Healthy Old Age: A Sourcebook on Health Promotion with Older Adults.* New York, N.Y.: Haworth Press, 1984.

Filner, B. and Williams, T.F. Health promotion for the elderly: Reducing functional dependency. In D.A. Hamburg (Ed.), *Healthy People. The Surgeon General's Report on Health Promotion and Disease Prevention. Background Papers.* Pub. No. 79-55071A, 1979, pp. 365–386.

Finch, C.E. and Hayflick, L. *Handbook of the Biology of Aging.* New York, N.Y.: Van Nostrand Reinhold, 1977.

Galbraith, J.K. *The Affluent Society.* 3rd ed., rev. New York, N.Y.: Houghton Mifflin, 1976.

Hogue, C. Epidemiology of injury in older age. In S.G. Haynes and M. Feinleib (Eds.), *Epidemiology of Aging.* Washington, D.C.: U.S. Department of Health and Human Services (NIH Publication No. 80-969), 1980, pp. 127–138.

Hulka, B.S., Cassel, J.C., Kupper, L.L. and Burdette, J.A. Communication, compliance, and concordance between physicians and patients with prescribed medications. *American Journal of Public Health,* 1976, *66,* 847–853.

Jeffers, F.C. and Verwoerdt, A. How the old face death. In E.W. Busse and E. Pfeiffer (Eds.), *Behavior and Adaptation in Late Life.* Boston, Ma.: Little, Brown, and Co., 1977, pp. 163–182.

Kane, R.L., Kane, R.A., and Arnold, S.B. Prevention in the elderly: risk factors. Paper prepared for the Conference on Health Promotion and Disease Prevention in Children and the Elderly, Foundation for Health Services Research, Sept. 16, 1983.

Kannel, W.B. and Gordon, T. Cardiovascular risk factors in the aged: the Framingham Study. In S.G. Haynes and M. Feinleib (Eds.), *Epidemiology of Aging.* Washington, D.C.: U.S. Department of Health and Human Services (NIH Publication No. 80-969), 1980, pp. 65–89.

Kaplan, B.H., Cassel, J.C., and Gore, S. Social support and health. *Medical Care,* 1977, *15*(Suppl.), 47–58.

Kasl, S.V. and Berkman, L.F. Some psychosocial influences on the health status of the elderly: the perspective of social epidemiology. In J.L. McGaugh and S.B. Kiesler (Eds.), *Aging: Biology and Behavior.* New York, N.Y.: Academic Press, 1981, pp. 345–385.

Klein, L.E., German, P.S., and Levine, D.M. Adverse drug reactions among the elderly: a reassessment. *Journal of the American Geriatrics Society,* 1981, *29,* 525–530.

Kreps, J.M. The economy and the aged. In: R.H. Binstock and E. Shanas (Eds.), *Handbook of Aging and the Social Sciences.* New York, N.Y.: Van Nostrand Reinhold, 1976, pp. 272–285.

LaPorte, R.E., Cresanta, J.L., and Kuller, L.H. The relation of alcohol to coronary heart disease and mortality: implications for public health policy. *Journal of Public Health Policy,* 1980, *1,* 198–223.

Larson, R. Thirty years of research on the subjective well-being of older Americans. *Journal of Gerontology,* 1978, *33,* 109–125.

Lawton, M.P. The impact of the environment on aging and behavior. In J.E. Birren and K.W. Schaie (Eds.), *Handbook of the Psychology of Aging,* New York, N.Y.: Van Nostrand Reinhold, 1977, pp. 276–301.

Lee, P.R., Franks, P., and Fullarton, J.E. *Lifetime Fitness and Exercise for Older People.* Washington, D.C.: Administration on Aging, 1983.

Leighton, A.H. Psychiatric disorder and social environment. In B.H. Kaplan (Ed.), *Psychiatric Disorder and the Urban Environment.* New York, N.Y.: Behavioral Publications, 1971, pp. 20–67.

Lipid Research Clinics Program. Lipid Research Clinics Coronary Primary Prevention Trial Results. I. Reduction in incidence of coronary heart disease, and II. The relationship of reduction in incidence of coronary heart disease to cholesterol lowering. *Journal of the American Medical Association,* 1984, *251,* 351–364, 365–374.

Lowenthal, M.P. and Haven, C. Interaction and adaptation: intimacy as a critical variable. *American Sociological Review,* 1968, *33,* 20–30.

Ludeman, K. The sexuality of the older person: a review of the literature. *The Gerontologist,* 1981, *21,* 203–208.

Maddox, G.L. Successful aging: a perspective. In E. Pfeiffer (Ed.), *Successful Aging. A Conference Report.* Durham, N.C.: Duke University Center for the Study of Aging and Human Development, 1974, pp. 5–11.

Markides, K.S. and Martin, H.W. A causal model of life satisfaction among the elderly. *Journal of Gerontology,* 1979, *34,* 86–93.

Marmot, M.G., Rose, G., Shipley, M.J., and Thomas, B.J. Alcohol and mortality: a U-shaped curve. *The Lancet,* Mar. 1981, *14,* 580–583.

Masters, W.H. and Johnson, V.E. Sex and the aging process. *Journal of the American Geriatrics Society,* 1981, *29,* 385–390.

Minkler, M. Applications of social support theory to health education: implications for work with the elderly. *Health Education Quarterly,* 1981, *8,* 147–165.

Morgan, J.N. What with inflation and unemployment, who can afford to retire? In M. W. Riley (Ed.), *Aging from Birth to Death.* Washington, D.C.: American Association for the Advancement of Science, and Boulder Co.: Westview Press, 1979, pp. 153–166.

Morrison, J.D. Geriatric preventive health maintenance. *Journal of the American Geriatrics Society,* 1980, *28,* 133–135.

National Institute on Aging. *National Plan for Research on Aging.* Washington, D.C.: U.S. Department of Health and Human Services, 1982.

Neugarten, B.L. Successful aging in 1970 and 1990. In E. Pfeiffer, (Ed.), *Successful Aging. A Conference Report.* Durham, N.C.: Duke University Center for the Study of Aging and Human Development, 1974, pp. 12–17.

New York State Journal of Medicine, 1983, *83,* 1245–1352. (Special issue on "The World Cigarette Pandemic.")

NIA Task Force. Senility reconsidered. Treatment possibilities for mental impairment in the elderly. *Journal of the American Medical Association,* 1980, *244,* 259–263.

Nichols, J.L. *Effectiveness and efficiency of safety belt and child restraint usage programs*. Washington, D.C.: U.S. Department of Transportation, National Highway Traffic Safety Administration, 1982.

Orme-Johnson, D.W. and Farrow, J. (Eds.), *Scientific Research on the Transcendental Meditation Program. Collected Papers*, Vol. 1. Livingston Manor, N.Y.: Maharishi International University Press, 1977.

Palmore, E. Sociological aspects of aging. In E.W. Busse and E. Pfeiffer (Eds.), *Behavior and Adaptation in Late Life*. Boston, Mass.: Little, Brown, and Co., 1969, pp. 33–70.

Palmore, E. Predictors of longevity. In S.G. Haynes and M. Feinleib (Eds.), *Epidemiology of Aging*. Washington, D.C.: U.S. Department of Health and Human Services (NIH Publication No. 80-969), 1980, pp. 57–64.

Pardini, A., Passick, R., Franks, P., and Rice, D. Health Promotion for the Elderly: Program and Policy Issues. San Francisco: University of California at San Francisco, Aging Health Policy Center, 1984.

Parker, E.S. and Noble, E.P. Alcohol and the aging process in social drinkers. *Quarterly Journal of Studies on Alcohol*, 1980, *41*, 170–178.

Peters, R.K., Benson, H., and Peters, J.M. Daily relaxation response breaks in a working population. II. Effects on blood pressure. *American Journal of Public Health*, 1977, *67*, 954–959.

Pfeiffer, E. Sexual behavior in old age. In E.W. Busse and E. Pfeiffer (Eds.), *Behavior and Adaptation in Late Life*. Boston, Ma.: Little, Brown, and Co., 1969, pp. 151–162.

Pfeiffer, E. Mental health check-ups in mid-career. *In Successful Aging*. Durham, N.C.: Duke University Center for the Study of Aging and Human Development, 1974, pp. 78–83.

Rowe, J. and Langer, E. Health and behavior in the elderly. Workshop summary. In: D.L. Parron, F. Solomon, and J. Rodin (Eds.), *Health, Behavior, and Aging*. Washington, D.C.: National Academy Press, 1981, 75–84.

Shapiro, A.P., Schwartz, G.E., Ferguson, D.C.E., Redmond, D.P., and Weiss, S.M. Behavioral methods in the treatment of hypertension. *Annals of Internal Medicine*, 1977, *86*, 626–636.

Satariano, W.A. and Syme, S.L. Life changes and disease in elderly populations: coping with change. In J.L. McGaugh and S.B. Kiesler (Eds.), *Aging: Biology and Behavior*. New York, N.Y.: Academic Press, 1981, pp. 311–327.

Shephard, R.J. *Physical Activity and Aging*. Chicago, Il.: Year Book Medical Publishers, 1978.

Siegler, I.C. and Costa, P.T., Jr. Health behavior relationships. In: J.E. Birren and K.W. Schaie (Eds.), *Handbook of the Psychology of Aging*. New York, N.Y.: Van Nostrand Reinhold, in press.

Sorlie, P., Gordon, T., and Kannel, W.B. Body build and mortality. *Journal of the American Medical Association*, 1980, *243*, 1828–1831.

Stamler, J., Farinaro, E., Mojonnier, L., Hall, Y., Moss, D., and Stamler, R. Prevention and control of hypertension by nutritional-hygienic means. *Journal of the American Medical Association,* 1980, *243,* 1819–1823.

Sussman, M.B. The family life of old people. In: R.H. Binstock and E. Shanas (Eds.), *Handbook of Aging and the Social Sciences.* New York, N.Y.: Van Nostrand Reinhold, 1976, pp. 218–243.

Treas, J. Family support systems for the aged. *The Gerontologist,* 1977, *17,* 486–491.

Truch, S. *The TM Technique and the Art of Learning.* Totowa, N.J.: Little-field Adams and Co., 1977.

Uhlenberg, P. Demographic change and problems of the aged. In M.W. Riley (Ed.), *Aging from Birth to Death.* Washington, D.C.: American Association for the Advancement of Science, and Boulder, Co.: West-view Press, 1979, pp. 153–166.

Vaisrub, S. Beware the lean and hungry look. *Journal of the American Medical Association,* 1980, *243,* 1844.

Vestal, R.E. Alcohol use as a health problem in aging: biological perspective. In: D.L. Parron, F. Solomon, and J. Rodin (Eds.), *Health, Behavior, and Aging.* Washington, D.C.: National Academy Press, 1981, 41–46.

Wallace, R.K., Dillbeck, M., Jacobe, E., and Harrington, B. The effects of the Transcendental Meditation and TM-Sidhi Program on the aging process. *International Journal of Neuroscience,* 1982, *16,* 53–58.

Weksler, M.E. Three great networks: the central nervous system, endo-crine system, immune system, and aging. In: D.L. Parron, F. Solomon, and J. Rodin (Eds.), *Health, Behavior, and Aging.* Washington, D.C.: National Academy Press, 1981, 57–63.

Wheeler, H. The democratization of longevity: reflections on closing the generation gap. In: E. Pfeiffer (Ed.), *Successful Aging. A Conference Report.* Durham, N.C.: Duke University Center for the Study of Aging and Human Development, 1974, pp. 33–42.

6

Social and Behavioral
Change Strategies

GUY W. STEUART[1]

Introduction

The most obvious reason for influencing behavior is the clear relationship between the overt behaviors of individuals and their
health status. Those behaviors are described in some detail in
Chapter 5. In public health programs for the elderly however, as
for other segments of a population, it is critical to recognize that
such behaviors do not occur in isolation from the mental health of
individuals nor from the broader social and physical environment
in which they live. This chapter deals with holistic strategies of
health-related social and behavioral change on behalf of the elderly, that include consideration of these additional factors.

While medical care and public health are complementary
rather than antithetical to one another, it is in this domain of
social and behavioral change, that public health confronts a more
formidable task.

In medical care, the individual and to some extent the family,
is in close, intimate association with the care giver. The parties to
the transaction share the priority of recovery and rehabilitation of
the client. There is professional dominance in "delivering" care to
the "consumer." In public health, on the other hand, the concern is

[1]I wish to express a general indebtedness to Hendricks and Hendricks (1977),
which, in addition to the specific citations in the text, provided the main background and orientation for major parts of this chapter.

for whole populations. Thus the units of practice extend well beyond the individual and family, and intimacy of relationship is not
possible. The professional priorities of disease prevention and
health promotion must compete with the contrasting priority concerns of that majority of all segments of the population, including
the elderly, who see themselves as well. The problems of achieving
patient compliance in medical care are serious enough. The problem of influencing health-related social and behavioral change in
the population at large is considerably more complex.

For both the elderly and for much younger adults, the impression that one feels younger than one's chronological age is very
common. Certainly among the elderly, including even the very old,
the claim to be in better health than is found by clinical examination is often heard (Hendricks and Hendricks, 1977; Kovar, 1977;
Linn et al., 1978).

Compounding the problem is the phenomenon of psychological
denial. This is seen most dramatically with those experiencing
early symptoms of disease and delaying going for diagnosis and
those confronting a clinical diagnosis of serious disease or a major
loss such as the death of a loved one. Denial is an emotionally
protective device. It is not susceptible to reasoned argument alone.
It may well contribute, along with other factors of course, to the
underutilization of medical and psychiatric facilities and indeed to
the non-compliance with prescribed regimens, which are common
among the elderly (Cantor and Mayer, 1976; Busse, 1977; Hendricks and Hendricks, 1977).

Even among that considerable proportion of the elderly who
report having at least one chronic condition, there is a majority
who seem to be able to pursue their daily lives without serious
disruption (Figa-Talamanaca, 1976; Hendricks and Hendricks,
1977). When there is added to these, the elderly who by self-report
and clinical examination, are in fact well, this probably constitutes
a majority of the elderly in most populations to whom health as
such, while it will be of some concern, is unlikely to have priority
over the more pressing ones of coping with the practical and social
concerns of everyday life.

Stereotyping and Intervention Implications

The problem of incompatibility between what people themselves,
including the elderly, see as their priority needs as against what
health professionals may see as priorities, is compounded by stereo-

typing. Stereotyping of the elderly is predominantly negative in nature (Butler, 1975; National Council on Aging, 1975; Butler and Lewis, 1982). It is indeed only rather recently that many of the stereotypes of the elderly as being ill, frail, dependent, senile, and lapsing into an introspective period of life awaiting death, are being seriously questioned and investigated.

To be sure, there comes a time in the life of every individual who survives to the so-called "later years," when a more marked decline in physical capabilities and social independence becomes a particular concern of health programs for the elderly. But the arbitrary designation of the age of 65 for "elderly," or of 75 for "aged," while of considerable pragmatic value, is misleading and distorting.

The elderly share the same generic natures, health status determinants, fundamental human needs, motivations and social-behavioral coping patterns with other age-cohorts. They do not, in short, become "different" people when they become elderly. Their lives and their behaviors have fundamental continuities with their pasts. Contrary to much public expectation, and indeed to professional expectation as well, while physical functions tend to decline, social and psychological functions often show little or no change. Those intellectual changes that have been reported (provided they are not a function of illness) are slight and have little effect if any on cognitive capacities in the problem-solving of everyday life. Indeed, there are very wide disparities in elderly populations in respect to physical, psychological, and social age (Palmore, 1970; Butler and Lewis, 1982).

There is considerable heterogeneity in terms of male-female, urban-rural, majority-minority ethnic, and socioeconomic backgrounds. This is associated not only with varied health status but with a range of social and behavioral patterns in respect to expectations, concerns, felt needs, roles, life satisfactions, and use of services (Cantor and Mayer, 1976; Eribes and Bradley-Rawls, 1978; Jackson, 1978; Kim and Wilson, 1981; Butler and Lewis, 1982; Gelfand, 1982). Age "is never merely a biological fact of life; everywhere it takes on cultural meanings that inevitably color the social definitions of people and the things they do" (Hendricks and Hendricks, 1977).

It is not only the public at large that tends to stereotype the elderly. Unconscious as the process may be, both scientists and practicing professionals are not above stereotyping. Thus stereotyping by a society itself is too often reinforced by its echoes in the attitudes, practices and even research directions of public health professionals and scientists whose emphasis historically has been upon the waning influence of the elderly, their physical infirmities, and their loss of mental acuity and senescence (Butler, 1975).

It could indeed be argued that even in respect to health status itself, heterogeneity increases rather than decreases with age (Butler and Lewis, 1982) and this would be at least equally true for psychological and social functioning. It is then perhaps not an exaggeration to suggest that a source of major stress to which the elderly are subjected in modern industrial societies is that of accommodating to or losing a struggle against the stereotypes imposed on them by their own societies (Botwinick, 1978).

Stereotyping tends to spawn intervention strategies that constrict the flexibility, sensitivity, and responsiveness that are a necessary ingredient of successful public health programs.

The view of the elderly as lacking the interest or capacity to engage in activities beyond their own personal concerns, of tending to lapse into introspective disengagement (Cumming and Henry, 1961; Botwinick, 1978; Midlarsky & Kahana, 1983), and as physically immobile and somewhat helpless, is incompatible with attempts to have the elderly be more active in helping themselves and in taking appropriate health measures. It is associated with a failure to see elderly people as a potentially active resource, not only for programs whose primary focus is their own needs, but for programs focusing on the needs of other segments of the population.

Interventions based on negative stereotypes will cause a considerable proportion of elderly people to resist or ignore the communications and persuasions that are expected to help them. Many of those who are particularly threatened by illness, infirmity, and dependence will resist through emotional denial, and those who are not will see such interventions as simply inappropriate for them. Stereotyping may lead to interventions that are likely to be limited to problems which may affect only a small proportion of the intended beneficiaries and simply neglect the needs and priorities of large segments of that population. There has, for example, been a consistent neglect, even avoidance, with respect to the elderly of the importance of sexuality not only in the physical sense but in respect to needs for loving and tender relationships (Loten and Evans, 1975; Griffitt, 1981; Traupmann and Hatfield, 1981; Weiler, 1981, Butler and Lewis, 1982).

Failure to recognize the wide social and cultural variations among elderly people results in messages and persuasions couched in language and referring to motivations which have meaning mainly for those of a social and cultural background similar to that of the professional programmers. Failure to recognize the needs of the well majority of the elderly leads to neglect of disease prevention and health promotion and of the wide range of socioeconomic, cultural, and environmental conditions that relate to physical and mental health states.

Health promotion needs are of special significance for the elderly. The later years of life are associated with an attitude, shared both by the public and by health professionals, that the elderly are worth less investment than the young. With the elderly, there is a temptation simply to "make the patient as comfortable as possible," to advise the individual to "learn to live" even with reversible conditions, and to help the elderly adjust as best they can to the circumstances of their lives without attempts to influence the circumstances themselves. In contrast, even in respect to the least capable elderly, serious questions are now being asked, for example, about alternatives to institutionalization, not only in terms of costs but of the beneficial health consequences of community residence, of home care, of day care services, and of other isolation-reducing possibilities (Problems of Older People, 1973; Butler, 1975; Trager, 1976; Kane et al., 1977; Kovar, 1977; Mason, 1978; Tobin, 1978).

Finally, stereotyping of the elderly leads to approaches that treat them as an entirely different and discrete segment of the population at the very time of their lives when the elderly themselves are striving to retain an integrated place in society. In this respect, it is important to consider both the practical and psychological consequences of advocating national health insurance for the whole population, including the elderly, thereby eliminating their identification as a distinct service group (Etzioni, 1976).

Rationale for Social and Behavioral Interventions

It could be argued that there is no such thing as "health behavior" in the sense that it is separable from other behaviors. The daily round of eating, drinking, smoking, alcohol and drug use, rest, exercise, work, and sleep, carelessness that results in accidents at home and in the street, self-care when ill, or the use of medical services—these and other personal activities make up the whole cycle of living, and are intimately related to the health of the individual.

Moreover, there is some compelling evidence of a relationship between physical health, and indeed mortality, and mental or emo-

tional health status. The association goes beyond such obvious relationships as those with alcohol or other substance abuse, with suicide, or with clinically identified mental illness and disability.
There is a considerable history of basic research into the physiological correlates of emotional states of fear, anger, love, grief, and other
intense emotions (Wolf, 1981). It would be somewhat surprising
then if the emotional experience of stress were not associated at all
with physical health status. But these studies, as pointed out in the
initial chapter, have neither proven causality as such nor the direction of causality. This evidence also does not detract from the significance of genetic, physical, environmental, or overt health-
related behaviors. Thus to the extent that emotional status may be a
contributing determinant, such effects are probably synergistic
rather than discrete. Moreover, emotional status seems to have a
generalized rather than disease-specific association with individual
morbidity which probably reflects idiosyncratic vulnerability. But
the evidence cited in the initial chapter shows that for the elderly,
"emotional balance" whether described as life-satisfaction, work-
satisfaction, or happiness, does have associations with physical
health; stress-inducing events that disturb that balance such as
retirement, bereavement, or relocation are in turn associated with
increased morbidity or limited longevity.

However, whatever the association, mental or emotional
health merits consideration in its own right. In public health, concerned so much with organic morbidity and the major causes of
death, mental health in the normative sense, as distinct from psychiatric illness, has not received much attention and has been
taken very much for granted.

What then, are the determinants of mental health? The evidence suggests that while constitutional vulnerability and stress
are the major negative factors, social support, successful modes of
coping with crisis, and everyday problem-solving competence are
the positive factors. The elderly in particular, face and experience
such potentially stressful events as loss of employment, bereavement, the onset of disabling illness, loss of mobility, waning economic power and social influence, loss of social support networks,
and the continuous threat of loss of control over their own lives.
Some have described the most serious mental health problem of
the elderly to be the threat of an identity crisis somewhat akin to
that of adolescence. As the elderly lose their supportive networks
"to which they could return for reaffirmation of the self-concept"
(Hendricks and Hendricks, 1977), what is at risk is no less than

"psychological survival," which is "equivalent to maintaining a sense of self-continuity, integrity and identity" (Lieberman and Tobin, 1983). The positive effects of affective and instrumental support relationships arise from feedback that one's efforts toward any particular ends are approved and have the desired consequences; that stressful experiences may be shared and mitigated by the understanding and emotional support of significant others; and that this support is reciprocal in that it is both received and given (Cobb, 1976; Kessler and Albee, 1977; Dunkel-Schetter and Wortman, 1981; Kahn and Antonucci, 1981; Traupmann and Hatfield, 1981; Wolf, 1981).

Moreover, the capacity to cope with crisis and to manage with confidence the everyday problems of living contribute to a vital sense that one's life and destiny are sufficiently under one's own control to prevent, or at least retard, what sometimes threatens to be drastic change (Sears, 1981; Hulicka, et al., 1983; Liebermann and Tobin, 1983). The realization that competencies that were effective in the past may no longer work, and that what is left of the future is unpredictable and beyond one's control, is particularly stressful.

The sense of emotional security of the elderly is based to a great extent on how much continuity with the past can be maintained and how predictable the future may be. In this respect, the elderly may be seen as more cautious about change, and may therefore experience greater emotional security in dense minority ethnic neighborhoods which may be changing slowly. The evidence suggests also that mental and physical health are to some extent a function of stable and predictable societies where individuals are clear about their status and roles; where there are warm, reciprocal, supportive relationships; and where change in social organization and expectations of roles and behaviors occurs at a pace which does not disrupt established patterns (Wolf, 1981).

Finally, there are apparently complex and intimate associations between a healthy social environment and a healthy physical environment. The "social diseases" of unemployment, overcrowding, crime, forced migration through economically deprived circumstances, and breakdown of community support systems and traditional coping styles tend to be associated, mainly in urban areas, with environmental deterioration. Such areas commonly have inadequate, unsanitary and hazardous dwellings, environmental pollution, and inadequate maintenance of streets, buildings, and public facilities. It is not poverty in itself that is necessarily associated with such conditions. Many poor communities, both urban and rural, maintain a level of neighborhood pride and identity, remain stable and close-knit, and display a level of daily problem-solving competence under what, to the external observer who has never lived under such circumstances, may appear to be the most formidable of economically deprived conditions.

Disproportionate numbers of the elderly are concentrated in inner cities where conditions of social and physical deterioration and disorganization are frequently found. The inner city elderly have a lower health status than their other urban peers and evidence more multiple health problems. They also experience major disincentives to utilization of health services due to poverty, fragmentation of services, and depersonalization in their delivery (Hammerman, 1974; Davis and Reynolds, 1975; Harris, 1975; Cantor and Mayer, 1976; Figa-Talamanca, 1976).

Social and behavioral change strategies need to include provision for these complex associations and not rely on attempts to influence the behavior only of the elderly of whom "countless numbers . . . cannot be held individually accountable for what happens to them" (Hendricks and Hendricks, 1977).

At the private and personal level, there is accordingly the need to influence the behavior of kin and the significant others of the elderly. This includes ways of providing affective support to the elderly, of endorsing roles that help them feel useful and wanted, of sheltering them from the economic hazards to which they may be subject, of tending to needs which they may be unable to meet by their own efforts, and where necessary, of easing the transition to institutional care.

There is also a need to influence the public behavior of those in influential positions who, by their actions and decisions, affect the health of the elderly in significant ways. These would include, for example, legislators who influence the distribution of goods and resources, retirement benefits, or urban renewal; public service officials who implement the policies of legislators and who locate and deliver human services so that they are accessible and responsive to the needs of the elderly; and leaders of commerce and industry who influence the physical environment and the adequate labelling of foods and medicines, and who, through advertising, project to the public a particular image of the elderly.

The expectations of social and behavioral inverventions are that people will themselves assume more active roles in contributing to their own health and that of others. Thus while there may be program-specific health outcome goals, a broader strategy model should inclulde, in achieving those specific goals, processes which themselves are directed toward the additional goal of the continuous development and strengthening of the general coping abilities, competence, and self-confidence of the intended beneficiaries. This is a necessary, if not sufficient, contributory condition for promoting mental health, self-confidence, and a belief among the elderly that they are capable of helping themselves both in their private lives and through public action that influences others upon whom their health and welfare may depend. This is particularly relevant for the elderly as they enter and experience a phase of feeling less confident, less capable, and less independent. These goals are not met by providing accessible and sophisticated technical services with all decisions being made essentially by professionals. This would tend to exacerbate feelings of helplessness and dependence and not be conducive to the self-activation that social and behavioral interventions are expected to achieve.

Beyond the Individual as the Unit of Practice

Behavior change of individuals is constrained or facilitated by the social systems of which they are members. Thus health strategies for the elderly need to address units of practice that extend well beyond the individual. These potential units of practice may be delineated when a population is described in terms not only of its quantitative demography but of its constituent subcultures and neighborhoods, kin and non-kin networks and groups, and schools, churches, and other activity and special interest groups and organizations.

These social structures are not simply aggregates of individuals but have at least some level of system-like integrity, with the membership sharing an identification and providing affective and instrumental support to one another. They have been described as mediating social structures (Levin and Idler, 1981) and as social units of identity and of solution (Steuart, 1975; Steuart, 1978).

It is important to discover how in various populations the elderly may be clustered in social units of identity and solution. It is also important to discover the extent to which there are isolated, lonely elderly people who are commonly the most in need.

The transition in role and social settings which the elderly and the aged commonly experience is one of lessening family ties and an increase in the need for supportive relationships with other elderly people. For the elderly, the most long-lived group experience of their lives is the family, first as infants, children, and teenagers in their original families of orientation, and later in their own families of procreation. The extent to which such family ties are maintained and are meaningfully supportive of the elderly varies widely according to urban or rural, cultural and subcultural, and socioeconomic status. But large numbers of the elderly, at a time of life when they are least capable of adapting comfortably to major change, have to seek and establish new social systems of identity and of solution. The isolated, lonely elderly tend not only to present the most serious health and welfare problems but the most formidable behavior change problems as well. Thus interventions need not only to focus upon existing support systems but also to facilitate the formation of new support systems and, as far as possible, decrease the proportion of isolated elderly in the population.

As with variations in individual competencies, some families, networks, and neighborhoods tend to exhibit a higher level of problem-solving competence in managing affairs of common interest to the membership and in providing needed reciprocal support. Some neighborhoods and communities have a substantial history of initiating and organizing their membership to meet the needs of the community as a whole or of particular segments within it. Such groups and neighborhoods in a population may be used in programs as sources of local expertise and as active participants in implementing programs. So far as the elderly are concerned, where such groups and neighborhoods have an experience of active helping roles on behalf of elderly and aged people, far from being left alone because they are managing so well, their potential role in effecting the diffusion of their own experience, skills, and commitment to other families and neighborhoods should be explored.

The relative urgency of facilitating the formation of support systems for the elderly will of course vary with different communities. In dense ethnic neighborhoods, the elderly often feel they belong, are members of extended families, are living in familiar and predictable cultural environments, and are objects of concern and support. But under conditions where more rapid change is taking place, even under the relatively benign conditions of carefully planned urban renewal, for example, the stress experienced by the elderly may be difficult to assuage. These stress levels become critical when loss of family continuity is accompanied by neighborhood disruption such as with inner city deterioration of housing, increased crime in the streets, forceable entry into homes, and movement away of long-time friends and associates. Under such conditions, conventional health-directed persuasions will have little meaning and must yield to the more pressing priorities of social, emotional, and economic survival.

It seems essential therefore that health program strategies include provision for close coordination between all possible human service agencies in order to pool a range of expertise and experience, and to develop at least complementary strategies, or at best, a common strategy. This may present a formidable task indeed, but is nonetheless a goal worth moving toward (Chapter 8). Strategies should also include provision for governmental involvement and support as well as that of political leadership, including some at local levels. In addition, individuals, groups and neighborhoods will commonly identify with populations beyond their dormitory and work-site borders. They may share with them the same ethnicity, socioeconomic status, concerns, and aspirations. Some identifications may be with formal organizations such as trade unions or the Gray Panthers. These extended units of identity, which have become units of solution as they formally organize and take action, are potentially significant agents of social change in ways not possible for local communities or groups alone. Moreover, they may provide some antidote to the feelings of helplessness of those on behalf of whom they are acting. When prominent, elderly Gray Panther or other activists achieve visibility and influence change, the elderly as a whole are able to identify with this leadership, feel that "we" did it, and be more responsive to local efforts at organized self-help by the elderly themselves.

Implications for Traditional Strategies

Perhaps the most common health intervention strategy in medical care, but still to some extent present in public health, follows what may be called a professional (or social) control model. Professional expertise is the dominant component; it is "delivered" to "consumers" along with education about health and exhortations to comply.

The priorities and design, the activities and evaluation of the program are professionally determined, and the program remains in effect under professional management for its duration. This occurs even with the presence of "consumer" boards, which usually have little power fundamentally to change the course of events.

Even the knowledge and attitudes deemed necessary to influence behavior change are defined by professionals, and the education of the public is done primarily, if not exclusively, by trained staff. Interagency coordination is unlikely to go beyond a simple individual referral system.

Community volunteers may be used in relatively rudimentary roles, client groups may be given considerable freedom to discuss the substance of educational sessions, and Senior Citizen Centers, elderly day care centers, "retirement communities," and other organizations may be used as points of access to elderly collectives. But professional control remains constant. Issues raised by the people themselves which are not clearly consonant with the health objectives and activities of the program already laid down, tend to be regarded as obstacles to be overcome rather than motivational opportunities to be exploited.

The focus is usually on individual behavior change outcomes somewhat narrowly defined for categorical health conditions with little or no attention to normative mental health or to the development of general problem-solving self-confidence and competence in the people themselves. The emphasis on categorical problems tends to militate against a "wide-angle" relationship with the people. Thus there tends to be a neglect of the fact that so many elderly people have increasing clusters of health problems such as failing eyesight, hearing, and physical mobility, along with multiple chronic conditions. Clearly, these require more specialized attention appropriate to such specific conditions, and membership in self-help groups of those suffering the same condition. But the more generalized affective and instrumental support fundamental to coping and adapting as handicapped elderly in a society from which they may feel alienated remains fundamental to their overall development of self-confidence, emotional security, and capacity for self-help.

The absence of a strong, active, decision-making role by communities, and of attention to competence-building in all client groups, means that future programs do not benefit from being introduced to already activated and increasingly competent communities and populations. The general use of the model for all age-cohort programs also means that adults in the middle-years and even younger have not been involved in the very coping and competence development activities that would serve them in good stead when they enter the ranks of the elderly.

The Social Change Strategy Alternative

The alternative to this prototypical professional and social control model is a social change model central to which is community competence development with professional support and consultation rather than control. It is fashioned to address health-related concerns which extend well beyond specific categorical health needs. Professionally defined health needs in a social change strategy are approached within the context of those larger environmental and social issues which constrain independent decisions, capabilities, and behavior change of the individual alone.

Community members, instead of being co-opted into a program already designed by professionals, would actively participate in representative groups of a variety of kinds. These would work at the local levels of socioeconomic and subcultural variation in the catchment population. They would play a major, even dominant, role in the initial decisions as to priorities, with minimal constraints pressing them toward selection of health-directed goals. The efforts of professionals as consultants and facilitators would be persuasive rather than directive. With the primary emphasis on group and community competence-building, the more traditional health and disease-categorical goals would be introduced and refined by professionals at those stages when they are seen to be most relevant to the directions community members designate as priorities. Thus, the experience of representative action groups in analyzing and validating their own community needs, with professional technical assistance, would take precedence over professionally independent needs assessments. While such early efforts might be scientifically fallible and professionally crude, the sense of communities, groups, and various mediating social structures that they are in control, and that professionals are there to provide them with the necessary expertise, would be a paramount concern. Later and successive needs assessments, refinements, and definitions of objectives, and the design of evaluation methods, would become increasingly more sophisticated. This does not preclude advanced technical work by professional groups themselves. It is only that such efforts would be put into operation as community groups see and are persuaded to accept the need and provide their endorsement.

For the elderly, this kind of involvement would be directed toward increasing their confidence that by joint action they can help themselves and that their local priority concerns can be addressed in socially and culturally appropriate ways. The program action would then, from the start, be based on existing motivational priorities, so that the health service does not face the usual task of trying to divert community priority concerns from those that are real for the elderly to those that are real for professionals. The elderly themselves, instead of being seen as relatively passive recipients of program benefits (which reinforces their own poor self-image), would become the driving force behind their own programs.

It may be argued that the professional control model may be preferred by certain groups and cultures. But while this may be seen as culturally preferable for medical care of the sick, it has to be remembered that all human communities are in the business of problem-solving, coping, and reciprocal helping, in both formal and informal ways independent of health and other human service activities. The social control model is not an imposed one. It is one of grafting program goals onto the existing motivational currents and problem-solving activities existing at the time of intervention.

Concerns of the catchment population for the overwhelming problems of poverty, unemployment, housing, safety in the street, or discrimination cannot adequately be addressed by health services as such. The linkage with other human service agencies so that they combine community and human services power and resources would need to be considered in addressing these broader issues. This does not imply exclusive engagement with these long-term problems for which some amelioration may be in sight only in the distant future. The elderly may be in dire straits economically; but this does not foreclose, while efforts are being made to explore sources for improving their meager incomes, their being offered assistance in budgeting and food buying for greatest nutritional benefit. Their dwellings may be dilapidated, and they may be engaged in action against exploitative landlords; but this does not foreclose efforts to help the elderly, by simple measures, to remove some of the major hazards in their rooms, apartments, or other dwellings.

Community members would also be called on to contribute various forms of expertise appropriate to human service and health programs. Such expertise may come from past employment and from past life experience, such as successful coping with the stress of retirement, bereavement, or relocation. Such expertise, supported and strengthened by professional expertise, would be a peer channel to the rest of the elderly population and would strengthen the complementary effects of communications from authorities to the public and between members of the public itself. The emphasis on competence development at all levels, from community to individual, would find expression in the specific activities and methods used in the program. The initial approach to every group, for example, would be one of eliciting the priority concerns of the membership and the competence with which they were already themselves attempting to address such concerns. Professional support and consultation would be directed towards strengthening that competence and the membership's self-image and self-confidence so that they can exercise some control over their circumstances and status.

This alternative social change model is not intended to jettison the generally accepted procedures in program development, such as needs assessment, the definition of measurable objectives and outcomes, and the design of evaluation procedures. Essential differences would reside in the sequence of these steps and in the acceptance of cruder efforts preceding more sophisticated ones. A major difference would be in the shared responsibility of communities and groups with professionals throughout the program and the maintenance of a sense by those communities and groups that they are in fact in control. Basically, the rule of action would be to do nothing that community members could do for themselves with professional backing; that whatever professional groups might do of a more advanced and technical nature would be done with the general understanding, advice, and consent of the community.

The broader social change strategy involves a focus wider than the discrete needs of a specific age cohort. Too narrow a focus in programs for the elderly may mean that whatever isolation or withdrawal from the rest of community life they may already be experiencing could well be reinforced. The elderly are to a great extent the victims of adverse social and economic circumstances, most of which in one way or another affect the whole population. At the same time, being led to dependence only on their own resources is often not enough. Thus the intention is that both the elderly as well as whole communities be involved in alleviating the elderly's health and welfare problems. Adopting a similar model for all health programs would mean that whole communities, including members of the elderly, would be involved in contributing to all segments of the population. Programs need the flexibility to meet the complementary and overlapping needs of a variety of population segments. Action on behalf of the elderly in inner city rooming houses would not exclude help for those in their 50s who are similarly isolated with chronic illness and malnutrition; programs for emotionally disturbed or mentally retarded children that have "adoptive grandparents" drawn from elderly volunteers and provide benefits for both child and adult; and all health programs that draw on the considerable experience and talent pool of the elderly to contribute to their development and implementation and also strengthen their own effectiveness as well as benefit the elderly who want to be of service.

The social change model is not easy to apply even if health professionals were enamored of it and ready to move. It represents a goal in the direction of which programs for the elderly, as well as programs for others in a population, need to move if we are effectively to enter disease prevention and health promotion in a comprehensive way.

Stability and Change in Social and Behavioral Systems

Intervention strategies represent planned attempts to induce social and behavioral change. However, their design depends upon the natural or unplanned determinants of stability and change. Since all behavior appears to be health-related, and "health behavior" is not a discrete and independent category, there is a need to consider these natural change determinants irrespective of their associations with health. This means stepping as it were, from the biomedical and public health domain as such, into the social and behavioral domain in its own right. Moreover, where the concern is for facilitating action by the people themselves, this involves a focus on the "inside" or emic view of the elderly and how they see their world, rather than the "outside" or etic view of the professional observer and practitioner. How people behave depends on their own feelings, and perceived needs rather than those of intervening professionals, no matter how well-intentioned the latter may be.

Health-Related Motivation

Of critical significance in understanding stability and change in individual behavior are the needs felt by people themselves and the motivations that drive their behavior. It is in the nature of human beings that they are not simply reactive to environmental stimuli. They are, in an important respect, stimulus-seeking. They have inner drives to experience, explore, understand, and find meaning in their social and physical environments. They are involved in a continuous process of meeting basic human needs for survival, for the avoidance of pain and discomfort, for the pursuit of sensual and sexual pleasures, for belonging and feeling wanted, for experiencing rewarding feedback from others, for some status and prestige, for maintaining a sense of physical and emotional safety and security in a predictable, stable world, and for a sense of control over their own destinies. These universal human needs are likely to be experienced in a more acute form by the elderly in highly industrialized societies like the United States precisely because they are commonly the most threatened in the later years of life.

Although they are related to health status they are usually not seen by the people in this particular light. They are seen rather as important in their own right in contributing to the quality of life. On the other hand, some behaviors such as seeking the assistance of traditional healers, of pharmacists, or of physicians are predominantly, if not exclusively, performed for "health" purposes (Chapter 5). These latter "health-directed" behaviors constitute only part, commonly a rather small part, of the whole range of health-related human behaviors. To the extent then that the individual eats certain foods as a result primarily of socialization, custom, palatability, and enjoyment, but without concern for the health implications as such, that food behavior is health-related. To the extent that food choices are made deliberately for health purposes, such behavior is health-directed.

This distinction has important practical implications for health programs which frequently ignore, or treat simply as obstacles to their success, those powerful and pervasive motivations of people that are not health-directed. Moreover, many behaviors which are ostensibly health-directed may be motivated by needs from the patients' viewpoints that are only tenuously concerned with health as such. Thus the lonely elderly may often use health services as a means of expressing to a sympathetic listener needs for emotional comfort and reassurance for all manner of daily living and relationship problems. Among the elderly and the aged generally, where it might be expected that physical health would be of paramount importance, the psychological and emotional satisfactions will frequently have precedence. Indeed, the reasons why such a large proportion of the elderly seek health advice from traditional healers as well as quacks, rather than from medical providers, may well be because these practitioners provide a more skillfully responsive sensitivity to these transcendent emotional needs in ways compatible with the cultural and social experience of their clients.

Thus, the achievement or maintenance of health, as seen by public health, may have relatively less priority and therefore less motivational power behind it, even with the elderly, than is often so optimistically assumed. With all population segments going through relatively stressful life phases, even when physical health is a strongly felt need, it is invariably accompanied, even dominated, by deep-seated emotional needs as well.

Of equal significance is the fallacy implicit in the common expressions of health professionals that they "have to motivate people" or that the people are "not motivated." Clearly it is not that people are not motivated; rather it is that their priority motivations are so often different from, or incompatible with, the motivations health professionals would like them to have. The act of noncompliance with a medical drug regimen may be as positive and "motivated" an act as that of compliance; the act of continuing to smoke in the face of urgent public health messages to the contrary, may be as positive and motivated an act as ceasing smoking.

Individual Behavior Patterns

The social-behavioral, like the physiological, make-up of the individual operates as a system. There are no free-floating behavior bits which are not compatible with the total social-psychological system that expresses the more or less unique personality of the individual. When there are severely conflicting feelings and behaviors that the individual is unable to reconcile with one another, the result is clinically identifiable emotional disturbance and disability. With the emotionally well, each individual personality is distinctively and inwardly experienced as having a recognizable identity—a sense of "who I am" and how "I am distinctive from those around me." From the emic viewpoint then, the individual may be considered a "unit of identity." The term "unit" does not here imply a uniform element as much as an intrinsically unitary nature.

The daily life style of the individual is patterned with system-like characteristics. It is not simply an assemblage of discrete behaviors. Behavior bits such as smoking, drinking coffee, flossing one's teeth, or going to bed each night at 10 p.m., do not occur randomly. They are each part of behavioral subsystems such as those clusters of behaviors involved in rising each morning and preparing to face the day or in the preparation, eating, and social setting of the main daily meal. Social and behavioral change strategies therefore have to take account of the fact that the behaviors they may specifically wish to target will in all likelihood be "tied in" with other behaviors which might need to be changed as well. Thus there are often close associations between eating, drinking, and smoking behaviors. Sometimes too, the behavior "sets" that professionals link with a health issue are each to some extent independently tied into different social-behavioral systems. An example from dental health is the fluoridation of water supplies, oral hygiene, snacking between meals, and regular use of the dentist. Thus fluoridation was, and in some communities still is, a major political issue; oral hygiene and teeth brushing may be tied into behaviors concerned with personal attractiveness to others; snacking may be an intrinsic element in a larger system of food and social behaviors; visits to the dentist may be linked to all those behaviors concerned with the utilization of professional services.

The daily life style of the individual consists of a behavioral system "motivated" to meet needs and fashioned by the constraints of the particular physical, social, and cultural environment. It is a product of a life-long process of socialization and enculturation which defines and redefines role expectations and behavior changes as maturing and aging occur. These forces establish the range of normative behavior for the various life-phases such as adolescence, young adulthood, the middle years, and later life. Impending stages and the sociocultural expectations of individuals within them are usually sufficiently predictable that individuals normally undergo an anticipatory adaptation to what is to come. Predictability and the expectation one can perform with some adequacy in a changing role provide a measure of emotional security.

On the other hand, rapid change where the individual is unable to adapt, and feels helpless to influence events, is emotionally disturbing and disruptive. The habitual nature of daily behavior, within a context of predictable expectations about the immediate future, is an expression of feelings of security that well-tried coping methods will continue to work. Thus the diurnal cycle of behaviors that covers most of the days of a week, the somewhat different diurnal cycle for "rest" days such as weekends, and the periodic special, festive holidays, are characterized in all societies by an extraordinary repetitiveness.

Microchange does occur over time, but macrochange, particularly from pressures or events beyond the individual's control, tends to be psychologically stressful and therefore resisted. Thus, social and behavioral change strategies that appear to be demanding or advocating dramatic change are likely to be seen as threatening and will stimulate strong resistance; strategies that are seen as directed toward easing inevitable transitions, slowing their pace, or offering alternatives in which the individual feels some control over events by being able to exercise a choice, will tend to attract supportive responses.

Elderly individuals have a long prior life experience of coping and of establishing habitual ways of managing life problems. Therefore their life styles will tend to be somewhat entrenched and resistant to change. They will tend also to experience stress as changes in the mores of their society occur over the course of their lifetimes. Thus their expectations, for example, as to the feelings, attitudes, and behaviors of the young toward the old which were socialized in them when they themselves were young, may dramatically have changed by the time they enter the socially defined phase of being "elderly." Generally then, the slower pace of change in rural, and particularly in non-technological societies, are in this respect at least more favorable to the mental health of the elderly than the more rapid changes characteristic of urban and highly industrialized settings.

Roles and Competencies

Not only will there be social and cultural variations in the experience, stresses, and coping styles of the elderly as whole, but within each culture and subculture, wide individual differences in their roles, competencies, and aspirations may be found. Some individuals, for example, who are more cosmopolitan in their attitudes and receptiveness, will tend to seek and to respond more rapidly to experiences and to communications, particularly the mass media, from outside the more immediate social system of which they are members, such as their own communities and interpersonal networks. Many will be members of interpersonal networks that are themselves predominantly cosmopolitan in outlook. Others are more local in their orientation, responding largely to interpersonal communications and persuasions from inside the social system of which they are members (Rogers, 1983).

These differences will be found among the elderly as they will in other age cohorts, although one might expect in different proportions. Urban, higher-educated elderly are more likely to have larger proportions of these cosmopolite individuals and networks than rural and lower-educated elderly. Thus, account needs to be taken of the selective responses to health communications coming from external professional sources and of the possibility that it may often be those most in need who are the least responsive to such communications.

Some individuals, often under the most unlikely of circumstances, seem to have a higher degree of expertise in the management of their daily lives, a high level of self-confidence and a pleasant feeling-tone. Such individuals frequently provide a model for others to emulate. Often too, they act as informal advice-givers who provide both affective and instrumental support to others beyond their own immediate family and circle of associates. Such advice-givers, opinion-leaders, or influentials may be modernist, progressive, and cosmopolitan in orientation. They may also be traditional, conservative, and local in their outlook and help reinforce existing behaviors and resistance to innovation from external sources.

During the earlier part of their lives, those elderly who played such influential roles may have influenced others in different age groups, both younger as well as older than themselves. In a rapidly changing or urban industrial society, this influential role is likely to become seriously eroded with age as these life-long skills have decreasing relevance for younger people. Their domestic arts, crafts, and self-help skills become outdated through technological advances; their local neighborhood and community knowledge is no longer meaningful to more mobile and cosmopolitan younger people; and their relegation to an elderly, less capable stereotypical category means that even their human relationship and stress management skills are less in demand. As they move into a category apart, their interpersonal networks will tend to be composed primarily of their age peers where their influential roles of the past may be perpetuated.

Again, social and behavioral strategies need to take account of these elderly influentials as themselves a vital program resource. It is they who may exert considerable, if not decisive, influence on a program's acceptance by the elderly and who may, as agents of the program, contribute their indigenous expertise in helping others in their age cohort.

With regard to communications and persuasions among the elderly themselves, and with health professionals, there are certain important considerations for program purposes. Homophilous communication is that between persons of similar background, education, social status, and other characteristics; heterophilous communication is that between persons of dissimilar background and experience. By far the greatest amount of human communication is homophilous—that is, occurring between individuals and in groups that are relatively homogenous. These kinds of communication appear to be most effective in influencing action. Heterophilous communications, however, for instance from professionals to the public, both in interpersonal situations and through the mass media, may be listened to with respect, and even intellectual and emotional acceptance. But actual behavior change appears to occur primarily as a function of homophilous communications where the source is more personally trusted and seen as a model for emulation (Rogers, 1983).

In respect to the mass media, it is the opinion leaders, those able to influence the attitudes and behaviors of others, who tend to respond to those messages and in turn exercise a critical influence on those in their personal networks of kin, non-kin, friends, and associates, the majority of whom may tend not to be influenced to behavior change from the media messages themselves (Katz and Lazarsfeld, 1955). Indeed, the more immediate impact of the mass media seems to be in introducing an idea and finally in reinforcing existing behavior. The intervening stage of actually changing behavior is largely a function of interpersonal, homophilous communication (Rogers, 1983). Effective behavioral change strategies then may depend on identifying such opinion leaders, soliciting their advice on the nature and appeals of mass communications, and working directly with them as sources of influence among their peers.

Local Program Development for the Elderly

In terms of practical program development at the local level with a specified catchment population, procedures with a social change strategy would be similar for the elderly as for any other segment of that population. The starting process of discovery on each occasion would be an analysis in broad terms of the social systems, particularly the communities and neighborhoods likely to be subculturally and socioeconomically distinctive. Within these, it would be necessary to glean a preliminary view of the kinds of mediating structures such as churches, social organizations, citizen groups, and kin and non-kin networks of which the elderly are members. It would be necessary also in respect to each community as well as to the catchment population as a whole to make an early identification of the power structure and citizen leadership.

The purpose of this relatively crude initial analysis is the identification of individuals, groups, and constituencies with whom the collaborative work of the health program might begin. This does not preclude the formation of new community groups having memberships with constituencies to which they may provide access and on whose behalf they may speak and act. From these communities, the membership of any central board may be drawn to take responsibility, in close collaboration with professional staff, for program policy on behalf of the whole catchment population.

The advantages of this early controlling and continuous participatory role by representative members of the total population and of each of the distinctive communities or neighborhoods are several. First, they are the means by which the program through all stages of its development may contribute to the self-help competency of each of the communities involved. Second, it averts from the start a serious incompatibility between community and professional goals respectively. Third, it provides the opportunity to graft professional health priorities onto existing motivational currents and activities. Fourth, it removes the need for lengthy preliminary diagnoses of cultural and subcultural belief, attitude, and behavioral systems since the representative community members would be expected to make culturally and socially appropriate decisions. Fifth, it reduces manpower pressure on a service because program responsibility will be shared and potential community resources mobilized through community representatives.

After these preliminary steps, diagnosis and action at every stage of program development becomes a shared community and professional endeavor, with each step being directed toward increasing the competence of the participants and their constituencies in addressing their priority needs and substantive health issues in this context.

While professional consultations would of course be directed towards various groups and sub-groups of the elderly themselves with a variety of needs, they would be directed also toward other groups whose activities have an impact on the health and welfare status of the elderly. Where such groups may not have adequate representation of elderly people, professional advice would be to increase such representation. The intention would be to provide them with immediate sources for a clearer perspective of priority needs felt by the elderly themselves and to identify special categories of the elderly with distinctive needs, disabilities, and health problems.

The intervention strategy will be concerned with the particular settings and methods for accomplishing the detailed behavioral changes described in Chapter 5.

Information dissemination is clearly essential for appropriate behavior to result. Information alone, however, is commonly not enough. Not only may other motivational priorities transcend more limited health-directed behavior changes, but both practical and psychological disincentives may be present such as lack of transport to use health care services or demeaning treatment when they are used.

Motivational and emotional factors are of fundamental importance in facilitating or retarding the transformation of knowledge into action. An illustration may be found in the case of weight control. Assume we have three categories of elderly women. One category might consist of majority culture women whose weights are within normal health and cultural limits and who wish to maintain or slightly reduce their weights; a second category might be women from a minority ethnic group whose weights, while detrimental to their health, are nonetheless culturally appropriate and aesthetic; a third group might be majority culture women who are obese and outside acceptable cultural limits and causing them considerable emotional stress.

Similar basic nutritional knowledge is relevant to all three groups. The first group, however, with the largely uncomplicated motivation of retaining their physical attractiveness is likely to respond to and to use information with peer support and perhaps some simple behavior modification techniques. The women in the second group, their physical appearance being culturally acceptable, are unlikely to change without a broader change in the values of their communities. The third group usually have rather complicated emotional problems and conflicts about food intake and present a problem not so much of information as of psychotherapy and strong emotional support.

The emotional support of peer groups is critical in attempting behavioral change except where problems are of a severity requiring individual treatment. The major vehicle of change is the group rather than the individual. Health service providers are more familiar and comfortable with groups in which the members are experiencing the same or similar health problems and needs. Such groups are of importance because they provide a sharing and support milieu of others with similar problems. But there are also more heterogeneous groups of family members, friends, and associates with whom the individual may interact in everyday life. These groups, discussing and dealing with change in complementary behaviors of the members, are of equal importance. Groups of family members discussing the dietary needs of elderly individuals among them, or the strengthening of the grandparenting role, would be groups of this kind.

Generally, leader-centered groups assembled for purposes of teaching the members, even when they allow time for discussion, are likely to build some dependence on the leader. Group-centered discussion on the other hand, is focused more on an effort to develop and strengthen the group itself so that it can function as a unit of identity and solution without external leadership. While professionals may play a major role in the stimulation of group formation and in getting the process started, lay facilitators should eventually take their place so that professionals can withdraw and be called in at those times when the group decides it needs professional advice or support. Once a group has built up some solidarity and confidence as a group, the members tend to feel less threatened and more free to put questions and even debate points with the professional guest.

These interpersonal modes of influencing behavior are at the core of every behavioral change strategy. The strong initiating, supporting, and reinforcing role of non-personal methods in the mass media needs to be recognized as well. But their power will depend to a considerable extent on their sensitivity to the social and cultural background of the target audience, on their reflection of favorable rather than derogatory images of the elderly, and, of course, on the clarity of the information they provide. It is helpful to have elderly people, "typical" of the target audience, assisting with the preparation of such messages or, at the very least, being involved in their pretesting prior to general use. This makes possible any modifications responsive to unintended misperceptions and adverse emotional reactions.

There are probably no important social and behavioral change needs of any segment of a population, including of the elderly, which do not require a range of interacting social systems as units of practice. Thus in dietary change, the elderly individual must both feel the need and find the alternatives acceptable; the family or household unit may have to provide special preparation arrangements; the local community might need to persuade food stores to stock particular foods at reasonable prices; or legislative bodies may be involved in changing food stamp regulations or other welfare grants. Thus, a not inconsiderable program effort has to be devoted toward behavior change among those who influence directly or indirectly the health and welfare of the elderly.

Programs for the elderly will then reach out to younger adults and even to young children, to radio and television executives, to public libraries, to school boards and the selection of textbooks, to architects and building contractors, to employers, to adult education centers, to public transport, street, sidewalk, and lighting authorities, to the police, and indeed to all major sources of influence on the image, social status, role, and physical and mental health of the elderly. In the social change strategy model however, as far as possible, both the elderly and other citizen groups would be the prime movers in exerting this influence rather than health or other human service professionals.

Finally, in all health programs ranging from the most comprehensive to the most narrowly categorical, health professionals need constantly to consider involving as planners, implementers, and as indigenous experts those of the elderly with particular talents, skills, and interests. In all social and behavioral change programs, there is a need to make use of all possible community resources, and especially those with interpersonal and communication skills. It is in these respects, particularly among the elderly, that there is an unmined lode of talent and experience.

Activism, Social Change, and the Elderly

No review of social and behavioral change strategies for the elderly is complete without a consideration of those social systems that extend beyond local population and community boundaries. The broader social and cultural environment, and the distribution of goods and services which are among the central concerns of social policy, are of fundamental significance for the health of the elderly.

Active community service has for a long time been associated with the young rather than the elderly who were seen as a relatively helpless and incapacitated category of the population. This impression is contradicted by the fact that, for example, in 1973, it is reported that four and a half million elderly people were actively involved in volunteer work (Midlarsky & Kahana, 1983). Also in recent years there has been a vastly increased interest in the influence of the elderly on the political process (Weaver, 1976; Hendricks and Hendricks, 1977; Cutler, 1981; Fox, 1981; Schlesinger and Schlesinger, 1981; Butler and Lewis, 1982; Pratt, 1983).

Even without organized action, the elderly as voters are assuming more visible power with modern technology in analyzing voter age cohorts and opinions. Almost 90 percent of the elderly are registered to vote and about two-thirds of these vote regularly, more than any other age group (Butler and Lewis, 1982). Moreover, this political influence is likely to grow as the age cohort increases in size (Cutler, 1981). The number of government programs and legislation directly affecting the elderly have also vastly increased. National health policy, as a highly relevant issue for the elderly, could eventually blunt the differences in the political views they bring from the past (Weaver, 1976).

This level of elderly activity and involvement is now, and in the future may increasingly become, of great significance for the health and welfare of the elderly. To the extent that elderly persons see themselves as sharing common disabilities, problems, and aspirations, they constitute a unit of identity and certainly therefore of potential solution. In the private interpersonal support systems that make up the more immediate life space of most individuals, mental health (and such physical health sequelae as there may be) is dependent not simply on the receipt of affective and instrumental support, but on its giving as well.

Organizations of the elderly, or predominantly of the elderly, may well prove more satisfying to their memberships by increasing their concern for the needs of non-elderly segments of the population; such groups may also suffer socially imposed disabilities in job discrimination, loneliness, alienation, and the like. Sophisticated activist leaders are constantly seeking new alliances or extensions of the social units of identity and solution of which they are members. Martin Luther King, Jr. provided a notable example in extending the black minority unit of identity and of solution to the poor, white and black.

Even at the local level, concerns of special immediacy for the elderly are serious enough concerns for the rest of the population as well. The maintenance of roads and of sidewalks, street lighting, police protection, and neighborhood decay affect numerous others besides the elderly. Thus, through relatively modest levels of action with local authorities, the elderly may expand their units of identity and of solution to other age groups, not to mention other ethnic groups, and establish themselves as a valued and integral part of the community as a whole.

The common experience of the elderly that their world and arena of activity is shrinking, that they are no longer valued, and have nothing to contribute to society, may to a great extent be counteracted by their increasing participation in activist movements and organizations of all kinds.

Since such activism is likely to contribute to change in the broader social and environmental conditions affecting the health of the elderly, as well as in itself being potentially promotive of their mental health, health services might be expected to support and encourage such participation.

The question remains, however, as to what extent public health professionals are prepared to go beyond the constraints of professional control strategies and enter the wider arena of social change strategies. Professionals in human services, including health professionals, represent a formidable behavior change problem in themselves. Not only have they tended to show a less than enthusiastic interest in the elderly and the aged, which is only now beginning to change, but they have clung to the security of low risk intervention models, in spite of their lack of promise for comprehensive and effective preventive and health promotive outcomes. There is therefore a significant educational task involved in the preparation of public health professionals themselves if a signal contribution is to be made to the health of elderly people and the aged.

References

Botwinick, J. *Aging and Behavior,* Second Edition. New York, N.Y.: Springer Publishing Company, 1978.

Busse, E. Health and mental illness after 65. *State Government,* Aut., 1977, *50* 231–236.

Butler, R. and Lewis, Myrna I. *Aging and Mental Health: Positive Psycho-*

social and Biomedical Approaches, Third Edition. Saint Louis, Mo.: C.V. Mosby Company, 1982.

Butler, R. *Why Survive: Being Old in America.* New York, N.Y.: Harper and Row, Publishers, 1975.

Cantor, M. and Mayer, M. Health and the inner city elderly. *Gerontologist,* 1976, *16,* 17–25.

Cobb, S. Presidential Address—1976. Social support as a moderate of life-stress. *Psychosomatic Medicine,* 1976, *38,* 300–314.

Cumming, E. and Henry, W.E. *Growing Old: The Process of Disengagement.* New York, N.Y.: Basic Books, 1961.

Cutler, N. Political characteristics of elderly cohorts in the twenty-first century. In Kiesler, S., Morgan, J., and Oppenheimer, V., (Eds.) *Aging: Social Change.* New York, N.Y.: Academic Press, 1981, pp. 127–157.

Davis, K. and Reynolds, R. Medicare and the utilization of health services by the elderly. *Journal of Human Resources,* 1975, *10,* 361–377.

Dunkel-Schetter, C. and Wortman, C. Dilemmas of social support: parallels between victimization and aging. In Kiesler, S., Morgan, J., and Oppenheimer, V. (Eds.) *Aging: Social Change.* New York, N.Y.: Academic Press, 1981, pp. 349–381.

Eribes, R. and Bradley-Rawls, M. Underutilization of nursing home facilities by Mexican-American elderly in the Southwest. *Gerontologist,* 1978, *18,* 363–371.

Etzioni, A. Old people and public policy. *Social Policy,* 1976, *7,* 21–29.

Figa-Talamanca, I. Health status and health care problems of the aged in an Italian community. *International Journal of Aging and Human Development,* 1976, *7,* 39–48.

Fox, R. The welfare state and the political mobilization of the elderly. In Kiesler, S., Morgan, J., and Oppenheimer, V. (Eds.) *Aging: Social Change.* New York, N.Y.: Academic Press, 1981, pp. 159–182.

Gelfand, D.E. *Aging: The Ethnic Factor.* Boston, Ma.: Little, Brown and Company, 1982.

Griffitt, W. Sexual intimacy in aging sexual partners. In Fogel, R.W. et al. (Eds.) *Aging: stability and change in the family.* New York, N.Y.: Academic Press, 1981, pp. 301–315.

Hammerman, J. Health services: their success and failure in reaching older adults. *American Journal of Public Health,* 1974, *64,* 253–256.

Harris, R. Breaking the barriers to better health care delivery for the aged—medical aspects. *Gerontologist,* 1975, *15,* 52–56.

Hendricks, J. and Hendricks, C. *Aging in Mass Society: Myths and Realities.* Cambridge, Ma.: Winthrop Publishers, 1977.

Hulicka, I.M., Cataldo, J.F., Morganti, J.B., and Nehrke, M.F. Perceptions of choice and importance by the elderly: implications for intervention. In Kleiman, M. (Ed.), *Social Gerontology. Interdisciplinary Topics in Gerontology,* Vol. 17. Basel, Switzerland: S. Karger, 1983, pp. 25–39.

Jackson, J. Special health problems of aged blacks. *Aging,* 1978, *287–288,* 15–20.

Kahn, R. and Antonucci, T. Conveys of social support: a life-course approach. In Kiesler, S., Morgan, J., and Oppenheimer, V. (Eds.) *Aging: Social Change.* New York: Academic Press, 1981, pp. 383–405.

Kane, R., Jorgensen, L., Teteberg, B., and Devenport, J. How a team approach improved the nursing homes in our area. *Medical Times,* 1977, *80,* 43d–49d.

Katz, E. and Lazarsfeld, P. *Personal Influence: The Part Played by People in the Flow of Mass Communications.* New York, N.Y.: Free Press, 1955.

Kessler, M., and Albee, G. An overview of the literature of primary prevention. In Albee, G.W., and Joffee, J.M., (Eds.) *Primary Prevention of Psychopathology,* Vol. 1. Hanover, N.H.: University Press of New England, 1977, 351–399.

Kim, P. and Wilson, C. Toward mental health of the rural elderly. Washington, D.C.: University Press of America, 1981.

Kovar, M. Health of the elderly and use of health services. *Public Health Reports,* 1977, *92,* 9–19.

Levin, Lowell S., and Idler, Ellen L. *The Hidden Health Care System: Mediating Structures and Medicine.* Cambridge, Mass.: Ballinger Publishing Company, 1981.

Lieberman, M. and Tobin, S. *The Experience of Old Age: Stress Coping and Survival.* New York, N.Y.: Basic Books, 1983.

Linn, B., Linn, M., and Knopa, F. *Very Old Patients in Ambulatory Care.* Miami, Fl.: Veterans Administration Hospital, 1978.

Loten, E. and Evans, B. Man was for woman made and woman for man. *New Zealand Medical Journal,* 1975, *82,* 201–204.

Mason, D. Elderly day care service in the U.S.A.—a viable option. *Nursing Homes,* 1978, *27,* 4–9.

Midlarsky, E. and Kahana, E. Helping by the elderly: conceptual and empirical considerations. In Kleiman, M. (Ed.) *Social Gerontology. Interdisciplinary Topics in Gerontology,* Vol. 17. Basel, Switzerland: S. Karger, 1983, pp. 10–24.

National Council on Aging. *The Myth and Reality of Aging in America.* Washington, D.C.: Louis Harris and Associates, 1975.

Palmore, E. *Normal Aging. Reports from the Duke Longitudinal Study, 1955–1969.* Durham, N.C.: Duke University Press, 1970.

Pratt, H. Political implications of aging. In Kleiman, M. (Ed.), *Social Gerontology Interdisciplinary Topics in Gerontology,* Vol. 17. Basel, Switzerland: S. Karger, 1983, pp. 144–156.

Problems of older people: forced idleness, impoverishment, ill health, isolation. *Bulletin of the New York Academy of Medicine,* 1973, *49* (12).

Rogers, E. *Diffusion of Innovations,* (Third Edition). New York: Free Press, 1983.

Schlesinger, J. and Schlesinger, M. Aging and opportunities for elective office. In Kiesler, S., Morgan, J., and Oppenheimer, V. (Eds.) *Aging: Social Change.* New York: Academic Press, 1981, pp. 205–239.

Sears, R. The Role of expectancy in adaptation to aging. In Kiesler, S., Morgan, J., and Oppenheimer, V. (Eds.) *Aging: Social Change.* New York: Academic Press, 1981, pp. 407–430.

Steuart, Guy W. The people: motivation, education and action. *Bulletin of the New York Academy of Medicine,* 1975, Second Series, *51,* 174–185.

Steuart, Guy W. Social and cultural perspectives: community intervention and mental health. In *Perspectives in Primary Prevention.* Proceedings of the Fourteenth Annual John W. Umstead Series of Distinguished Lectures, 1978, North Carolina Division of Mental Health and Mental Retardation Services, Raleigh, North Carolina.

Tobin, S. Mystique of deinstitutionalization. *Society,* 1978, *15,* 73–75.

Trager, B. *Adult Day Facilities for Treatment, Health Care, and Related Services.* Washington, D.C.: Government Printing Office, 1976.

Traupmann, J. and Hatfield, E. Love and its effect on mental and physical health. In Fogel, R.W. et al. (Eds.) *Aging: Stability and Change in the Family.* New York: Academic Press, 1981, pp. 253–274.

Weaver. J.L. The elderly as a political community: the case of national health policy. *Western Political Quarterly,* 1976, *26,* 610–619.

Weiler, S. Aging and sexuality and the myth of decline. In Fogel, R.W. et al. (Eds.) *Aging: Stability and Change in the Family.* New York: Academic Press, 1981, pp. 317–327.

Wolf, S. *Social Environment and Health.* Seattle, Wa.: University of Washington Press, 1981.

PART IV

HEALTH SERVICES FOR THE ELDERLY

In both planning and organizing services, the public health approach is to regard the community as a whole, and to view community services from a systems perspective. Ideally, such an approach implies that goals will be formulated primarily for the good of the population to be served, and that services will be designed so as to best implement these goals. It also implies the existence of an intelligent central mechanism to receive input and feedback from all those who are affected. Such a system would strive to use available resources in the most effective and efficient way. It would also have the capacity to respond to changing conditions so that yesterday's solutions do not become tomorrow's problems.

However, in reality, policies and services have been instituted in piecemeal fashion, with no such overall perspective. Individual agencies and organizations have their own goals, which often compete and may conflict with the goals of the community as a whole. Piecemeal policies have resulted in an inefficient collection of programs which often leave serious gaps and promote waste.

Public health, working with the existing service situation, strives for more effective coordination of the diverse official, informal, and voluntary support systems. Ultimately, an efficient and responsive system will require an accommodation of its components, either through voluntary change or through political action.

The first two chapters in this section present the range of services theoretically available to the elderly, and discuss strategies for planning and coordinating services. Chapter 7 maps out the desirable functions to be accomplished by the system of health care. Chapter 8 reviews the problems of coordinating the highly individualistic providers of care. Chapter 9 critically reviews current health policies for the elderly in the United States and offers guiding principles for reform.

7

Organizing Community Health Services for the Elderly

HARRY T. PHILLIPS

Introduction

At the present time, health and health related programs for the elderly of the United States provide a patchwork of inefficient, unevenly distributed, and poorly coordinated services. Moreover, they are often inappropriate to the needs of individual clients and patients (Brody, 1973). A relatively small proportion of old people are well served by virtue of personal wealth, religious ties to strong organizations, inclusion in demonstration projects, or other exceptional circumstances. In general, however, health and related community support services for the elderly are less than ideal, with many valleys between the peaks of high quality care.

The purpose of this chapter is to outline public health approaches to the organization of health services for elderly populations. The most pressing problem for both elderly people and society as a whole is satisfying the need for long-term care. Consequently, this aspect of health care is presented as a special case for public health consideration.

However, before considering *organized* community services, it is important to recognize that dependent people of all ages are primarily supported by their families, friends, and neighbors—the *unorganized* informal, natural, support system of the community. It is reported that 80 percent of the home care given to those 55 and over is given by family members living in the household (U.S. House of Representatives, Select Committee, 1980, p. 67).

The number of frail elderly people is increasing, and many have few or no family members to provide needed assistance because of smaller family size, mobility of children, increase in the proportion of women who work, and high incidence of divorce. Moreover, the expectations and potential costs of health care have risen. The outcome of these trends is that the informal support system is becoming less able to satisfy the needs of the growing number of frail dependent people. Organized or formal services, supported by government, are increasingly being called upon to augment or replace the care given by families and voluntary groups.

Formal Services

Briefly stated, formal services are those which are provided by people who are outside the individual's normal social network. Generally, they are delivered by professional or other trained workers, or by volunteers who are part of an organized agency (Gelfand and Olsen, 1980; Lowy, 1980; Furukawa and Shomaker, 1982).

Aims of Formal Health Services for the Aged

From a public health standpoint, the primary goal is to maintain the well-being of as many elderly people in the community (state, region, nation) for as long as possible. To prevent, postpone, or lessen the burden of physical and mental disability, the community must provide a range of accessible, high quality health and supportive services. These must be offered in a variety of settings to afford choices which best meet the needs and wishes of the older person and his family at different levels of dependency. Maintaining the well-being of the elderly may require such diverse services as housing, transportation, social, cultural, recreational, and educational services, and of course, financial supplements, if income is lacking. It is generally accepted that to the extent that it is feasible and desired old people should be assisted in remaining in their own homes and communities, rather than in institutions.

Guiding Principles for Developing Health Services

Emphasis on Prevention. Services should emphasize prevention of disease and disability.

1. *Primary Prevention.* Comprises intervention before any disease develops, such as immunization against influenza, or cessation of smoking.

2. *Secondary Prevention.* Consists in detecting early evidence of disease, often asymptomatic, and treating it effectively; for example, screening for hypertension, and controlling it, if present.

3. *Tertiary Prevention.* Is applied to the practice of avoiding complications and disability; for example, early ambulation after surgery, and first aid.

Preventive care also takes the form of social interventions such as construction of housing and other amenities which reduce the risk of isolation or injury, or organizing social groups, or promoting educational programs for the elderly.

Integration of Services. Health services for the elderly should be integrated into the general system of care, unless there is a good reason for keeping them apart. Medical care should be coordinated with other related services, and continuity of care ensured.

Spectrum of Services. The spectrum of health services should be wide, providing care at different levels. It should include:

1. *Primary Care.* Generally provided in doctor's offices, health centers or hospital out-patient clinics. Primary care affords entry into the health care system, and ideally the provider maintains continuity between the different modalities of care, makes appropriate referrals, and serves as the manager and coordinator of the individual's formal care (Madison, 1983). Primary care functions are, in the United States, often shared between family physicians, nurses, and social workers.

2. *Secondary Care.* Is provided by medical specialists, usually in a hospital setting. It includes laboratory and radiological diagnosis, general surgery, and other forms of treatment using advanced medical technology.

3. *Tertiary Care.* Covers highly specialized medical diagnosis and treatment in medical centers.

Settings of Care. Services should be provided in a wide variety of settings. A consideration of where care is to be delivered is important for all persons, but particularly so for the elderly.

1. *Home Care.* As stated earlier, for the 2 to 4 million elderly people confined to their homes, 80 percent of all care is informal and provided by family and friends (U.S. House of Representatives,

Subcommittee on Human Services, 1980, p. 67). Organized care in the home is provided mainly through home care programs by public health nurses, supported in some cases by physical therapists, social workers, or aides of various kinds (Brickner, 1978). Care at home may not be cost effective in terms of several important criteria, but it promotes patient contentment (Weissert et al., 1980) and should be available as an option. Although this care is "physician directed" according to most regulations, physicians in the U.S. do not frequently make house calls.

In recent years organized hospice care has been added as a new dimension to home care in the United States (Cohen, 1979). It provides a range of health and related services to terminally ill patients and their families. (There may also be an in-patient component to this program.)

Foster care for elderly isolated people provides another way to remain home-based when independent living alone is no longer possible. Thus the setting does not necessarily have to be the older person's own home.

2. *The Community.* This includes doctors' offices, clinics, neighborhood health centers, health maintenance organizations, mental health centers, day hospitals, rehabilitation centers, halfway houses, and multipurpose centers. These provide a mixture of medical, social, and psychiatric services where the patient or client lives at home and comes to a locus where necessary space, personnel, or equipment are available. Services may range from health promotion to acute care, chronic care, or rehabilitation.

3. *Institutional Care.* This includes short-term hospitals and a variety of long-term care facilities ranging from long-term care hospitals (generally for special categories of disability such as mental illness), through skilled nursing facilities and intermediate care facilities (both defined under the Medicare/Medicaid regulations), to homes for the aged, boarding homes, and similar residential facilities.

Coordination with Related Services. Health services must be coordinated with related services. Particularly in the case of the elderly, who are prone to be subject to multiple and long-term deficiencies, it is essential that social, housing, transportation and similar non-medical resources be made available and used. Moreover, the system must have a sound and equitable source of funding.

Community Health Planning. Services for the elderly must be planned at the community level. By definition, a public health approach necessitates a rational, conscious effort to base community action on the needs and resources of the population, rather than permitting services to develop in response to market forces.

Rational Planning

Regional planning of health services has long been a dream of community leaders. Starting with the Committee on the Cost of Medical Care in 1932, there have been a series of recommendations, and later, laws, aiming at a more rational process for organizing health services. The most recent legislation, the National Health Planning and Resources Development Act of 1974 (P.L. 92-641), projected a set of ideal structures and processes for planning health services at the national, state, and local levels. Although the law is still in effect, its thrust has been severely reduced by lack of political and budgetary support. Nevertheless, this law sowed seeds which, when the political climate is favorable, could grow into an effective structure to support community health planning.

Briefly and simply stated, the *rational* process for addressing health needs of a community consists of the following steps:

1. *Defining the Needs.* Ideally, this is an epidemiological exploration and analysis of the distribution and health needs of the population at risk. Valuable information for this purpose can be obtained or derived from census data, surveys by the National Center for Health Statistics, studies by health planning agencies, local government, or other sources.

2. *Identifying and Evaluating the Resources.* An inventory of facilities and personnel, and financial and other resources available to the community of solution are compiled.

3. *Presentation and Review of Feasible Solutions.* Medical, economic, social, environmental, and political constraints are reviewed.

4. *Developing a Plan.* Needs and resources are matched. A plan comprises statements of goals and objectives, as well as proposed organization, deployment of available resources, and generation of new resources, to achieve these goals.

5. *Obtaining Political Acceptance of the Plan.* The transmission of information in a manner which enhances the plan's chances

of acceptance by those whose control community resources can lead to adoption.

6. *Implementing the Program.* Essentially, this is the job of program administrators, who may be employed by the agencies making the decisions, as in many state and local programs, or by the private sector, whose employees and institutions may be offered incentives and rewards to implement needed programs.

7. *Program Regulation and Evaluation.* This is implicit in the planning process, in order to maintain the purpose of the program.

The Case of Long-Term Care

The need to provide appropriate long-term care is considered by many to be the biggest and most difficult health issue of our time (Kingson and Scheffler, 1981; Somers, 1982). Long-term care may be needed by people of all age groups; the need, however, is greatest among the elderly, and particularly among the very old.

Chronic diseases and their accompanying disabilities are the epidemics of today. Thus the delivery of long-term care is reviewed here to illustrate public health approaches to a community health problem. The important issues in long-term care have been discussed in greater depth in a number of excellent reviews (Pollak, 1978; Kane and Kane, 1980; Vladeck, 1980; U.S. Health Care Financing Administration, 1981).

Lowy has defined long-term care as consisting of "those services designed to offer diagnostic, preventive, therapeutic, rehabilitative, supportive, and maintenance services for individuals of all age groups who have chronic physical, developmental, or emotional impairments. This care is provided in a variety of institutional and non-institutional, health and social care settings, including the home, with the goal of promoting the optimal level of physical, social, and psychological functioning" (Lowy, 1980, p. 100).

Although it is estimated that 5 percent of people aged 65 and over are in long-term care institutions at any one time, 20 to 25 percent of old people are likely to be in a long-term institution at some time before they die (Dunlop, 1976). In addition, in a national probability survey in 1975, it was found that 14 percent of non-institutionalized people aged 65 and over had severe levels of disability and were being taken care of by their families, friends, and neighbors (Shanas, 1979). Only a lesser part of long-term care, therefore, is provided in institutions such as nursing homes.

As seen in Chapter 1, human survival curves are becoming more rectangular in shape—people are living longer on the average, even though the ultimate span of life seems not to be increasing. This means that more people are living into the eighth, ninth, and tenth decades, with inevitable increase in frailty and dependence. Assuming this trend will continue in the coming decades, there will be even greater need for long-term care, particularly for the very old and frail.

Despite this increase in survival, the application of the community health planning models outlined above can do much to ensure timely care in appropriate settings, postpone dependency, and control the need for long-term care in institutions. Strategies to achieve this objective are outlined below.

Strategies for Appropriate Long-Term Care

Postponement or Avoidance of Long-Term Disability. Much disability and dependence in old age can be postponed or eliminated by health promotive measures applied earlier in life. To this end, public policies should promote physical fitness programs, opportunities for meaningful work and recreation, nutrition education and food subsidization, preretirement programs, and similar strategies. Likewise, encouraging preventive programs against disease by education about the harmful effects of smoking, physical inactivity, and excessive drinking can lead to a healthier old age. In treating disease, much education is needed to counteract such matters as ignorance about the pharmacological action of prescribed and non-prescribed drugs, and the dangers of wonder cures for cancer, arthritis, and other diseases which resist conventional medical treatment. In dissemination of information which helps people to prolong their years of good health, official health agencies such as health departments, and voluntary organizations such as the American Heart Association and the American Cancer Society, have major roles to play. (See Chapters 5 and 6.)

Provision of a Comprehensive Range of Alternatives. Because there is a large variety of situations facing frail, older people and their families, what is needed is the availability of a wide range of options to best meet these individual situations. Of paramount importance is accessibility to good primary care (Somers, 1982), as well as referral to other appropriate social and medical services.

An effective planning authority is essential for the rational analysis of health needs, for the allocation of resources, and for implementing or insuring implementation of goals.

Strengthening Informal Social Support Systems. Natural social support systems can be assisted in maintaining and strengthening their function of supporting relatives, friends, and neighbors with disability. This is a most important strategy, not only because it builds upon a pre-existing natural structure, but because long-term institutional care is as often the result of the inability of the social support system to continue to cope as it is of the need for medical care. Admission to nursing homes is often precipitated by the illness or death of the caretaking spouse.

The informal support system can be more effective through the following strategies:

1. *Education of the Public.* Training in ways to manage elderly parents is an important aid to troubled families. Numerous books have been written to assist the families of disabled elderly (e.g., Silverstone and Hyman, 1981; Gray and McKenzie, 1980).

2. *Organized Agency Outreach.* Official and voluntary health and social service agencies can assist families in maintaining elderly parents at home by supplying homemakers, chore workers, bedside nursing, and meal services. Other important services include the provision of fuel in winter, insulation of houses, home repair, installation of ramps, and other assistance for continuation of living at home.

3. *Integration of Formal and Informal Support Systems.* This is a fairly recent innovation which has steadily increased. Some informal support groups have actually been organized by formal agencies to extend their role and ease the function of family support by supporting these supporters. Examples include the community support groups developed in New York City (Community Service Society of New York, 1981) and the mutual support groups organized by the Alzheimer Disease and Related Disorders Association, as well as many others. The hospice movement in the United States is a striking example of support groups organized to assist families in dealing with terminal care of a family member.

4. *Respite Care.* Services of various kinds have been well developed in Britain, and could be usefully developed in the United States as a way of helping families cope with the continuing burden of a disabled family member.

a. *Home Helps* are one of the most popular forms of respite care. They may relieve the caregiver or assist an elderly person living alone, for a specified number of hours a week. A special type of home help is the "night watch," who is available on a recurring basis for one or more nights a week to stay overnight with a difficult family member, thus enabling family members to enjoy a good night's sleep. Night watchers may also be used during the period of transition after discharge from hospital to home when the patient needs assistance to tide him over the early period of recuperation.

b. *Adult Day Care Centers* for the elderly are another form of respite care. These are available in some communities in the United States, but, being poorly supported by public funds, are insufficient in number. Day care centers and day hospitals (almost unknown in the U.S.) can also render services enabling families to cope with the needs of disabled elderly members (Weiler and Rathbone-McCuan, 1978). In Britain, day care centers (and day hospitals) provide, among other services, regular podiatry services. Podiatry services, essential to ambulation of the elderly, are a much neglected service in the U.S.

c. *Temporary Admission* to a nursing home or other institution is another method whereby respite can be given to caregivers so that they might enjoy a needed vacation or undertake an important business trip. This method of support is currently being used in the United States, but is available only to families who can afford such services. If the program were made available to those less affluent, many more families could continue the burden of caring for disabled elderly relatives. Respite admissions have been used for a number of years in the United Kingdom (Robertson et al., 1977). This type of respite is also used by psychiatrists who are treating disoriented patients in need of psychiatric care, but whose care can be shared with family members (Salber and Phillips, 1980, p. 34; Arie, 1981). Admissions for respite care can be planned on a regularly recurring basis, for example, a week in each month. In this way expensive institutional beds can serve several times the number of patients who might otherwise occupy these beds on a permanent basis. To work efficiently, however, the service has to be responsive to cries for help without long waiting periods before admission. "If a service is sluggish or niggardly in its responses people will invariably make more strident demands and generate 'crises' in order to provoke the services to action" (Arie, 1981, p. 30.).

5. *Checking Systems* of various types, first developed in Great Britain, have been shown to be effective and are being used in some locations in the U.S. One type is an electronic device which alerts people in a central office if an elderly person living alone falls or becomes unconscious. Not only does this system help in situations of actual emergency; it increases the confidence of persons living alone to know that help will come if needed (McCann, 1981). Telephone reassurance services are another type of checking system.

6. *Assistance with Incontinence* can provide immense relief to families. Incontinence is often the straw that breaks the camel's back and convinces the family that the old person has to be institutionalized. Several methods can be used to reduce this burden. In Britain a number of local authorities have been providing an "incontinence laundry service." In this service soiled linen is collected on a regular basis by the local authority, laundered in the hospital's laundry, and fresh, clean linen is delivered to the home (Salber and Phillips, 1980, p. 74). A great deal of emphasis is placed on the need for nurses and physicians to be more aware of methods for controlling incontinence through training of the patient and his or her caretakers, and/or in the use of appropriate devices. Specially trained and equipped "incontinence nurses" have been used to spread this knowledge and teach the skills needed.

7. *Financial Incentives* have been used to assist in maintaining old people at home. The most commonly recommended incentive, in partial use, is the tax rebate which subsidizes families who take care of disabled members. However, much more can be done in this area to encourage families to continue the care of older persons at home. At present, while there is little or no incentive, there are sometimes disincentives for continuing care at home. For example, Medicaid in most states covers the total costs of caring for the patient (including food and shelter) in a nursing home, but in the home setting there are severe limitations on the use of physicians and medications and most expenses must be paid by the family.

Continuity of Care. Access to primary care for all older people has been emphasized by Somers (1982). Primary care, as mentioned earlier, includes the provision of preventive as well as long-term services for chronic disability. However, in addition to providing access to the system, primary care should insure continuity between the various modalities of service, a function which is needed especially by elderly people with chronic illnesses. Primary care probably can be best furnished by a solo physician who cares for his patient, in both senses of the word. However, a well-organized group practice, such as health maintenance organization (HMO), can also efficiently provide these kinds of services. The federal government has recently funded a demonstration project to test the feasibility of social health maintenance organizations that combine acute and long-term health care and social services for the elderly (Diamond and Berman, 1981). The HMO has great potential for maintaining continuity of care.

A Supportive Environment. Ways in which the environment can be made safe for vulnerable people such as the elderly have been described in Chapters 4 and 5. Here it is only necessary to add that because of the increasing number of older people in the community, if for no other reason, we should be more aware of the need to design micro- and macro-environments in such a way as to reduce hazards and barriers to comfortable living. Engineers, architects, town planners, and others can make major contributions to creating a more comfortable living environment for disabled people and thus make it easier for the frail to continue living at home.

Included in this environment should be planned access to shopping, health care facilities, and other amenities of life. Where services cannot be brought to the residence of older people, transportation linkages between their homes and these resources should be furnished. Services that must be made more widely available are congregate feeding, health screening by nurses, alarm systems in case of emergency, and the like.

Provision of a range of appropriate, alternative kinds of housing for the elderly is of paramount importance in maintaining their independence (Acheson, 1982). While it is true that a high proportion of older people own their own homes, it is also true that these homes are often in poor condition (see Chapter 5). In addition to independent housing units for healthy older people, there is need for a variety of types of accommodation which can facilitate continuing independence or semi-independence for the more frail elderly.

In-Home Services. Most chronically ill elderly, if given the choice, would remain in their own homes rather than move to a nursing home or other long-term care facility. (Bell, 1973). Since physicians' house calls are rare, professionally trained nurses, including geriatric nurse practitioners, could make home visits to administer needed medical care and to supervise other care givers, thereby prolonging independent living. Home health agencies, certified under Medicare and Medicaid, not only provide in-home skilled nursing, but make available such services as physical, occupational, or speech therapy, social services, and care by home health aides. Homemaker and chore services, permitted under Title III of the Older Americans Act and Title XX of the Social Security Act, are invaluable in assisting the chronically ill older person with the activities of daily life, but are not as available as they should be.

In many cases, in-home services are less expensive than institutional care, particularly when institutional care is used as a substitute for unavailable social, as opposed to medical, support (Doherty et al., 1978; Hammond, 1979). However, in calculating the cost of in-home services, it is essential to specify whether or not costs include the expense of maintaining the patient at home. There is also evidence that, in many cases, there is the potential for such services to improve outcomes of care such as health functioning abilities, independence, and life satisfaction of the elderly (Doherty et al., 1978; Mitchell, 1978; Skellie, 1979).

Long-Term Institutional Care. It is clear that a range of options should also be available for people who for medical or social reasons can no longer live in their own homes in the community, either alone, with their families, or with substitute families. Home care is not *invariably* better than institutional care. Constant nursing or medical needs, or extremely unfavorable physical and social home conditions, may make institutionalization the better choice. Psychological or even physical abuse or neglect of old people at home is not as rare as one would hope.

The spectrum of institutions and levels of care should range from boarding homes for the elderly where shelter and meals are provided, but with only a minimum of health care, to intermediate care and skilled nursing facilities where various levels of medical and nursing care are provided. Ease of movement between these levels of care, as appropriate, needs to be assured.

For people who prefer to be in an age-segregated and very

comfortable environment, these modalities of care can all be supplied as required in a multilevel retirement center. At present such resources are accessible almost exclusively to middle and upper income groups; they could and should be made available to a wider segment of society.

When older people are institutionalized, it is important that there be ready access to the family and community at large. When the need arises, linkages to other parts of the medical system should be available, and financial or professional barriers should not stand in the way of necessary transfer. It has been shown that when nursing home beds are fully occupied there is resistance from providers of care to accepting patients with heavy nursing needs (Robbins, 1982). Financial incentives should be available to facilitate such transfer when patients are occupying more expensive hospital beds for administrative rather than medical reasons.

Financing Long-Term Care. In addition to all the service-delivery problems of long-term care, there is deepening concern about the cost of such care. Particularly expensive, of course, is in-patient long-term care, which is mainly provided in intermediate care facilities, skilled nursing facilities, and long-term hospitals. Relatively small sums of public money are spent on other types of long-term care.

Costs of care are shared mainly by the individual or family, and government. Relatively little Medicare money (1.6 percent in 1981) is spent on nursing home care; but 44 percent of Medicaid money was used to pay for such care (White House Conference Report, 1982, p. 73). Since Medicaid is limited to the poor, it follows that a high proportion of people in nursing homes, especially if their stay is long, will be paupers. In fact, many people enter nursing homes on private pay, but become pauperized after a period because of the high costs.

Medicare and Medicaid spent only 2.2 and 1.0 percent of their funds, respectively, on home care in 1978 (White House Conference Report, 1982, p. 85). Very few people have private insurance that covers long-term care of any kind.

The costs of long-term care are high, no matter where delivered, and especially if the care is adequate and of high quality. But no system of comprehensive services can be planned and delivered without attention to the financing of services.

Conclusion

If all of the strategies discussed above are to be employed in order to improve the availability and utilization of needed resources by the elderly, and for that matter by people of all age groups, it is evident that we have to increase the role of collective action, while at the same time maintaining the very important responsibility of individuals and agencies in meeting the needs of our nation. Thus far we have not done as much as we could and should to meet the long-term care needs of our chronically disabled and frail. All the resources needed for an effective, efficient, and humane approach should work in unison, rather than in competition with each other. Doing better entails a strong partnership at the community level, "community" being broadly interpreted to mean the community of solution.

References

Acheson, E. D. The impending crisis of old age: a challenge to ingenuity. *The Lancet,* Sept. 11, 1982, 592–594.

Arie, T. The demented patient: making services work. In Wilson, J. M. G., (Ed.), *Conference. Appropriate Care for the Elderly: Some Problems.* Edinburgh, Scotland: Royal College of Physicians, 1981, pp. 27–31.

Bell, W. G. Community care for the elderly: an alternative to institutionalization. *The Gerontologist,* 1973, *13,* 349–354.

Brickner, P. W. *Home Health Care for the Aged.* New York, N.Y.: Appleton-Century Crofts, 1978.

Brody, E.M. A million procrustean beds. *The Gerontologist,* 1973, *13,* 430–435.

Cohen, K. P. *Hospice.* Germantown, Md.: Aspen Systems Corporation, 1979.

Community Service Society of New York. *Strengthening Informal Supports for the Aging.* New York, N.Y.: Community Service Society, 1981.

Diamond, L. M. and Berman, D. E. The Social/Health Maintenance Organization: A single entry prepaid long-term care system. In Callahan, J. J., and Wallack, S. S. (Eds.), *Reforming the Long-Term-Care System.* Lexington, Ma.: D. C. Heath and Co., 1981, pp. 185–213.

Doherty, N., Segal, J., and Hicks, B. Alternatives to institutionalization for the aged: viability and cost effectiveness. *Aged Care and Services Review,* 1978, *1,* 1–16.

Dunlop, B. D. Need for and utilization of long-term care among elderly Americans. *Journal of Chronic Disease,* 1976, *29,* 75–87.

Furukawa, C. and Shomaker, D. *Community Health Services for the Aged.* Rockville, Md.: Aspen, 1982.

Gelfand, D. E. and Olsen, J. K. *The Aging Network: Programs and Services.* New York, N.Y.: Springer Publishing Co., 1980.

Gray, J. A. M., and McKenzie, H. *Taking Care of Your Elderly Relative.* Boston, Ma.: Allen and Unwin, 1980.

Hammond, J. Home health care cost effectiveness: an overview of the literature. *Public Health Reports,* 1979, *94,* 305–311.

Kane, R. L. and Kane, R. A. Long-term care: can our society meet the needs of its elderly? In *Annual Review of Public Health, Vol. I.* Palo Alto, Ca.: Annual Reviews, 1980, pp. 227–253.

Kingson, E. R. and Scheffler, R. M. Aging: issues and economic trends for the 1980s. *Inquiry,* 1981, *18,* 197–213.

Lee, D. R. and Estes, C. L. Eighty federal programs for the elderly. In C. L. Estes, *The Aging Enterprise.* San Francisco, Ca.: Jossey-Bass Publishing Co., 1979, pp. 76–117.

Lowy, L. *Social Policies and Programs on Aging.* Lexington, Ma.: D. C. Heath and Co., 1980.

Madison, D. L. The Case for Community-Oriented Primary Care. *Journal of the American Medical Association,* 1983, *249,* 1279–1282.

McCann, J. Implications for the future. a panel discussion. In Wilson, J. M. G. (Ed.), *Appropriate Care for the Elderly: Some Problems.* Edinburgh, Scotland: Royal College of Physicians, 1981, pp. 86–87.

Mitchell, J. B. Patient outcomes in alternative long-term care settings. *Medical Care,* 1978, *16,* 439–452.

Pollak, W. Long term care. In Feder, J., Halahan, J., and Armor, T. M. (Eds.), *National Health Insurance: Conflicting Goals and Policy Choices.* Washington, D.C.: The Urban Institute, 1978, pp. 475–520.

Robbins, F. D. A study of discharge delays in Rhode Island hospitals. *Pride Institute Journal of Long Term Home Health Care,* 1982, 5–11.

Robertson, D. R., Griffiths, A., and Cosin, L. Z. A community based continuing care program for the elderly disabled. *Journal of Gerontology,* 1977, *32,* 334–339.

Salber, E. J. and Phillips, H. T. *Services to the Elderly in England: Impressions from a Sabbatical.* Chapel Hill, N.C.: Department of Health Administration, University of North Carolina, 1980.

Shanas, E. The family as a social support-system. *The Gerontologist,* 1979, *19,* 169–174.

Silverstone, B. and Hyman, H. K. *You and Your Aging Parent.* New York, N.Y.: Pantheon Books, 1981.

Skellie, F. A., The impact of alternatives to nursing home care. *Journal of the American Health Care Association,* 1979, *5,* 46–53.

Somers, A. R. Long-term care for the elderly and disabled. *The New England Journal of Medicine,* 1982, *307,* 221–226.

U.S. Health Care Financing Administration. *Long Term Care: Back-*

ground and Future Directions. Washington, D.C.: U.S. Department of Health and Human Services, No. HCFA 81–20047, 1981.

U.S. House of Representatives, Subcommittee on Human Services of Select Committee on Aging. *Future Directions for Aging Policy: A Human Service Model*. Washington, D.C.: U.S. Government Printing Office, 1980.

Vladeck, B. C. *Unloving Care: The Nursing Home Tragedy*. New York, N.Y.: Basic Books, 1980.

Weiler, P. G. and Rathbone-McCuan, E. *Adult Day Care: Community Work with the Elderly*. New York, N.Y.: Springer Publishing Co., 1978.

Weissert, W. G., Wan, T. H. H., Livieratos, B. B., and Katz, S. Cost-effectiveness of home-maker services for the chronically ill. *Inquiry*, 1980, *17*, 230–243.

White House Conference. *Final Report of the 1981 White House Conference on Aging*, Vol. 1. Washington, D.C.: U.S. Government Printing Office, 1982.

8

Interorganizational Coordination of Services to the Elderly

ARNOLD D. KALUZNY AND BRUCE J. FRIED

Introduction

Health care delivery in the United States has often been described as a confusing and expensive patchwork of uncoordinated services resulting in multiple service gaps and duplication. Among the factors contributing to this situation are fragmentation of funding sources, the competitive nature of our society, the high value placed on individualism and personal freedom, and, perhaps most important, the growth of health technology leading to specialization of personnel and agencies. In attempts to gain maximum efficiency, we have often failed to build connective links which would provide a more organized, comprehensive, and perhaps effective service delivery system. Achieving and assuring such linkages should be a major goal for health services managers. Implementing the concept of coordination represents a major challenge to those involved in the delivery of health and human services.

Researchers and health service managers, using ideas and findings derived from organizational theory, are attempting to deal with the theoretical and practical implications of coordinating health care delivery. The objective of this chapter is to review the status of coordination of health care services, with special emphasis on services to the elderly. First, we define coordination, with consideration of its various forms and rationale, as well as the political context within which coordination must occur. Next we describe the barriers to effective coordination. The chapter concludes with guidelines for enhancing efforts to achieve coordinated services for the elderly.

What Is Coordination?

Coordination is usually defined as a process that occurs *within* organizations and which involves integrating or linking together different components of an organization to accomplish a collective set of tasks and goals (Mintzberg, 1979). For example, a hospital or nursing home must coordinate the activities of its nursing staff with those of the dietary and other departments and units. Without coordination, each subunit of the organization would function as if it were a totally independent entity, rather than part of a complex dynamic social system. The result would be inefficiency, if not collapse, of the organization.

In regarding the community as the unit of public health practice, coordination is seen as an *interorganizational process*. The purpose of interorganizational coordination is to promote the effective and efficient delivery of services through collaboration of a number of different organizations. As will be shown, such an approach is particularly relevant to providing health services to the elderly, for whom the services of several different agencies are often required.

Why Coordination Is Important

In the commercial world, market forces such as competition and the need to make a profit provide major incentives or disincentives for production of goods and services. However, in the provision of social programs such as services to the elderly, market forces are usually not applicable. Here, a high value is placed upon the availability and efficient use of a comprehensive range of services to meet the special needs of the population. Coordination is an intermediate goal for implementing these programs.

In recent years, strong political pressures have developed in response to the growing demand that the elderly be treated whenever possible in the community rather than in institutions. Congress has recently responded in numerous ways by modifying existing laws such as Medicare and Medicaid. Despite these efforts, often very expensive to both patient and taxpayer, services to the elderly continue to be structured in a largely unplanned, piecemeal fashion. Four major defects in services persist—fragmentation, unnecessary duplication, gaps in services, and inaccessibility (Marmor and Kutza, 1975); these are discussed below.

Fragmentation. Frail elderly people, especially the chronically ill, often need a broad spectrum of services to meet their needs. In addition to primary medical care, at times they may require hospitalization for acute episodes of illness, care in a long-term facility, home-care services, social services, or assistance with housing or transportation. They may need access to these services over a short period of time; or as their condition changes over weeks or months, they may need adjustments to their services over a longer period.

Single agencies, generally for very good reasons, cannot provide the whole spectrum of services for their patients or clients. Consequently, linkages and transfers have to be made which, even under the best of circumstances, are not easy for either the agency or patient to make. Community agencies often do not have the capacity or the incentive to ensure that the patient's needs are met by the most appropriate service; doing so can be costly in terms of effort, time, and money. Moreover, it may be difficult or impossible to provide the appropriate kind of care because the person is not eligible for the service on grounds of age, income level, or kinds of services needed, and consequently the agency would not be able to receive third-party reimbursement.

Duplication of Services. Duplication arises when a number of different agencies in a community provide the same services, or perform the same function. Some degree of duplication of commonly used services, such as primary health care, may be justifiable to satisfy the goal of accessibility. Minimizing excessive duplication improves service efficiency and effectiveness, but what is excessive is difficult to define without certain value assumptions. For example, one must determine an acceptable standard for travel to primary medical care. What is considered duplication by one standard may in fact be viewed as increasing accessibility by another standard. The determination of whether a service system is duplicative is thus partially dependent on the political posture and value assumptions of the observer.

Joint decision making among providers offers one approach to reducing excessive duplication and enhancing efficient resource allocation. This strategy assumes the existence of a cooperative spirit among organizations and the realization that organizations may benefit from a more efficient use of resources (Aiken and Hage, 1968). While joint decision making may limit the autonomy of individual organizations, it usually enhances the overall collective impact of the participating organizations as they compete for limited resources in the community.

Service Gaps. Gaps become an issue when services needed in a community are not available. Several factors contribute to this problem, including the lack of available funds or personnel as well as appropriate incentives to initiate and maintain needed services. An important issue in this area is the degree to which communities of differing sizes should provide various modalities of care. For example, the efficiency of small rural hospitals comes into question here. Another concern is related to problems inherent in attempting to combine private enterprise and the profit motive with public priorities and goals. Incongruity between public and private interests is a matter of ongoing policy debate.

Because of the fragmented nature of services, the existence of gaps is often unknown or overlooked for extensive periods of time. Providers and consumers may assume the existence of certain services which in reality do not exist, or they may assume that nothing can be done to alleviate the situation and so make do with what is available. Periodic needs-assessment and service inventories are important approaches to identifying service gaps and providing needed services.

Inaccessibility or Difficulty in Procuring Services. Inaccessibility of services is a problem for many people, but it is especially crucial for the elderly for two reasons. First, the elderly often have problems with physical mobility. Thus, even if services are available in the community, conventional transportation is often of limited use. There may also be barriers due to architecture and limited hours of service. Second, service organizations often view the elderly as nonfavored recipients of services (Tobin et al., 1976). Nonfavored status may be due to the financial status of patients, to cultural differences often involving language barriers, and to providers' perceiving patient expectations as unrealistic. Providers may also find the physical setting in which health services are delivered or the financial arrangements unattractive, as in the case of nursing homes. These factors may decrease accessibility to needed services.

To lessen the problem, consideration needs to be given to establishing more formal coordinating mechanisms between service organizations. Specifically, formal agreements may be required mandating one agency to accept certain clients of other agencies under specific financial and other terms. Formal arrangements could facilitate access and result in improved services for clients.

Other responses to the problem of inaccessibility are a function of situational factors (Marmor and Kutza, 1975). These include provision of necessary information through information and referral services when lack of information is the problem; the provision of a case manager or ombudsman to guide the individual through the system when lack of access is a function of complexity; and the development of multipurpose neighborhood service centers (co-location of services) when inaccessibility is a function of distance.

Political Context of Coordination

A decision to initiate an interorganizational coordinative strategy is a major policy choice in the provision of services to the elderly. Whether such a decision is made at the local, state, or national level, coordinative initiatives may involve reallocation of resources from other important activities, particularly from the provision of direct services. For example, a hospital that decides to divert scarce resources from patient care activities to coordination functions, such as the decision to establish a local coordinating council or to hire a nurse or social worker to coordinate patient referrals, may in fact reduce the amount of direct patient care that a community hospital provides, and consequently reduce the income of the institution. Obviously, coordination is not merely an ancillary concern but may involve substantial opportunity costs. Therefore, it is important to consider the costs and benefits of coordination to organizations, and the incentives and disincentives they face.

The Older Americans Act (U.S. House of Representatives, 1978) mandates coordination as a major function of health service delivery systems. However, the law is diffuse and ambiguous with little guidance in the legislation or regulations to aid local area agencies in operationalizing the concept. As an example of the "new federalism," the Older Americans Act favors decentralization of decision making and resource allocation. Estes (1979, p. 37) argues that this strategy enabled President Nixon to channel the demands of special interest groups to local governments; by mandating coordination of services at the local level, the federal government sought to alleviate pressures from powerful interest groups at the national level.

Local provider agencies may support the notion of coordination for their own strategic reasons (Marmor and Kutza, 1975). For example, well-established coordinative strategies reaffirm the local agencies' virtually exclusive claim to their respective domains, thus protecting agencies from competitors by institutionalizing domains and interrelationships. Similarly, local agency concern about coordination implicitly assumes that the types of services currently provided are adequate and appropriate, and that radically different services are not required. This latter concern has received considerable attention from critics who claim that current policies and programs are based on a social construction of reality which views the elderly as sick, dependent, and troublesome. Estes (1979, pp. 24–26) for example, argues that the programs of the 1960s and 1970s, including those supported by the Older Americans Act, function as social control mechanisms to maintain the elderly in a dependent state and divert attention from more substantive problems requiring a redistribution of income. It is suggested that programs for the elderly proliferate as a result of pressures from professional groups rather than the client population. According to Estes, the Older Americans Act places the

> ... professional perspectives and interest of planners and providers between the problems experienced by the aged ... and the amelioration of those problems, and it proposes that the appropriate intervention strategy is planning-coordination-bureaucratic reform, not structural reforms that might threaten the beneficiaries of current political and economic arrangements (Estes, 1979, p. 19).

This provider orientation is reinforced by the manner in which coordinative strategies have been evaluated. Typically, such measures as degree of interaction between actors in the system, involvement of other individuals and organizations, cross-referral of clients, joint efforts in service delivery, and the extent to which services match needs have been used in assessing the success of coordination. These measures provide little information about the actual improvements in the system of delivering services for the elderly (Estes, 1979, p. 125). Needless to say, they tell us even less about the impact of coordinative strategies on client satisfaction and well-being (i.e., outcomes), which are the ultimate measures of program effectiveness.

Barriers to Coordination

Why is it difficult to achieve coordination among the various organizations providing services to the elderly? The need is great and legislation advocates mechanisms for coordination of programs and agencies. What factors at the local, state, and national level inhibit coordinative efforts?

National Legislative Problems

The Older Americans Act assumed that better coordination of services to the elderly would lead to increased effectiveness of services and subsequent improvement in the quality of life for the elderly. Local Area Agencies on Aging were established to accomplish the coordinative task. The fundamental problem with this approach lies in the fact that a local planning agency is charged with the responsibility of establishing effective and efficient procedures for coordination between numerous programs, each of which is responsible to different and sometimes multiple constituencies. Furthermore, programs are usually financed by a variety of funding sources, each with its own particular accountability requirements. For example, an Area Agency on Aging may need to coordinate with other federally mandated programs such as a community mental health center (accountable to the National Institute of Mental Health); Title V employment programs (accountable to the Department of Labor); and a housing authority (accountable to one or more divisions in the Department of Housing and Urban Development). Moreover, federal programs are typically organized on a categorical rather than a client-centered or functional basis. On the local level, federal programs frequently have different eligibility criteria for service recipients. Some criteria are based on age alone; others, on income; yet still others on age and income. Attempting to assure continuity of care in such an environment is likely to frustrate a local coordinating agency.

Further complicating the problem, Area Agencies on Aging

also received the mandate to establish mechanisms to coordinate non-federal programs serving the elderly, including services of hospitals, nursing homes, home health agencies, and other proprietary and non-profit programs—all with allegiances and values of their own.

Area Agencies on Aging were provided with little power to facilitate the process of coordination. The coordinative component of the Older Americans Act defines coordination loosely and ambiguously, and gives Area Agencies no authority to enforce coordination; it thus may be viewed as largely symbolic. Coordination under these conditions does not necessarily provide either a statement of or a solution to the problem, but it may be a way of avoiding both when accurate prescription would be too painful (Pressman and Wildavsky, 1973, p. 134).

The basic problem in this situation is the lack of a clear national policy on aging. By placing responsibility for planning and coordination at the local level, the federal government avoids making politically high-risk decisions. Local coordinating agencies are left without guidance, power, or even the means of evaluating their coordinative initiatives. In a study of Area Agency directors, Tobin et al. (1976) found that directors viewed the following terms used in the Act to be ambiguous: effectiveness, linkage of services, pooling untapped resources, comprehensiveness, coordinated services, gap filling, and monitoring. Such vagueness poses enormous problems for Area Agencies on Aging.

Organizational Barriers to Coordination

Organizations seek to obtain an adequate supply of resources from the environment (Yuchtman and Seashore, 1967). This is essentially a strategy of survival, for without funds, materials, personnel, information, and clients, human service organizations cannot function. The extent to which an organization must procure these resources from other organizations determines in part the nature and degree of its interactions with other organizations. Theoretically, were all the essential elements in infinite supply there would be little need for organizational interaction and cooperation as an ideal (Levine and White, 1961). In reality, however, resources and time are limited and organizations must obtain needed resources from the environment, i.e., other organizations. One perspective suggests that organizations exist to meet their own goals, and that the extent of coordination with other organizations is directly related to the degree to which such interactions will further these goals. Thus, an organization's effectiveness is dependent upon its ability to use its environment in the acquisition of scarce and valued resources (Yuchtman and Seashore, 1967; Pfeffer and Salancik, 1978).

In order to acquire resources from the environment, organizations engage in a process of exchange. The process of exchange lies in any voluntary activity between two or more organizations, which has consequences, actual or anticipated, for the realization of their respective goals or objectives (Levine and White, 1961). This view has a very rational tone, and one might suppose that because organizations are interdependent, they will interact and coordinate their activities. However, the fundamental problem remains: What happens when the individual organizations in an interorganizational network function effectively (i.e., they have each acquired all the inputs required for performing their functions), but the system of service delivery is ineffective? "Market failure" in economics presents a simple analog for interorganizational analysis: various components, or all components as a whole, may be ineffective; that is, the degree of interaction or coordination among organizations may be optimal for specific organizations, yet suboptimal for the system as a whole. Instead of choosing to cooperate, organizations may decide to refrain from doing so, or actively resist cooperation.

To understand the process by which organizations choose whether or not to cooperate, it is necessary to explore the motivations that organization managers face. Benson (1973) describes administrators as seeking resources to satisfy four action orientations: (1) fulfillment of program requirements, (2) achievement of domain consensus, (3) maintenance of resource flows, and (4) promotion and defense of the agency perspective. Each factor bears heavily on organizations' willingness to coordinate, as discussed below.

First, administrators work toward *fulfillment of program requirements*. Organizations are primarily oriented to maintenance of order and effectiveness in their established programs. Thus, agency administrators are often reluctant to undertake tasks or to tolerate practices of other agencies which interfere with the fulfillment of current programs. For example, an organization whose eligibility criteria are age and income-related would not suddenly accept all elderly clients simply because such change is in the interests of the service-delivery network (and clients). Such a change would be highly disruptive to the internal functioning of the agency.

A second motivational orientation of program administrators is the striving toward maintenance of a *domain consensus* for the organization—that is, the agency's goals and services are agreed upon by other agencies in the network. Organizational domain refers to claims which an organization stakes out for itself in terms of problem or disease covered, population served, and services rendered (Levine et al., 1963), and is characterized by one or more of the following attributes: (a) exclusiveness—a claim untrammelled, unchallenged by other organizations; (b) autonomy—a claim permitting the performance of activities independently, without supervision, direction, or shared authority by another agency; (c) dominance—a claim permitting authoritative direction of other agencies operating in a specific sphere (Benson, 1973).

By their very nature, coordinative activities threaten the domain of some or all participating organizations. Where there is domain consensus the chances of successful coordination are enhanced. If agreement on each organization's domain is not established, coordinative strategies will likely fail (Van de Ven, 1976).

Besides posing barriers to coordination, domain dissensus also leads to competition or conflict among agencies. Conflict may arise either because one organization invades the turf of another, or because one organization judges that another organization is not doing as much as it should (Levine et al., 1963).

Issues of domain have been particularly troublesome in service delivery to the elderly. For example, conflicts between agencies which provide homemakers and home health aides have not been uncommon. Other conflicts have been noted between Area Agencies on Aging personnel and Title XX staff members over the delivery of social services. These conflicts exist not only on the local level, but may be traced to state and federal levels, where conflict over domain is a chronic problem.

Administrators work toward maintenance of orderly, reliable patterns of *resource flow*. Where there is uncertainty in the supply of resources, organizations are typically mistrusting and reluctant to engage in coordinative activities. The following discussion of an unsuccessful attempt at building a coordinated geriatric health system illustrates the problem:

The health center, hospital, and nursing home existed within the context of a larger environment that surrounded and affected their relationship. The environment of the organizations was continually changing, at increasing rates and towards greater complexity, thereby creating the stress of uncertainty . . . The intensity of each organization's effort to adapt to an uncertain environment had a cumulative effect on the outcome of the organizational relationship. (Bleiweiss and Simson, 1976, pp. 150–151).

In short, environmental uncertainty is a constraining factor in the development of coordinative relationships among agencies.

Administrators promote the *application and defense of the agency's perspective* and defend the organization's way of doing things. One negative outcome of this defensive posture is interprofessional and professional-lay conflicts. A classic study of coordination among health and welfare agencies by Levine et al. (1963) still has relevance today. For example, they found strong conflict between professionally trained social workers and those staff members with no formal training who were called social workers. They also found intraprofessional conflict arising from organizational affiliation, which influenced professional roles:

In some communities, trained nurses may be employed by the health department, the Visiting Nurses Association, and the school department. Professionally, these nurses might be in considerable agreement in their approach to the patient and his problems, but the respective organizations for which they work may have divergent policies regarding ways of handling the patient and of referring him to other agencies (Levine et al., 1963, p. 1193).

Bleiweiss and Simson (1976) describe the problem of service orientation with respect to coordinating services provided by a health maintenance organization (HMO), a hospital, and a nursing home in providing comprehensive care to the elderly:

The staff at the HMO and hospital were oriented to providing three levels of care—primary, secondary, and tertiary—which utilized multiple services. . . . In contrast, the staff at the nursing home was oriented toward providing nursing care in a self-contained manner that was not dependent upon outside services. These differences caused tension between the organizations' staffs. The HMO and hospital staff saw their major task as expanding and upgrading medical care. The nursing home staff perceived this medical orientation as an attempt to supplant their nursing role. The staffs could not coordinate their different orientations in order to deliver comprehensive geriatric services (Bleiweiss and Simson, 1976, pp. 149–150).

Approaches to Interorganizational Coordination: Structure and Process

Interorganizational coordination of health services to the elderly has taken numerous forms, with variability in both structure and process.

Structure

Three structural dimensions of interorganizational relations have been identified (Van de Ven, 1976): formalization, centralization, and complexity. Each is discussed below.

Formalization. Formalization refers to the degree to which rules, policies, and procedures govern the agreements between organizations (Van de Ven et al., 1979). For example, using a uniform patient record system to facilitate referrals between organizations reflects a highly formalized relationship, whereas incidental or random referral of patients between organizations not having a uniform patient record system is indicative of a less formalized, or informal relationship.

Organizations typically adapt to each other in a mutually adjusting fashion. Referral of patients, for example, is often accomplished without highly formalized arrangements between organizations. Where such procedures are insufficient to achieve the desired level of coordination, organizations may standardize the means by which patients are referred by use of common forms or other procedures. Arrangements between organizations become more formalized when they are written, contracted, or mandatory.

Centralization. Centralization refers to the locus of decision making in an interorganizational network. When organizations join together, they continue to strive towards the attainment of their individual goals. Concurrently, certain decisions affecting individual organizations are made by the collectivity of agency representatives. The extent to which this core of individuals, analogous to the board of directors in a single organization, makes decisions binding upon the member agencies determines the degree of network centralization.

Three alternative models, which vary in the degree of centralization, are presented in Figure 8.1 (adapted from Tobin et al., 1976).

1. *The hierarchical model* reflects the presence of a leading local agency that serves a coordinating function. The leading organization may receive funds to purchase services from other agencies, in which case it attains power over organizations in the network. In this instance, a highly centralized interorganizational network concentrates decision making and resource allocation in the local coordinating agency. The Triage Project was a centralized, single-entry system of care for the elderly. The Triage team assessed the needs and resources of patients who had been referred, and a member of the team contacted the appropriate service providers to initiate services. All charges were processed by Triage, which continuously monitored the quantity and quality of care provided under its auspices (Quinn, 1982).

2. The *egalitarian model* is exemplified by local planning organizations such as hospital planning councils and community human service consortia which convene agencies relevant to the planned effort. The organization serves as a catalyst or facilitator in establishing a working group of agencies, while control over consortium decision making is retained by the participating agencies. This structure represents a decentralized interorganizational network.

3. The *reciprocal model* develops in a situation in which a planning organization delegates policy making powers to its constituent agencies, but retains its leadership function. The planning agency functions as the implementor of the coordinative strategy agreed upon by participating organizations. Using the organizational analogy, the group of agencies corresponds to the board of trustees, while the planning agency represents the executive director. One might view this model as a compromise between the highly centralized hierarchical model and the decentralized egalitarian approach. For example, in many multi-hospital systems, individual hospitals retain considerable autonomy and decision making authority but allocate certain areas of responsibility to the larger corporate system (Starkweather, 1981).

Complexity. The complexity of a coordinative network refers to the number of differentiated elements that must be integrated in order for an interorganizational network to act as a unit. Two measures of structural complexity are important: the number of participating organizations and the number of different issues or tasks confronting the network.

The number of organizations involved in an interorganiza-

FIGURE 8.1   Three models of coordination

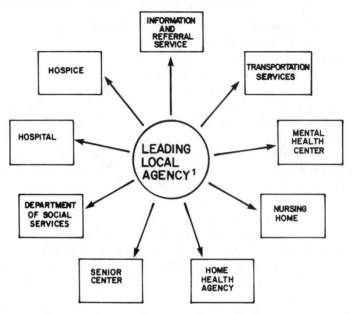

HIERARCHICAL MODEL OF COORDINATION

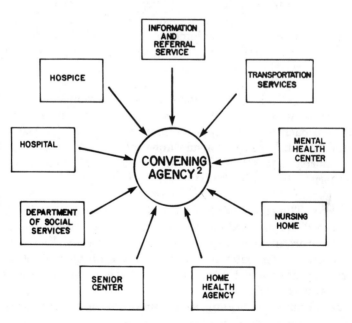

EGALITARIAN / CONSORTIUM MODEL OF COORDINATION

FIGURE 8.1, continued

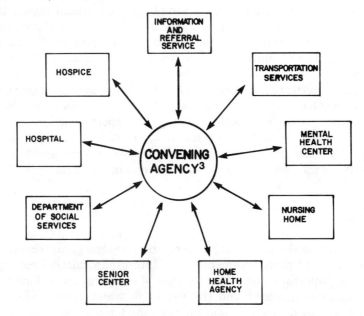

RECIPROCAL / FEDERATION MODEL OF COORDINATION

[1] FOR EXAMPLE, DEPARTMENT OF SOCIAL SERVICES, COUNCIL ON AGING

[2] FOR EXAMPLE, COUNCIL ON AGING, AREA AGENCY ON AGING

[3] FOR EXAMPLE, COUNCIL ON AGING, AREA AGENCY ON AGING

Source: Adapted from Tobin, S.S., Davidson, S.M., and Sack, A. *Effective Social Services for Older Americans.* Ann Arbor, Mi.: Institute of Gerontology, University of Michigan and Wayne State University, 1976, p. 95.

tional network is an important consideration in devising a coordinative strategy. As can be expected, the larger the number of organizations, the more complex the network, and the more difficult to manage.

In most cases, the size of the network is closely related to the second measure of structural complexity, i.e., the number of different issues or tasks on which the network is based. An interorganizational network may consist simply of two organizations that have chosen to share continuing education facilities and programs. At the other extreme, several organizations may coordinate because they are required by law to do so, or because of mutual interest or concern with a number of issues. As an example of a mandated network, an Area Agency on Aging promotes coordination of services to meet the varied and complex needs of the elderly population, such as health, housing, transportation, and safety, largely by contractual arrangements with Councils on Aging at the local level. On the other hand, resistance to the enactment of restrictive laws may unite a disparate group of agencies.

Process

In addition to the structural dimensions of interorganizational networks, several process dimensions of interorganizational coordination are important, including the flow of resources and information between organizations and the extent to which relationships between organizations are voluntary or mandated.

Resource flows involve the exchange of money, equipment, facilities, clients, and staff personnel, and are measured in terms of their direction, intensity, and variability (Van de Ven, 1976). For example, a central coordinating agency may provide grant-development consultants to constituent agencies. These agencies, in return, may pay the salaries of some of the planning agency's personnel and provide services to clients referred through the coordinating agency.

Information flows are messages or communications about the units of exchange or the nature of the relationship, transmitted between organizational parties through a variety of media, such as reports, letters, phone calls, discussions, and meetings. Information flows may be assessed in terms of direction and intensity.

Another important process dimension of interorganizational coordination is the voluntary or mandated nature of the involvement of participating organizations. Most agreements in the health and social services sector are voluntary, although there is a growing trend towards mandated relationships as programs consolidate and larger institutions achieve dominance. Development of mandated relationships implies that all participants may not be interested in interaction and may require some encouragement, if not coercion

(Raelin, 1980). In a reciprocal mandated relationship, formal agreements are established between organizations willing to participate in mutual advancement. In a legally or politically mandated network of relationships, the larger society imposes interaction on a set of organizations to achieve stated objectives. For example, the Joint Commission on Accreditation of Hospitals (JCAH) has established a written set of principles to which community mental health programs must adhere in order to receive accreditation. One requirement specifies the establishment of case management services "aimed at linking the service system to a consumer and at coordinating the various system components in order to achieve a successful outcome" (JCAH, 1976, p. 20). The skill of superordinate organizations in shaping the network may have great bearing on the probability of achieving successful coordination. Much of the current lack of coordination among providers of care can be attributed to the lack of clear and specific guidelines for coordination associated with programs such as Medicare and Medicaid.

Action Guidelines for Interorganization Coordination Strategies

Effective coordination requires a perspective that emphasizes the role of the *community* as problem solver rather than the sovereignty of individual providers and provider organizations. This perspective must also recognize the structural and procedural complexity of interorganizational relationships. From this viewpoint, delivery of appropriate and flexible services for the elderly can be effected through (a) recognizing that many providers are linked with parts of larger organizational entities—particularly at regional and/or state levels, and (b) providing services based on a detailed knowledge of each community and close cooperation of relevant providers at the community level.

The following guidelines for coordination strategies are presented as reference points for agencies and individuals interested in facilitating the process of coordination. These guidelines focus on two sets of factors: (a) characteristics of the coordinating organization and (b) characteristics of the community and its service providers. Following the discussion of these community and organizational considerations, the concept of case management is presented as a useful model for enhancing coordination among provider organizations.

While coordinating organizations are charged with the general legislative mandate to coordinate services, they differ widely in the resources and power at their disposal. At one extreme are agencies with a high degree of control over resources in that they actually fund local services, or act as entry points into the system for the elderly population. The channeling demonstration project in Connecticut, Triage (Quinn, 1982), was one example, but there are now numerous similar programs based upon the same model and supported by Medicare and Medicaid waiver arrangements. This type of coordinating organization controls the flow of clients and funds needed by service providers. In such a position an agency has a great many options for coordination. For example, if service gaps are a problem, the agency can coerce a local provider organization into expanding an existing program to include the needed services. It may also have the power to mandate certain interorganizational processes, i.e., communication and referral, and to influence the internal dynamics of participating organizations. At the other extreme are coordinating organizations with little control over needed resources. In this situation the organization attempting to institute formal coordinative mechanisms by decree will probably meet with failure. Such an organization would obtain better results through informal approaches to voluntary coordination.

There is no rule that informal relationships are less effective than formalized arrangements, although certainly the formal approach has greater stability. The basic point is that coordinating organizations should avoid overstating what is feasible, given a set of practical or political constraints. In some cases informal coordinative initiatives are the only possible options. Furthermore, interorganizational networks are dynamic entities, easily subject to deterioration, but also capable of growth and development. What begins as an incidental, informal mechanism of coordination may in fact evolve into a formal, stable relationship.

In addition to local, political, or practical constraints, coordinating agencies must consider a number of community characteristics in deciding upon a coordinative strategy. These include the following.

Goals and Purposes of Coordination

The term "coordination" too often is used without establishing feasible goals and without ensuring a clear understanding of the problems to be solved through coordinated activity. It is necessary to define the problem realistically and to articulate clearly the desired actions of organizations and individuals relevant to problem resolution. For example, if the problem is defined as inconsistent referral between the various provider agencies, the first step may be to document the situation, that is, to provide evidence of the problem, identify the organizations involved, and decide what they should do to resolve the problem.

Awareness of Other Organizations

Once the relevant organizations are identified, the coordinator determines the degree to which organizations are aware of each other's existence. If there is high mutual awareness, the coordinator should determine whether organizations tend to evaluate each other positively. Agencies are more willing to cooperate when the other organizations are positively evaluated. Affiliation with other effective organizations may in fact enhance the reputation of a given organization.

When there is a low level of knowledge about the other organizations, the coordinator may explore the reasons for this situation and develop an initial strategy aimed at ameliorating the condition. It is impossible to effectively coordinate a group of agencies that are individually unaware of services provided by other organizations in the group.

One should also explore the local history of coordination in the community as well as the current state of affairs. It is likely that some other organization has previously attempted to coordinate community services. In this case much can be learned from past mistakes and successes. Where organizations are currently coordinated in some fashion, it is usually best to build on and refine pre-existing relationships rather than to institute totally new arrangements foreign to the community or relevant organizations.

Domain Consensus

Organizations that agree on mutual service domains tend to be more receptive to coordinative initiatives. Mutual recognition of organizational areas of competence and expertise is an important prerequisite to successful coordination. Where this recognition does not exist, the coordinator should determine if the situation is competitive or if there is evidence of negative evaluation of services provided by the agencies. Either case poses serious problems for a coordinating agency. In the first instance, agencies may embark on competitive, conflictual behavior not conducive to coordination. They may be reluctant to participate in joint ventures, referral, and other cooperative arrangements. In the latter situation, organizations may be unwilling to cooperate with organizations viewed as incompetent.

Resource Dependency

Organizations are typically dependent upon their environment for resources necessary for their continued operations and survival. A high degree of resource dependency among organizations may balance out preconditions that militate against coordination and cooperation. The degree of resource dependency should be explored to see if this is a reasonable foundation on which to base a coordinating strategy. If some form of coordination is currently in progress, it is probably based on resource dependency, e.g., mutual referral, sharing of facilities. A skillful coordination effort capitalizes on interdependencies and creates additional sources of interdependency. For example, resources could be allocated among organizations such that cooperation is incumbent to assure effective use of those resources. Alternatively, a coordinating agency could explicitly define the benefits accrued to individual agencies by coordinating, e.g., additional resources or clients, or use of others' facilities.

Value Consensus

It is generally easier to achieve coordination if the organizations share a common philosophy and service orientation and have similar structural characteristics. With respect to organizational philosophy, one would examine profit vs. non-profit status; public vs. private affiliation; age-segregated vs. age-integrated programs; and medical vs. social service orientations. In terms of structural characteristics, considerable attention needs to be given to the existence and qualities of boundary-role personnel. These are individuals from one organization who interact with others both in their own organization and in other organizations (Adams, 1976). Such individuals frequently communicate organizational values and priorities to other organizations and are thus critical actors in interorganizational networks. Other structural characteristics that may determine the probability of successful coordination are similarities and differences in operating hours, routinization and formalization of rules and policies, and organizational size. The presence or absence of similarities along these dimensions may affect the feasibility of coordinating services for the elderly.

The Case Management Function

Case management has been loosely defined as a way to provide multiple services to clients with various and complex needs. Case managers perform the function of linking together organizations in the interests of a client or group of clients. As such, they potentially represent the personification of coordination strategies. However, because of the frequently ambiguous nature of the functions of case managers, careful attention needs to be given to the development of case management roles and responsibilities.

Although there are many examples of informal care management, from the friend who transports a neighbor to the physician's office, to the clergyman who visits people in need, there is a growing trend toward the institutionalization of the case management function. Usually employed by human service agencies, case managers typically reach out to clients to promote awareness of services, conduct individual needs assessments, develop service plans, and assure that clients receive needed services. The acceptance of the case management function has been widespread, due in part to the fact that it has not been viewed as a systemic reform, but as a function that is easily incorporated into and non-threatening to current service delivery systems (Austin, 1983). However, when case managers are given the authority to control the allocation of resources, there is the potential for such persons to act as change agents by altering the patterns of resource dependence among provider organizations. This suggests that case management roles should be structured so that persons occupying these roles are given the authority and power to control the allocation of resources perceived as valuable by service providers, thereby reducing the discretion of service providers. That is, permitting those individuals who understand the total needs of a client population to influence the manner in which resources are distributed is a necessary and critical component of a client-centered service delivery system.

As boundary role occupants, case manager roles should also be structured so that they are shielded from co-optation by their own agency's requirements to create service demand.

> Not surprisingly, case managers in health agencies develop service plans emphasizing health services; the service plans of case managers in social service agencies are slanted toward meeting a client's social needs. If case managers located in provider agencies succeed in efforts to develop a plan that truly meets client needs, they soon become sensitive to strain in their roles. Their continued employment hinges upon agency case load; on the other hand, the development of cost-effective service plans emphasizes appropriate service provision rather than agency sponsorship (Wylie and Austin, 1978).

There is currently widespread debate over the roles case managers should play. Much of this debate centers on the extent to which case managers should provide services involving direct contact with clients as opposed to brokerage activities. Four models of case managment have been developed which vary along this and other dimensions (Case Management Research Project, 1980).

The *minimal model* places strong emphasis on diagnostic assessment, client monitoring, and documentation. Minimal to moderate emphasis is placed on follow-up and follow-along monitoring of services provided to clients by external agencies, and on individual therapy and counseling with clients.

The *coordinated model* places moderate emphasis on follow-along monitoring with external agencies, evaluation of client status, and on recording and reporting activities. Some emphasis is placed on individual therapy and counseling, while extensive emphasis is placed on follow-up and advocacy with external agencies.

The *mixed model* views client contact as central to the case management role. Minimal emphasis is placed on referral, follow-up, follow-along, advocacy, and recording and reporting activities. Essentially, this model combines traditional case management functions with therapist roles.

The final model of case management is the *comprehensive model*. In this view, there is little direct client contact, but extensive follow-up and follow-along contact with other agencies to assure the success of referrals. Heavy emphasis is placed on evaluation and reporting and recording activities.

The choice of a case management model to employ in a given situation is dependent upon a number of factors, as illustrated in Figure 8.2. *Individual personnel characteristics* refers to the per-

FIGURE 8.2 Factors affecting pattern of case manager activity

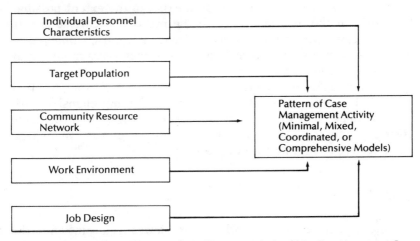

Source: *Adapted from* A Comparative Analysis of Twenty-two Settings Using Case Management Components. *Austin, Tex.: Case Management Research Project, School of Social Work, University of Texas at Austin, 1980.*

sonal traits of the person occupying the case manager role—training, education, experience, etc. The nature of the *target population*—its size, socioeconomic status, and so forth—will also affect the structure of the case manager's role.

A third factor that should be considered in structuring the case manager's role is the nature of the *community resource network.* This was discussed extensively earlier in this chapter and refers to such things as the number and types of provider agencies, the nature of their interdependence, and the extent of cooperation among community organizations.

The case manager's *work environment,* specifically the place of employment, affects the activities in which s/he is engaged. For example, in a mental health agency, it is likely that the case management role will be structured more around the therapy/clinical role than in an Area Agency on Aging, which is likely to promote more of a brokerage role. Related to the work environment is the actual *job design.* Frequently, the job description is dictated by organizational or regulatory requirements that may be irrelevant to the needs of the community or to the organization. What is important to realize here is that the official job design, while certainly affecting the activities carried out by case managers, is often not reflective of the activities actually carried out by case managers. Because case management is often a dynamic and necessarily ambiguous position, there should exist, to the extent possible, flexibility in the manner in which the function is carried out. In fact, the case management function frequently varies among case managers in the same agency, and even among cases managed by the same case manager.

In summary, the nature of the case management role, whether it is of the minimal, mixed, coordinated, or comprehensive varieties, is dependent upon several important factors. In structuring positions and in developing job descriptions for case managers, these factors should be carefully considered.

Conclusion

For many years, coordination has been viewed as a solution to the problems in our health and human service delivery systems. Initial concern for clients getting lost in the complex web of fragmented programs and services gave way to managerial assurances that programs were indeed coordinating their services. Although systematic problems were often cited as the root cause of such problems as poor follow-up and service fragmentation, the response more often than not has taken the form of symbolic rather than substantive changes. For various reasons legislative mandates have not been successfully implemented.

The elderly often face more difficulties responding to poorly coordinated service systems than other population groups because of their limited resources and their need for long-term care. Solutions reside not solely in new state or national legislation, but in strategies which first address communication gaps among federal, state, and community levels. This requires development of a strong national policy on the elderly, with delegatory provisions for state and local responsibility. However, it is essential that these policies be based on sound data to determine where and why coordinative efforts have succeeded and with what costs and benefits.

In implementing a national policy for the elderly, local communities must be aware of certain key community characteristics. Those pursuing interorganizational cooperative goals must have an understanding of the problems facing the elderly in their community. They must also be aware of certain qualities of organizations serving the elderly. These qualities, endemic to all service organizations, include the need for resources (clients, funds, and personnel), the need to establish and protect a philosophical domain, and professional protectionism. In particular, agents of coordination must be aware of the ways in which these qualities are manifested in their own communities, and the manner in which and degree to which these qualities restrict the provision of high quality services of a comprehensive nature.

Case management has been suggested as a useful and proven tool for the effective coordination of services. Careful structuring of the case management role is essential to its successful employment. Attention should be given to such factors as the nature of the community resource network, the characteristics of the target population, the work environment, the official job description, and the particular qualities of the case management role occupant in structuring the case management role.

References

Adams, S. J. The structure and dynamics of behavior in organizational boundary roles. In Dunnette, M. D. (Ed.), *Handbook of Industrial and Organizational Psychology*. Chicago, Il.: Rand McNally, 1976, pp. 1175–1199.

Aiken, M. and Hage, J. Organizational interdependence and intraorganizational structure. *American Sociological Review*, 1968, *33*, 912–930.

Austin, C. D. Case management in long-term care: options and opportunities. *Health and Social Work*, 1983, *1*, 16–30.

Benson, J. K. The interorganizational network as a political economy. *Administrative Science Quarterly*, 1973, *20*, 229–249.

Bleiweiss, L. and Simson, S. Building a comprehensive geriatric health care system: a case study. *Journal of Community Health*, 1976, *2*, 141–152.

Case Management Research Project. *A Comparative Analysis of Twenty-Two Settings Using Case Management Components*. Austin, Tx.: Case Management Research Project, School of Social Work, University of Texas at Austin, 1980.

Estes, C. L. *The Aging Enterprise*. San Francisco, Ca.: Jossey-Bass Publishing Co., 1979.

Joint Commission on Accreditation of Hospitals. *Principles of Accreditation of Community Health Programs*. Chicago, Il.: 1976.

Levine, S. and White, P. E. Exchange as a conceptual framework for the study of interorganizational relationships. *Administrative Science Quarterly*, 1961, *5*, 583–610.

Levine, S., White, P. E., and Paul, B. D. Community interorganizational problems in providing medical care and social services. *American Journal of Public Health*, 1963, *53*, 1183–1195.

Marmor, T. and Kutza, E. *Analysis of Federal Regulations Related to Aging: Legislative Barriers to Coordination Under Title III.* Chicago, Il.: University of Chicago, 1975.

Mintzberg, H. *The Structuring of Organizations.* Englewood Cliffs, N.J.: Prentice Hall, 1979.

Pfeffer, J. and Salancik, G. *The External Control of Organizations.* New York, N.Y.: Harper and Row, Publishers, 1978.

Pressman, J. L., and Wildavsky, A. B. *Implementation.* Berkeley, Ca.: University of California, 1973.

Quinn, J. L. *Triage II: Coordinated Delivery of Services to the Elderly, Executive Summary.* Wethersfield, Ct.: Triage, Inc., 1982.

Raelin, J. A mandated basis of interorganizational relations: the legal-political network. *Human Relations,* 1980, *33,* 57–68.

Starkweather, D. B. *Hospital Mergers in the Making.* Ann Arbor, Mi.: Health Administration Press, 1981.

Tobin, S. S., Davidson, S. M., and Sack, A. *Effective Social Services for Older Americans.* Ann Arbor, Mi.: Institute of Gerontology, University of Michigan and Wayne State University, 1976.

U.S. House of Representatives. *Older Americans Act of 1965, as Amended: Comprehensive Older Americans Act Amendments of 1978. (Public Law 95-478, as Amended.) Conference Report No. 95-1618.* Washington, D.C.: U.S. Government Printing Office, 1978.

Van de Ven, A.H. On the nature, formation, and maintenance of relations among organizations. *Academy of Management Review,* 1976, *1,* 4–36.

Van de Ven, A. H., Walker, G., and Liston, J. Coordination patterns within an interorganizational network. *Human Relations, 32,* 1979, 19–36.

Wylie, M. and Austin, C. Policy foundations for case management: consequences for the frail elderly. *Journal of Gerontological Social Work,* 1978, *1,* 7–17.

Yuchtman, E. and Seashore, S. E. A system resource approach to organizational effectiveness. *American Sociological Review,* 1967, *32,* 891–903.

9

National Health Policies
for the Elderly

HARRY T. PHILLIPS

Introduction

In previous chapters a public health approach to the needs of the
elderly, and the biological, environmental, behavioral, and health-
care determinants of well-being in the elderly, have been reviewed.
A common theme throughout has been the advantage of regarding
aging of the population in collective rather than in individual
terms, both conceptually and in practice.

Because so many biological and social needs can best be met
through social action, people have always formed groups to act in
their collective interest. In western democratic societies, although
a wide variety of action groups are to be found in all communities,
from the local to the national, the most generally present and
accepted social organization is government. Although the United
States constitution assigns major legal powers to the individual
states, the fiscal and political influence of the federal government
vis-à-vis the states has grown. Consequently, the central government today largely determines the size and shape of all important
health and social policies and programs.

In this chapter the roles of government in protecting the
health of the community, and the nation's current policies and
programs for the health of the elderly, are briefly reviewed. The

features of an ideal program for the elderly which reflects public health values are outlined.

Public Health Roles of Government

Since public health is dependent largely, although not entirely, on government support, it is important first to examine the roles of government relevant to public health in the U.S. Six functions are briefly described below:

1. *Monitoring the health status* of the nation. (Examples are conducting and reporting national health surveys, census enumerations, and epidemiological studies.) Government agencies or government-subsidized non-government agencies perform this function.
2. *Providing and developing resources.* These include: (a) resources needed to protect the overall public health. (Examples are federal grants for manpower education and construction of facilities.) This is primarily the function of the federal government. (b) resources to support health care for vulnerable groups. (Examples are provision of medical care for the elderly, the poor, migrant workers, and people living in under-doctored areas.). This is a function of all levels of government.
3. *Promoting a planning capacity* for the allocation and use of public resources for health care. (Examples are state and regional planning programs.) This is funded mainly by the federal government.
4. *Developing regulations and setting standards* to safeguard the public health. (Examples are environmental protection and licensing of hospitals and professionals.) These are functions of both federal and state governments.
5. *Acquiring and disseminating knowledge through research* to improve the health of the public. (Examples are establishing centers such as the National Institutes of Health and other centers for research in biomedical science, mental health, and health services research.) Funds are supplied almost entirely by the federal government.
6. *Providing funds* to support the activities mentioned above through collection of taxes. Many, if not all, of these functions have a direct bearing on the health of the elderly.

All money earmarked for programs for the elderly does not by any means end up in the pockets of the elderly. As can be seen from Table 9.1, 26.4 percent of the federal budget in 1981 was devoted to programs which benefit people aged 65 and over (White House Conference Report 1982, p. 41). Although the elderly are indeed the primary beneficiaries through Social Security, pension funds, veterans benefits, Medicare, and some social programs, their

TABLE 9.1
Federal Outlays Benefiting the Elderly[1]

PROGRAM	FY 1981 (Actual) $ (Millions)	Percent of Elderly Budget	Percent of Total Budget
Totals[2]	173,345	100.0	26.4
OASDI (Social Security)	97,096	56.0	14.8
Medicare	35,752	20.6	5.4
Other Retired Disabled and Survivors Benefits[3]	22,847	13.2	3.5
Medicaid	5,967	3.4	0.9
Housing	3,562	2.1	0.5
Supplemental Security Income	2,598	1.5	0.4
Other Federal Health Care	2,229	1.3	0.3
Old Americans Act Programs	993	0.6	0.2
Food Stamps	906	0.5	0.1
Miscellaneous	701	0.4	0.1
Title XX Social Services[4]	595	0.3	0.1
ACTION	85	0.1	0.0
National Institute on Aging	70	0.0	0.0
White House Conference on Aging	4	0.0	0.0

Source: Office of Management and Budget, Health and Income Maintenance Division, in White House Conference on Aging, 1981: Final Report, Volume 1, p. 13.

[1] *Reflects outlays, including effects of proposed legislation, for recipients aged 65 and over in most cases. These are estimates based on Federal agency information—which may be administrative counts, samples, or less accurate estimates from Federal, State and program staff. Other Federal programs that assist the elderly (e.g., consumer activities, USDA extension services, National Park Services) have been excluded due to data limitations.*

[2] *Totals may not add due to rounding.*

[3] *Includes Veterans Compensation and Pensions.*

[4] *Includes Energy Assistance.*

families are thereby often relieved of financial responsibility, and tens of thousands of direct and indirect providers of care also benefit greatly. Thus the 26.4 percent of the federal budget devoted to programs for the elderly benefits a proportion of the population significantly larger than the 11 percent who are 65 or older.

It should be noted that currently in the United States, numerous individuals and agencies other than government actually deliver health services. Government money, however, provides much of the fuel to drive the machinery. Besides state and local governments, there are literally thousands of fiscal and operational intermediaries, including health insurers, hospitals, and physicians, between the national government and its beneficiaries. Such a fragmented system of services results in a proliferation of administrative rules and cumbersome paper work.

Given that society and its most powerful arm, the government, have important responsibilities in maintaining the well-being of its older members, there is still much room for dispute regarding the precise nature and extent of these responsibilities. In a democratic pluralistic society, resolving the issues which emerge is part of the political process. Pressure groups play an important role in this balancing act, and include not only the elderly (not a politically homogeneous group), but also the indirect beneficiaries of policies and laws. Many difficult questions face health policy makers, and numerous authors have expressed their concerns and opinions about these matters (Binstock, 1978; Hudson, 1978; Morris, 1979; Somers, 1980; Estes, 1979).

A guiding assumption in our society is that whenever possible individuals and their families should rely on themselves to maintain their health and well-being. When this is no longer feasible, the local community should be reponsible for assisting its citizens. When local resources are insufficient, responsibility should be assumed by the state and finally by the nation.

While intervention at each level should undoubtedly aim at enhancing the independence of elderly citizens, there is a fine line between compassion and paternalism (Halper, 1980). It is not always easy to be sure that support enhances independence.

Age as a Criterion for Entitlement

A major question in public health is whether age *per se* should be a criterion for eligibility for public support. The answer to this question is not simple. There are points for and against age-based programs, some of which will be discussed here (Neugarten, 1982). The points in favor of programs specifically for the elderly are:

1. Because the elderly as a group have more health problems and fewer resources than the population as a whole, they should receive priority when funds are limited.
2. Using age eligibility as a criterion limits the number of people entitled to benefit and thus conserves public monies.
3. The combination of serving the elderly and limiting the benefits to those who through no fault of their own cannot be expected to be self-sufficient has political appeal. There is sympathy for old people and we all hope to reach old age one day.
4. Age limited programs, particularly Medicare, relieve many groups of enormous expenditures. Consequently, such programs attract political support from a wide range of constituencies. Apart from the families of sick elderly, potential beneficiaries include health insurers (relieved of a high-risk group), hospitals and other providers (relieved of bad debts), and the people and agencies referred to as the "aging enterprise" (Estes, 1979).
5. Disabled people, of whom the very old form a major segment, need special medical and social services designed to reduce barriers to independent living.
6. Using age as a criterion for eligibility is administratively simple and less demeaning than applying a means test.

The points against separate programs are:

1. Segregation of the elderly encourages ageism (negative stereotyping of the elderly) and segregation promotes intergenerational rivalry and antagonism (Etzioni, 1977).
2. To benefit older age groups, many health services, both preventive and curative, should be available and in use early in life, and not postponed until a particular age is reached. An unhealthy childhood and middle age predicate an unhealthy old age.
3. Separate programs are both difficult and expensive to deliver; the fragmentation engendered leads to high administrative costs. At each level bureaucrats have to exercise control, make changes, collect money, apply regulations, and duplicate work that could be greatly reduced if the programs were integrated.

4. By using age as the criterion for eligibility, many patients or clients who are in great need are excluded because they have not yet attained the magic age of 65.
5. Health programs, fragmented by such arbitrary criteria as attained age, force people into services because they are financially covered, rather than because these services are most appropriate to their care. This problem applies to all eligibility criteria which are not based on need (Brody, 1973).

Since politics is the art of the possible, and the elderly have stronger political support than the needy, it seems that age will continue to serve as a major criterion for eligibility for publicly supported care.

Most aging-related policies adopted in the U.S. in the past few decades have had a bearing on health. Some of these laws affect health significantly, albeit indirectly. Examples of such legislation are those concerning income maintenance, retirement, housing, social services, volunteerism, employment, and similar subjects (Binstock and Shanas, 1976, pp. 511–663).

Major Health Policies Serving the Elderly

Apart from the veterans' health program, which serves an aging population and is a bureaucratic empire on its own, health care for the elderly is supported mainly through the following two federal programs (combining the two policies of age eligibility and need eligibility): Social Security Act, Title XVIII—Medicare, and Social Security Act, Title XIX—Medicaid. Federal expenditures in 1981 for these and other federally funded programs benefitting the elderly are shown in Table 9.1. It can be seen that Medicare is by far the most expensive health program supported by the federal government. Medicaid is a joint federal and state program; individual states contribute between 17 and 50 percent of the program costs. Through the Social Services Block Grants Act, a state program funded by federal money, and the Older Americans Act which provides federal funds for a national program operated through state and local agencies, limited health sevices can also be provided. (These two programs will be discussed under the heading of Social Services.)

While each of these health programs has alleviated the health burdens of the elderly to some degree, both have serious limitations, especially when related to the medical and financial needs of the populations they serve.

Medicare

Medicare provides financial support for selected medical services to about 26 million people over the age of 65, and to three million severely disabled people of all ages.

Part A of Medicare provides partial protection against the costs of inpatient hospital services, home health services, and post hospital skilled nursing facility services, with specified deductibles and coinsurance. It is financed through payroll taxes.

Part B of Medicare, the supplementary medical insurance program, is voluntary. It provides protection against the costs of physician services. Participants pay a monthly premium and are also responsible for a deductible cost set annually. Three-quarters of the cost of Part B is met from general revenue funds.

The cost of both parts of Medicare have increased markedly since the inception of the program in 1965. Outlays have gone up from $3.2 billion in 1967 to $49.8 billion in 1982, an annual average rate of increase of 17.6 percent (U.S. Senate Special Committee on Aging, 1982a, p. 1). Despite these huge outlays, Medicare pays physicians only 75 percent of their "usual and customary" charges. More importantly, it covers less than half (45%) of the total medical care costs incurred by the elderly. The average per capita annual costs to the elderly *not covered* by Medicare rose from $503 in 1970 to $1436 in 1980. ($1436 is equivalent to 19.1 percent of the average annual income of people aged 65 years and older (U.S. Senate Special Committee on Aging 1982a, p. 2).

Although the Medicare program has undoubtedly increased the ability of older people to obtain medical care, there are many drawbacks. The program covers only acute care and has severely restricted time limits. Deductibles and coinsurance costs are high and increasing, serving to discourage use of services. As Roemer (1982) points out, physicians order or prescribe the services which account for 80 percent of health expenditures. How reasonable, then, he asks, is it to place financial deterrents on the *patient* for services ordered by the *doctor?*

Medicare, like other third party payment programs, has been blamed for encouraging inflation of medical care costs. These programs help pay for needed medical care, but may also encourage physicians and other health care providers to render or order services which are not essential. They also tend to encourage in-patient rather than less expensive ambulatory care. For most of its history, Medicare has paid hospitals, physicians, and other service providers retrospectively, with little or no prior agreement on charges to be rendered. This system encourages inflation, abuse, and at times even fraud. In addition, because Medicare pays only 75 percent of their customary charges, an increasing number of physicians are now opting not to accept Medicare rates of payment and are billing patients privately, usually at substantially higher rates. The patient then claims the allowable amount from Medicare.

In recent years, new payment methods have been introduced with the aim of containing the cost of Medicare. An example is the recent decision to pay hospitals for patient care a set amount for each of a number of diagnostic categories.

Medicaid

The Medicaid program provides matching funds to states to finance medical care costs of low income people. Of the 22.1 million Medicaid recipients, it is estimated that 3.6 million are elderly. Federal outlays for this program increased seven-fold between 1970 and 1982. However, if nursing home costs are disregarded, the annual rate of increase was 11 percent, which is lower than the general increase in national health expenditures of 13 percent and the Medicare rate of 17.6 percent. (U.S. Senate Special Committee on Aging, 1982b, pp. 26–27). Program expenditures are heavily weighted towards in-patient care. Federal and state outlays for nursing home care alone, in 1980, amounted to $23.3 billion—42 percent of total program spending. Hospital care absorbed 28 percent; the remaining 30 percent went to physician care and medications. In the last few years, strenuous measures have been applied to cut Medicaid costs at both national and state levels.

Without Medicaid, millions of poor people would receive no or little medical care. However, the program as it is now administered has many problems. Benefits vary greatly from state to state. Medicaid rules favor institutional care; many items of care not covered for the patient living at home are covered in the nursing home. A substantial number of chronically ill patients who enter nursing homes as private paying patients end up as Medicaid patients, their financial resources depleted by the high costs of nursing home care. To be eligible for Medicaid the patient is first pauperized. Since spouses are deemed to be responsible for expenses, they, too, can be reduced to penury. As a result of this policy, in order to escape loss of all their assets, some spouses reluctantly divorce their partners after many years of marriage (Vladeck, 1980, p. 24).

Social Services for the Elderly

Since social and health services are closely related to the well-being of the elderly, reference is made here to the main sources of social support provided through national policy. These services are supported by:

1. Social Security Act, Title II—Old Age Survivors and Disability Insurance (OASDI);
2. Social Security Act, Title XVI—Supplemental Security Income (SSI);
3. Social Security Act, Title XX—Social Services Block Grants (as amended, 1981);
4. Older Americans Act, Title III Programs—these are administered through a network of state and local agencies.

Old Age, Survivors, and Disability Insurance

Clearly, the most important, and costly, social service is income maintenance. Although alternative pension plans exist, some of which are provided by the federal government, the major public source of income in retirement is the Old Age Survivors and Disability Insurance program of the Social Security Act, commonly referred to as Social Security. In 1981, $97.1 billion were spent on this program representing 56 percent of federal outlays benefiting the elderly, and 14.8 percent of the total federal budget. Other benefits to the retired, disabled, or survivors of deceased beneficiaries amounted to $22.8 billion.

Social Security payments are of major importance to the support of older people. Eighty-nine percent of all those 65 and over receive retirement benefits. For 66 percent of beneficiaries, social security payments make up more than half of their total income, and for 28 percent, such payments constitute 90 percent and more of their total income (Social Security Administration, 1980, pp. 22–26).

The political repercussions of the rising costs of entitlement programs, coupled with a depressed economy, foreshadow major changes in the income maintenance programs in the near future.

Supplemental Security Income

Under the Supplemental Security Income (SSI) program, $2.6 billion were paid to ensure a minimum income for old, blind, or disabled people (White House Conference Report, 1982, p. 13).

Title XX—Social Services Block Grants

In 1975 Title XX was added to the Social Security Act. It provides funds for a range of social services to be administered by the states. In 1981 this law was amended to establish the Social Services Block Grant Act. The major purposes of the law are to reduce dependency and promote self sufficiency for all ages in all low-income groups. Within broad limits the individual states have discretion over the way this money is used and as a consequence, benefits to the elderly vary widely among states.

In 1981, the costs of those Title XX Social Services which benefited the elderly were estimated to be $595 million (White House Conference Report, 1982, p. 13). Since 17 percent of the population aged 65 and over—about 4 million people—have incomes below the poverty level, on the average only about $150 per elderly poor person per year are available for social services under this act.

The Older Americans Act

Social services to the elderly are provided also under the Older Americans Act (OAA). First passed in 1965, the law has been amended by nearly every Congress since then.

OAA was passed in an attempt to coordinate policies, programs, and services at the national, state, and local levels. As is often the case, the preamble to the legislation is rhetorical and idealistic; however, it provides a set of objectives to which advocates of the elderly could all aspire. The preamble to the law states:

> The Congress hereby finds and declares that, in keeping with the traditional American concept of the inherent dignity of the individual in our democratic society, the older people of our Nation are entitled to, and it is the joint and several duty and responsibility of the governments of the United States and of the several States and their political subdivisions to assist our older people to secure equal opportunity to the full and free enjoyment of the following objectives:
>
> 1. An adequate income in retirement in accordance with the American standard of living.
> 2. The best possible physical and mental health which science can make available and without regard to economic status.
> 3. Suitable housing, independently selected, designed and located with reference to special needs and available at costs which older citizens can afford.
> 4. Full restorative services for those who require institutional care.
> 5. Opportunity for employment with no discriminatory personnel practices because of age.
> 6. Retirement in health, honor, dignity—after years of contribution to the economy.
> 7. Pursuit of meaningful activity within the widest range of civic, cultural, and recreational opportunities.
> 8. Efficient community services, including access to low-cost transportation, which provide a choice in supported living arrangements and social assistance in a coordinated manner and which are readily available when needed.
> 9. Immediate benefit from proven research knowledge which can sustain and improve health and happiness.
> 10. Freedom, independence, and the free exercise of individual initiative in planning and managing their own lives. (U.S. Congress, 1982)

These objectives provide a basis for national policy. National goals are limited to improvement of *opportunities for access* to resources which can enhance the quality of extended years of life, without actual promise of availability of necessary resources.

With the enactment of the OAA a *new* hierarchy of agencies was established, with a network of state and local agencies to plan and deliver services, to promote coordination of services, and to serve as advocates for the aged. Local programs may include a broad range of services: nutrition, information and referral, homemaker and home health aide, visiting and telephone reassurance, chore, maintenance, and legal services. Co-location and coordination of services was encouraged through establishment of multipurpose senior centers. Although no means test was applied to participants, preference was to be given to the elderly in areas of greatest need. Provision was made for grants to support services for congregate and home-delivered meals to the elderly.

In addition, under Title IV grants were made available for education and research purposes, as well as for establishing or supporting multidisciplinary centers of gerontology to encompass research, training, and consultation functions. Under Title V, provision was made to provide jobs for low income older workers who had difficulty in finding employment.

Ironically, it is quite possible that OAA, by establishing a new hierarchy of agencies, has helped to increase the fragmentation which weakens the impact of federal programs for the elderly. OAA agencies certainly do not have the legal or the fiscal power to achieve any significant degree of coordination of programs for the elderly. Coordination of services is difficult to achieve without some superordinate power to enforce central direction and cooperation. Especially in an era of reduction of resources, improved methods for integrating related programs are sorely needed.

In 1981, Congress allocated $672 million to support programs implementing the provisions of OAA. This sum equalled $22 per capita, if the total population 60 and over (OAA target) were included, or about $140 per annum if only the elderly poor were to be served. This sum is hardly adequate to achieve the goals stated in the preamble to the Act.

OAA contains components other than the social programs. Functions such as data gathering, training, and employment of older citizens were also included, but these components were reduced by Congress in the early years of the Reagan administration. One is forced to agree with critics of the program that often the main beneficiaries of OAA are the intermediaries—the bureaucrats and social workers (Estes, 1979).

Proposed Policies for a Public Health System for the Elderly

Ideal systems of care have been projected by a number of writers, some for the total population (Torrens, 1978, pp. 107–120; Roemer, 1978, pp. 551–560); others for certain aspects of health care (Somers, 1980; Portnoi, 1979).

It may seem naive to set forth ideals which will take many years, perhaps in the face of serious national crises, to reach, but doing so serves a useful purpose in setting goals for which to strive. Since public health is largely in the public arena, and its support is determined largely through the political process, compromises are inevitable in setting policies. Small gains may be the best one can expect in the short term, but having a set of long-term goals can serve as a guide for each short-term choice along the way. For a public health program for the elderly the following goals are suggested. These are based upon the mission and values which underlie the philosophy of public health and which are reflected in the goals and strategies stated in the introduction to this book.

Organization of Services

Health and social programs for the elderly should ultimately be integrated with programs for everyone else, and be based on need rather than age alone. (However, since the aged evoke more political sympathy and support than the needy, and there is considerable overlap between old age and dependency, age-based policies are reasonable compromises.)

The use of health resources should be guided by sound planning. Information on health of the people should be systematically developed, and priorities for services based on proven research findings. Weak planning favors only those who benefit from ignorance and chaos at the cost of consumers of care.

At all levels of the system, consumer interests must be paramount. Policies should emphasize that health care programs are for the benefit of the public. Incentives should be developed to maximize this benefit, and to eliminate misuse and exploitation by both providers and consumers.

The central government should develop major policies to minimize regional differences in the care of the elderly and the needy. Since demand will always outstrip supply, it is essential that allocated resources be distributed evenly and fairly.

Delivery of Services

Concepts of regionalization and coordination must be applied in planning for more accessible, comprehensive, quality services. Quality must be safeguarded by establishing systems of feedback between providers and consumers of care.

Highest priority must be given to health promotion and disease prevention programs, but public financial support should be given for these as well as therapeutic programs only if there be reasonable expectation of effectiveness.

Each person should have a primary care giver, usually a physician, to provide entry into the system, maintain continuity, and refer to related services when necessary. In many instances, however, nurse practitioners could, with benefit, be the primary source of care, for example, to patients in nursing homes.

Effective linkages should be established at all levels between the different parts of the health care system—community care, ambulatory services, in-patient and long-term care. Current fragmentation must be eliminated by bringing all branches of health care under one administration, at least at the local delivery level.

Effective linkages should also be established between health, social, and housing programs at the local level, since they are mutually supportive.

Long-term care, to be humane and effective, should be coordinated with other component services. There needs to be a continuum of health services integrated with acute care, home care, and community-based resources. There must also be close ties to social and housing programs, to enable patients to be cared for in the setting least restrictive and most appropriate for them and their families.

Financing of Services

The health care system must be financed through public means such as a national health insurance or a tax system, or a combination thereof. Using national guidelines, each region should be given its allotment of funds based on a formula reflecting the demographic composition and needs of the area.

There must be one system of funding for all, with no financial barriers in access to modalities of care which are appropriate for the individual.

Health professionals should accept responsibility for ensuring that the resources of the system are used judiciously by their patients. By eliminating the present "fee-for-service" system, costs of care would be reduced and administration simplified.

Resource Development

Adequate funds for research should be made available to assess population needs, and to evaluate the success of alternative delivery modalities.

Research to provide a better understanding of the processes of aging should be supported.

Research to explore methods for improving care of the elderly should also be supported.

Government funds to launch demonstration delivery projects and to evaluate their effectiveness should be provided.

Where health services research has demonstrated the need, government funds should be made available to develop and provide new resources. Funding could be used for training of personnel (especially in geriatrics), facility construction, and necessary equipment. In this way regional delivery systems would be made more effective, balanced, and equitable.

Conclusion

Striving for an ideal public health system of care for the elderly is not unrealistic. Many components of such a system are already in place in parts of our country, and more complete and good models exist in several countries with democratic systems of government akin to ours (Kane and Kane, 1976; Exton-Smith and Evans, 1977; Maddox, 1977). Implementation will not be easy, for presently in the United States health services are provided by government for a number of special groups through special programs. Thus we see services or subsidies for Indians, veterans, migrant workers, the poor, the elderly, the chronically and permanently disabled, the mentally ill, and people with advanced kidney disease. Programs for each of these groups are administered, funded, and frequently organized separately. But this incremental process for developing health services, carried to extremes, eventually diminishes the programs it sets out to assist. There is no economic or administrative logic to a system which is so cumbersome, wasteful, and difficult to administer. The nation would be better served, and receive better value for its money (Abel-Smith, 1974), were these programs coordinated at the national, state, and local levels, through a single system accessible to all in need of care.

References

Abel-Smith, B. Value for money in health services. *Social Security Bulletin,* 1974, July, 17–28.

Binstock, R. H. Federal policy towards the aging. *National Journal,* 1978, *10,* 1838–1845.

Binstock, R. H. and Shanas, E. (Eds.) *Handbook of Aging and the Social Sciences.* New York, N.Y.: Van Nostrand Reinhold Company, 1976.

Brody, E. M. A million Procrustean beds. *The Gerontologist,* 1973, *13,* 430–435.

Estes, C. L. *The Aging Enterprise.* San Francisco, Calif.: Jossey-Bass Publishing Co., 1979.

Etzioni, A. Old people and public policy. In F. Reismann (Ed.), *Older Persons: Unused Resources for Unmet Needs.* Beverly Hills, Ca.: Sage Publications, 1977, pp. 38–51.

Exton-Smith, A. N. and Evans, J. G. (Eds.) *Care of the Elderly: Meeting the Challenge of Dependency.* New York, N.Y.: Grune and Stratton, 1977.

Halper, T. The double edged sword: paternalism as a policy in the problems of aging. *Milbank Memorial Fund Quarterly,* 1980, *358,* 472–499.

Hudson, R.B. The graying of the federal budget and its consequences for old-age policy. *The Gerontologist,* 1978, *18,* 428–440.

Kane, R. L. and Kane, R. A. *Long-Term Care in Six Countries.* Washington, D.C.: U.S. DHEW Publication No. (NIH) 76-1207, 1976.

Maddox, G. L. The unrealized potential of an old idea. In Exton-Smith, A. N. and Evans, J. G. (Eds.). *Care of the Elderly: Meeting the Challenge of Dependency.* New York, N.Y.: Grune and Stratton 1977, pp. 147–161.

Morris, R. *Social Policy of the American Welfare State.* New York, N.Y.: Harper and Row, 1979.

Nelson, G. Social class on public policy for the elderly. *Social Science Review,* 1982, Mar., 85–107.

Neugarten, B.L. (Ed.) *Age or Need? Public Policies for Older People.* Beverly Hills, Calif.: Sage Publications, 1982.

Portnoi, V. Sounding board: A health care system for the elderly. *The New England Journal of Medicine,* 1979, *300,* 1387–1390.

Roemer, M. I. *Social Medicine.* New York, N.Y.: Springer Publishing Company, 1978, pp. 551–560.

Roemer, M. I. Market failure and health care policy. *Journal of Public Health Policy,* 1982, *3,* 419–431.

Social Security Administration. *Income and Resources of the Aged.* SSA Publication No. 13–11727. Washington, D.C.: U.S. Government Printing Office, 1980.

Somers, A. R. Rethinking health policy for the elderly: A six-point program. *Inquiry,* 1980, *17,* 3–17.

Torrens, P. R. *The American Health Care System.* Saint Louis, Mo.: C. V. Mosby Co., 1978.

U. S. Congress. *Compilation of the Older Americans Act of 1965 and Related Provisions of Law.* Washington, D.C.: U.S. Government Printing Office, 1982.

U. S. Senate, Special Committee on Aging. *Health Care Expenditures for the Elderly: How Much Protection Does Medicare Provide?* Washington, D. C.: U. S. Government Printing Office, 1982a.

U. S. Senate, Special Committee on Aging. *Congressional Action on the Fiscal Year 1983 Budget: What it Means for Older Americans.* Washington, D.C.: U.S. Government Printing Office, 1982b.

Vladeck, B. C. *Unloving Care: The Nursing Home Tragedy.* New York, N.Y.: Basic Books, 1980.

White House Conference on Aging. *Final Report, the 1981 White House Conference on Aging,* Vol. 1. Washington, D.C.: 1982.

Epilogue

In summary, in preceding chapters the authors have presented:

1. An epidemiological overview of the health of our aging population;
2. The biological bases for aging and its functional consequences;
3. The status of the elderly in relation to nutrition, housing, and injury prevention, and current organized responses to their needs;
4. The relation between behavior and health of the elderly;
5. Ways in which behavior can be modified to improve the health of the older population;
6. The wide range of existing health and related policies and services for the elderly and the desirability of coordinating these efforts.

The question arises: What can be done to promote a more effective public health response to the challenge of an aging population?

Some Future Directions for Promoting a Public Health Approach to Aging

1. Establishing public priorities and allocating national or local resources is a political process. Since public health is by definition an outcome of organized societal action, it follows that promotion of public health policies requires political action. Public health workers can influence this process by

producing, analyzing, and communicating health information to the decision makers—usually politicians and their staffs, preferably ones who are sympathetic to the goals and philosophy of public health.

2. In order to influence the political process with scientific information, it is necessary to conduct relevant research. This should include basic health research, epidemiology, and health services evaluation. Researchers and teachers have the responsibility for mobilizing the necessary support and designing the studies which can, in many ways, be used to promote public health action.

3. Education of future professionals is another potential channel of influence. The curricula of the health schools should include not only geriatric and gerontology topics, but also alternative ways of delivering services at the community level.

4. Establishing alliances with like-minded groups or individuals is a way of educating the public, organizing for political purposes, and arousing the consciousness of community leaders.

Commerce and industry have contributed greatly to the economic wealth of this nation, providing the means whereby public health measures could be instituted, reducing premature mortality, and causing our present demographic situation. These measures included organized programs for disease prevention, reduction of environmental hazards, health education of the public and the professions, organization and support of health care services, and research.

In a period when health care has become increasingly commercialized, it is crucial that public health rise to the challenge of burgeoning health and social needs of our aging society. It can be assumed that the nation's goals have included the prevention of premature mortality. This is now being achieved in large measure, through collective or public health measures. The same perspective and strategies can and should be applied to promoting the quality of life in the years which have been added.

Author Index

Subject Index